A PICTORIAL HISTORY OF THE

POSTWAR YEARS

FROM 1946 TO THE 1990s

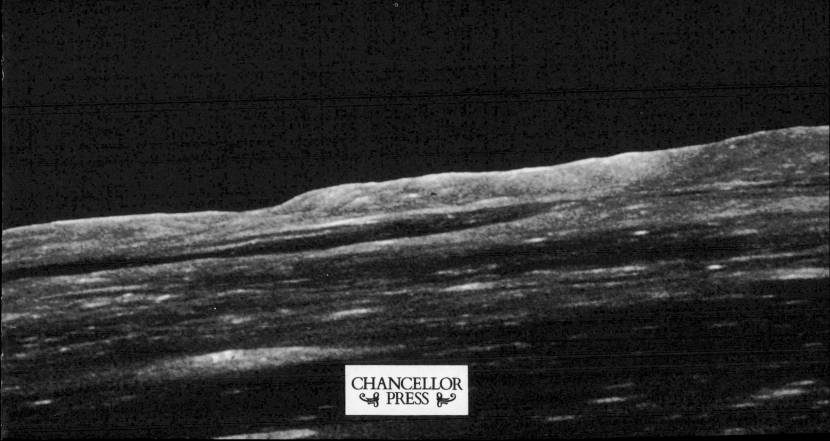

A PICTORIAL HISTORY OF THE

POSTWAR YEARS

FROM 1946 TO THE 1990s

CHANCELLOR PRESS

Chief contributor: **Neil Wenborn**

Other contributors: Helen Dore, Jake Douglas, Ian Jackman,
Tony Kingsford, Alan McIntosh, Brian Murphy, Sonia Porter

Title pages: Earth from the moon, July 1969
(Popperphoto)

Published in 1992 by
Chancellor Press
Michelin House, 81 Fulham Road, London SW3 6RB
part of Reed International Books

The material in this book previously appeared in *The 20th Century: The Pictorial History*
first published in 1989 by The Hamlyn Publishing Group,
part of Reed International Books

ISBN 1 85152 203 4

Printed in Hong Kong

CONTENTS

1946–1949

The 1940s

The 1940s were the decade in which the contours of today's political world map were drawn. It was a decade which began with the great European powers locked in military struggle and ended with relations between the world superpowers – the United States and the Soviet Union – frozen in the no less entrenched positions of the cold war. As the political battle-lines were drawn up in Berlin – the city from which Hitler had sought to spread his Reich throughout Europe – a new power bloc was formed by the signing of the North Atlantic Treaty. Just as the First World War had given birth to the League of Nations, so the Second provided the crucible for its successor, the United Nations.

Outside Europe and the United States, too, momentous changes were taking place in traditional patterns of power. In China Mao Tse-tung emerged victorious from the long drawn out civil war between the Nationalists and the Communists. In Asia the death knell of colonialism was sounded by the granting of independence to India after more than 160 years of British rule. And in the Middle East the seeds of a new and lasting conflict were sown by the formation of the Jewish state of Israel.

The aftermath of war

Scarcely one generation after the 'war to end all wars', the world had found itself plunged once again into bloody conflict. The scale and technological sophistication of the fighting were unprecedented, as were the number of casualties: the total of dead has been estimated at over 55 million, including civilians as well as combatants. The greatest human cost was borne by the Soviet Union, where some 20 million people died – a tragedy that was to leave an indelible mark on the national psyche. Millions of Jews had been murdered by the Nazis in the territories under their occupation, and by the end of the war, as the full horrors of the Holocaust were revealed, only a small minority of the Jewish population of Europe remained alive. The inauguration of the new United Nations in January 1946 was aimed at negating war and creating social justice and security. But Europe faced years of reconstruction, both in terms of whole cities which had been razed to the ground in the bombing, and of ruined national economies. Clement Attlee, Britain's new prime minister following Labour's landslide win in the general election on 5 July 1945, warned of serious financial trouble and announced post-war austerity measures, with rationing resulting from a world food shortage, which would demand similar sacrifices to those made during the war years.

The Iron Curtain

In March 1946 Churchill spoke of an Iron Curtain that had descended across Europe. It was perhaps the most telling image of the new confrontation which emerged from the Second World War – the political stand-off between the United States and her allies on the one hand and the Soviet Union and her newly-acquired satellite states on the other – a confrontation which came to be known as the cold war. In the aftermath of the agreements at Yalta and Potsdam, which divided the war-ravaged territories of Europe between the great powers along lines reflecting the military position on the eve of victory, Stalin acquired Bulgaria, Romania, Hungary, Poland and Yugoslavia. Russian forces remained in Prague, Vienna and Berlin. The guiding force of American foreign policy, which had been isolationist for so many years, shifted to fear of Russian expansionism. Berlin became the front line of this new battle. In 1948 the West defeated a Russian blockade of the divided city by mounting an historic airlift of supplies. In 1949 NATO was born.

India

After years of unrest and struggle, the people of India won independence from British rule in 1947. It was the first major loss to an Empire which at the beginning of the century had covered a fifth of the earth's land mass and a fitting symbol of the waning of British influence in a world now dominated by Russia and the United States. It was also the beginning of a new era of conflict on the Indian sub-continent itself. With the former British territory partitioned between India and Pakistan, independence lent fuel to the bitter intercommunal struggle between Hindus and Moslems.

Israel

The appalling sufferings of European Jewry under Nazi rule gave new political impetus to Zionist demands for a Jewish homeland. In 1948 the state of Israel was created in the former British mandated territory of Palestine. It was a birth preceded by acts of terrorist violence and was to prove the cause of many more in the years to come. With the creation of a Palestinian refugee problem of enormous dimensions, the foundations were laid for a struggle that was to change the relatively stable Middle East into a political powderkeg. A new focus of international tension was already developing.

The shadow of the Bomb

In August 1945 the United States dropped the first atomic bombs on the Japanese cities of Hiroshima and Nagasaki. The immediate effect was to bring the Pacific War to a sudden end and to shift the balance of international military power conclusively in favour of the Americans. In the longer term, the face of world politics was changed irrevocably. The wheels of the nuclear arms race had been put in motion, and with them the development of a weapon system which, for the first time in history, would give mankind the power to destroy itself. The relationship between political and military power had entered a new and terrible phase. The nuclear age had begun.

Pages 6–7: The atom bomb explodes at Bikini Atoll, 1946.

1946

Jan	7	The West recognises the Austrian Republic
	11	Albania deposes King Zog; declares a People's Republic
	20	France: De Gaulle resigns; Gouin becomes President
	30	London: UN General Assembly meets for first time
Feb	1	UK: 1st civilian test flights from Heathrow airport
	1	Norwegian Trygve Lie elected UN Secretary General
	1	Hungary declares itself a Republic
	7	Germany: Hess on trial at Nuremberg for war crimes
	14	UK: Bank of England is nationalised
	24	Argentina: Juan Perón is elected President
Mar	5	Winston Churchill speaks of an 'Iron Curtain'
	10	Britain and France start to withdraw from Lebanon
	15	USSR embarks on fourth 5-year plan
Apr	18	Geneva: League of Nations Assembly is dissolved
	21	E Germany: Social Democrats merge with Communists
May	5	Italy: Victor III abdicates; Umberto II is King
	25	Transjordan proclaims its independence
Jun	2	Italy: Referendum in favour of a Republic
	3	Italy: King Umberto II leaves the country

	28	Italy: Enrico de Nicola becomes President
Jul	4	Philippine Republic established
	7	Mexico: Miguel Alemán is elected President
	21	UK: Bread is rationed
	27	US author Gertrude Stein dies in Paris
Sep	1	Greece: Plebiscite in favour of a monarchy
	28	King George II returns to Greece
Oct	15	Cardinals win World Series in St Louis
	15	Goering commits suicide
Nov	4	China and US sign friendship pact
	5	US Republicans regain control of Congress
	6	UK: British National Health Act comes into force
	15	Holland recognises Indonesian Republic
Dec	5	New York chosen as permanent site for UN
	16	France: Socialist Léon Blum forms goverment
		The Arts
		Nikos Kazantzakis' novel *Zorba the Greek*
		Eugene O'Neill's play *The Iceman Cometh*
		William Wyler's film *The Best Years of Our Lives*

India pays the price of freedom

In September 1945, Clement Attlee, the new Labour Prime Minister, had promised India her independence at the earliest possible date. But this prospect, instead of uniting the nation in nationalistic rejoicing, ended up splitting it asunder. With the common enemy departing peacefully, the various sects and religions that had united against Britain now began to regard each other with suspicion, fear and hatred.

In February there was a mutiny in the Indian Navy. The mutiny was quickly suppressed but the turmoil in this well-disciplined force boded ill for the more volatile population of the sub-continent. More riots broke out later in February and the following months saw even more violence. The Muslims refused to join with the Hindus and demanded their own State of Pakistan. Massacres took place as neighbouring communities turned on each other in murderous sectarian rage.

Below left: Riots in East Bengal forced many villagers to abandon their homes and flee from affected areas. Here, an evacuee from Ibrahimpur waits with his household possessions to be ferried to safety, while one of the women carries a shotgun.

Below right: M. A. Jinnah, President of the All-India Muslim League and future leader of Pakistan (right) with Mr Chundragar, President of the Bombay Provincial League.

Riots in Calcutta

Top: Dead bodies were a common sight on the streets of Calcutta during the clashes between Muslims and Hindus. These corpses are lying on the main thoroughfare in north Calcutta.

Left: A dead Hindu lies among the Muslims who have killed him. They carry *lathis* – wooden sticks that can be lethal in trained hands.

Above: This was once a crowded and prosperous shopping centre in Calcutta, but Muslim–Hindu clashes have left it looking like a bomb site.

Mao's new war

The Chinese Communists had always regarded the Sino–Japanese war as an interruption in their long struggle to take over China. The Japanese were therefore no sooner defeated than Mao (top left) renewed his old war against Chiang Kai-shek and the Chinese nationalists. Mao was now in a much stronger position, with a million men in uniform, a straightforward strategy and tactics refined in 20 years of battle. The Kuomintang Nationalist Party under Chiang Kai-shek was divided and uncertain. Mao was so confident of the outcome that in August he declared war on his old enemy.

Above: Chiang Kai-shek (1887–1975) accompanied by his wife, greets an American WAC supply sergeant during a tea at their summer home in Chungking.

Strange fruit

Because it was not possible to import 'luxury' items during the war, a whole generation of British children had never seen an orange or a banana and the arrival of these mysterious fruits caused great excitement in most families. Many of the children did not know how to cope with them at first, and tried to eat them skin and all!

Dockers are shown handling the first bananas to reach Britain since before the war. They arrived from the West Indies at London's West India Dock on the banana boat *Jamaica Producer* and were on sale in the streets of London within hours.

We demand Pakistan!

This was the slogan that greeted British and Indian politicians on the streets of London and Delhi when they attended talks on Indian independence. The Muslims were convinced that they would not get a fair deal from the Hindus who made up the majority of the population of the sub-continent. They therefore wanted their own Muslim country. There was a large contingent of Muslim Indians in London at the time, many of them students and passionate nationalists, so these Muslim marches became a common sight on the streets of the capital. Here, a group from the All Indian Muslim League make their way to a meeting in Kingsway Hall after the police refused them permission to call on the Prime Minister in Downing Street.

Strike at General Motors

Workers at General Motors picketing the headquarters in Detroit give a wild welcome to news of the wage increases which will end their strike. The 113-day strike, which was the longest and most costly in the automobile industry's history, brought work to a standstill at hundreds of plants in 18 states. The settlement between management and the United Automobile Workers was for a wage increase of just over 18 cents an hour.

The company was founded in 1908 by William Crapo Durant. He acquired 75 per cent of Oldsmobile stock which, combined with Buick Motors which he had bought in 1904, became the General Motors Company.

The trade union movement

Members of the National Group of the Amalgamated Furnishings Trades Association march from Shoreditch Church (in London's East End) as a protest against the Board of Trade's decision to allow imports of processed glass from the beginning of the following year – a striking demonstration of the determination of working people to protect their jobs at any cost.

Bikini Atoll

Bikini Atoll, one of the American Marshall Islands in the Pacific Ocean, was almost unknown until the Americans decided to use it for testing their nuclear weapons. They removed the entire population to another island and conducted their first test, shown here, on July 25th. As targets, they used some of their own obsolete warships, such as the old battleship *Arkansas* and some warships captured from enemy navies such as the German cruiser *Prinz Eugen*. None of the ships survived the bomb and Bikini continued to be used as a testing site for many years. Its original inhabitants still want to return some day.

Spaak listens

The veteran Belgian statesman Paul-Henri Spaak (1899–1972) was elected President of the United Nations and presided at its very first session, shown here. He then went on to become Secretary-General to the North Atlantic Treaty Organisation (NATO) ten years later.

GI brides

Many thousands of American soldiers had fallen in love with British girls and a great number of them eventually married their sweethearts. These British girls are shown on the transatlantic liner taking them to their new homes in the USA. Unfortunately some were to find their new homes a great deal less desirable than the Hollywood-style houses they had expected.

13

1947

Jan	1	Britain nationalises its coalmines
	7	George Marshall appointed US Secretary of State
	16	Vincent Auriol becomes President of France
Feb	7	Arabs and Jews reject UK plans for Palestine's partition
Mar	3	Bulganin replaces Stalin as Soviet Defence Chief
	19	Paul Spaak forms coalition government in Belgium
	19	Communist HQ at Yunan falls to Chinese Nationalists
	29	Nationalist uprising against France in Madagascar
Apr	2	Britain passes Palestine problem to United Nations
	7	Death of Henry Ford
	19	Explosions in Texas City kill 377
May	23	British govt agrees to partition India
	29	Indian Parliament bans 'untouchables'
Jun	5	US: George Marshall calls for 'Marshall Aid' in speech
	17	Burma opts for independent Republic
Jul	6	Spain to have a King when Franco dies
	20	Dutch troops attack Indonesian forces in Java
Aug	1	UN Security Council asks for ceasefire in Indonesia
	15	India becomes independent, with Nehru as PM
	15	Pakistan comes into being with Ali Khan as PM
	27	British govt announces cuts to deal with economic crisis
	31	Communists win Hungarian elections
Sep	14	Concordat with Catholic Church denounced in Poland
	16	John Cobb breaks world land speed record at 394 mph
	30	Pakistan and Yemen join United Nations
Oct	5	Warsaw: Communist conference establishes Cominform
	26	Kashmir joins India despite Pakistan's protests
	29	Belgium, Netherlands and Luxembourg set up Benelux
Nov	14	United Nations recognises independence of Korea
	20	UK: Princess Elizabeth marries Philip Mountbatten
	22	Iran renounces oil agreement with USSR
	25	USSR demands war reparations from Germany
	27	Australian banks nationalised
	29	UN announces plans for partition of Palestine
Dec	19	Friendship pact between Rumania and Yugoslavia
	22	New constitution in Italy offers elected Senate
	27	Greek government bans Communist Party
	30	Kashmir problem goes to United Nations
	30	King Michael of Rumania abdicates
		The Arts
		Discovery of the Dead Sea Scrolls
		Malcolm Lowry's novel *Under the Volcano*
		Albert Camus's novel *The Plague*
		Robert Graves's book *The White Goddess*
		Tennessee Williams's play *A Streetcar Named Desire*

End of Empire

Lord Louis Mountbatten (1900–1979) was appointed the last Viceroy of India on February 20th. He and his wife arrived in India to find that the leaders of the two great religious groups, Hindu and Muslim, had informally agreed to partition the country into India and Pakistan. But their people were divided by hatred and religious bigotry. Worse, the religious groupings were inextricably mixed, with many pockets of Muslims in what was to become India and many pockets of Hindus in what was to become Pakistan.

Now the long trek of these displaced persons to their new countries began – and with it the indiscriminate slaughter. Towns and villages where the two religious groups had once lived in peace under the British Raj, became bitterly divided. Families who had lived side by side as neighbours were now deadly enemies. In spite of the most earnest pleas of the new Viceroy and the leaders of Congress, both Hindu and Muslim, the defenceless convoys slowly making their way across India continued to suffer ambushes and armed attacks.

A nation in turmoil

Horror stories abounded. Whole trainloads of refugees were stopped and their passengers hacked or beaten to death. Parties of children were ruthlessly murdered. Neither age nor sex was any protection against the senseless rage that had suddenly overtaken previously peaceful people. No count was ever made of the dead, although the final estimate ran into many hundreds of thousands.

Above: Lord and Lady Louis Mountbatten are enthroned as the last Viceroy and Vicereine of India.
Below: The Mountbattens had excellent relations with the leaders of both parties in India. Here, they talk to Mahatma Gandhi.

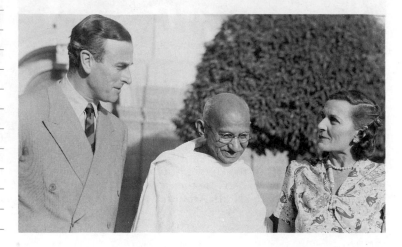

Right: After the riots the city of Amritsar looks as though it has been bombed.

Below: These refugees from murderous riots found temporary safety in the outskirts of Delhi. Feeding and sheltering them gave the government enormous problems.

Bottom: Rioting took place even in the centre of Delhi. Here, a lone soldier mans a Bren gun at a key crossing.

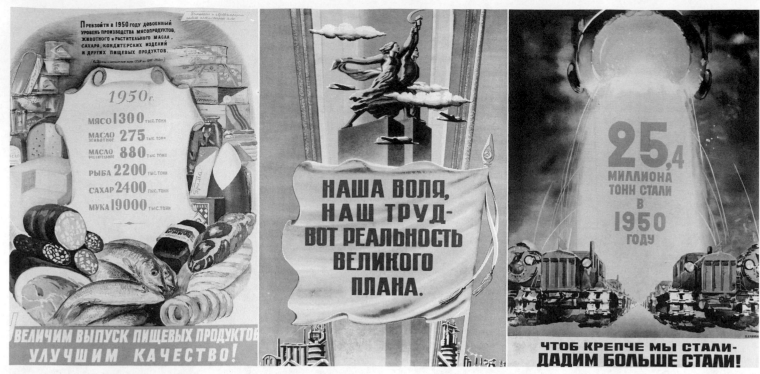

Soviet Union's five-year plan

The first post-war five-year plan for the reconstruction of the Soviet Union's war-torn infrastructure was halfway through when these patriotic posters appeared on the walls in the Soviet zone of Berlin. The one on the far left exhorts Soviet citizens to produce more and better food. The one in the centre proclaims

'Our Will and our Effort is the Essence of Our Five-Year Plan'. And the one on the right is aimed at steelworkers and encourages them to produce more steel. Although the designs are very powerful, their practical effect on the workforce was difficult to measure.

The royal wedding

The gloom of post-war Britain was briefly lightened by a fairytale royal romance. Princess Elizabeth had first met Philip at her parents' coronation. His father was Prince Andrew of Greece and his mother was the sister of Lord Louis Mountbatten, so there was a strong family connection.

Philip and Elizabeth met again when they were both grown-up, and he was a lieutenant in the Royal Navy. Their romance had flowered very quickly and the King and Queen were delighted that their daughter had chosen such a suitable match. They became engaged on July 9th and were duly married on November 20th, immediately after Philip had been ennobled as the Duke of Edinburgh by King George at a private ceremony.

Above: The Princess and her husband on honeymoon.

Left: The Princess's coach passes through Admiralty Arch on the Mall on its way back to Buckingham Palace after the wedding.

Al Capone

Born in New York of Italian immigrants, Capone early gained his nickname 'Scarface' while working as a bouncer for a Brooklyn brothel. Driven out of the city under suspicion for the murder of a policeman, he went to Chicago and joined mafia gangster Johnny Torrio. They soon headed the city's underworld along with the rival gang of 'Deanie' O'Banion. In the gangland war for supremacy during the Twenties, more than a thousand were wiped out. O'Banion was killed, and Torrio 'retired' leaving Capone to take over a thriving $5 million-a-year empire built on prostitution, bootlegging, extortion and gambling. He escaped attempts on his life but was finally caught on a tax evasion charge. Eleven years in prison broke him. Sliding into madness from syphilis, he went into hiding on his Florida estate on his release. He died on January 25th.

The return of Eros

On June 28th London's best-loved statue returned to its rightful place at the centre of Piccadilly Circus (top left). The graceful winged figure which was said to symbolise the Angel of Christian Charity, tops an elaborate bronze fountain. It was designed by Sir Alfred Gilbert as a memorial to the 7th Earl of Shaftesbury.

Kokoschka's choice

The Austrian-born artist and dramatist Oskar Kokoschka (1886–1980) became a British citizen in 1947. He had studied at the Vienna School of Applied Art and was a pupil of Gustav Klimt before moving to Berlin in 1907, where he worked on portraits and as an avant-garde illustrator produced some striking posters and lithographs. He was wounded during the First World War. In the early 20s he taught at Dresden Academy, but the vigorous and highly individual expressionist style that he developed eventually earned him the antagonism of the Nazis. After some extensive travelling he settled in Britain in 1937.

Jan	1	British railways nationalised		15	British leave Palestine; Egyptian troops enter
	4	Burma becomes an independent Republic		16	Chaim Weizmann named first President of Israel
	30	US aviator Orville Wright dies		26	Jan Smuts defeated in S African elections
	30	Mahatma Gandhi assassinated in India	Jun	3	Malan forms new Nationalist government in S Africa
Feb	4	Self-governing Dominion status for Ceylon		7	President Beneš resigns in Prague
	7	Omar Bradley succeeds Eisenhower as US Army Chief		19	Selective Service Bill in US for men aged 19 to 25 years
	25	Communists seize power in Czechoslovakia		24	Russians stop road and rail traffic to and from Berlin
	28	Last British troops leave India	Jul	13	14th Olympic Games open in London
Mar	7	Juan Perón wins election in Argentina		15	UN Security Council orders ceasefire in Palestine
	11	Offices of Jewish Agency in Jerusalem blown up	Aug	15	South Korea becomes a Republic
	15	US coal miners go on strike for better pensions	Sep	4	Queen Wilhelmina abdicates in Holland
	29	Chiang Kai-shek elected President of China		9	North Korea becomes a Republic
	31	US Congress passes 'Marshall Aid' bill	Nov	2	Harry S. Truman wins US Presidential election
Apr	1	Britain nationalises electricity industry		15	Canada: Mackenzie King retires; Louis St Laurent PM
	12	Roosevelt memorial unveiled Grosvenor Square, London	Dec	15	Indonesia: Dutch troops seize Jakarta
	16	Organisation for European Economic Cooperation set up			*The Arts*
	19	Americans test new type of atom bomb			Alan Paton's novel *Cry the Beloved Country*
May	5	Ben-Gurion chairs provisional Israeli govt in Tel Aviv			Vaughan Williams' *Sixth Symphony*
	14	Arab Legion invades 'Palestine' from Jordan			Jackson Pollock's *Composition No. 1*

The Berlin airlift

The Berlin airlift was not only concerned with bringing supplies in, it was also concerned with flying people out, thus reducing the number of mouths to be fed. Here, on one of Berlin's many lakes, a Sunderland flying boat is about to take a party of children to the safe and well-supplied haven of Hamburg.

When the Soviets began to slow down and then to halt all surface transport to West Berlin, the Western powers had a clear choice – to supply the city by air or to abandon it. They chose the first alternative but were immediately faced with enormous logistic problems. By means of careful planning, almost continuous work by pilots, loaders and air traffic controllers, and the use of flying boats as well as conventional aircraft, food and other essential supplies began and continued to flow into the beleaguered city, at one point reaching 7,000 tons a day.

The Berlin airlift lasted about a year; in May 1949 the Soviets allowed trains and lorries through again and the airlift finally ended in September. The airlift had a symbolic importance to the people of Berlin: their freedom would not be threatened again.

Formation of Israel

Thirty-one years after Britain's endorsement in the Balfour Declaration of the Jewish right to a national home in Palestine, and only hours before the expiry of the British Palestinian Mandate, the formation of the State of Israel was proclaimed by David Ben-Gurion on May 14th. Ben-Gurion himself became Prime Minister in the new State's provisional government, and Chaim Weizmann (above), for many years an embodiment of the Zionist cause, was named as its first President.

Zionism had drawn great strength from the genocidal persecution of the Jews under Nazism, but Israel's birth pangs were marked by terrorist outrages perpetrated by both Jews and Arabs. Events such as the terrorist group Irgun's bombing of the King David Hotel in Jersualem in 1946 and the Arab-organised explosion in the same city in 1948 (above left) created deep unrest, and the mass exodus of Arabs after Irgun's massacre in the village of Deir Yasin sowed the seeds of the Palestinian refugee problem.

The international reaction to the declaration was not slow in coming. President Truman immediately recognised the provisional government, as did Stalin. Egypt, Syria, Lebanon, Iraq and Jordan instantly mobilised their troops against the new State (left), but the Arab attack was uncoordinated and by the end of the year the Israeli Army, by now 100,000 strong, had achieved conclusive victory.

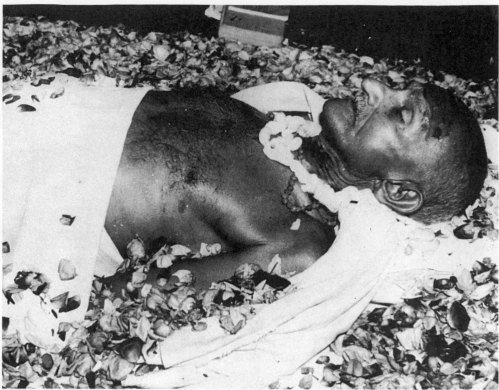

Gandhi assassinated by Hindu fanatic

On January 30th, Mahatma Gandhi, who had been seriously weakened by a fast for Hindu–Muslim friendship, was shot dead as he was helped towards a prayer meeting. His assassin, Nathuram Godse, was a Hindu member of an extremist sect who totally rejected Gandhi's message of goodwill, peace and love.

Gandhi had been heartbroken by the death and violence that had so badly stained the birth of India and Pakistan, and he would have been even more grieved if he could have foreseen the further

violence caused by his death. Riots erupted the moment the news reached Bombay, and the police had to fire on the rioters before order could be restored. In the event, the new leaders of India and Pakistan managed to contain the unrest. Under no circumstances did they want a return to the horrors of 1947.

Gandhi had won the affection and loyalty of gifted men and women, old and young, of Europeans of every religious persuasion and of Indians of almost every political line.

Above left: The man who, more than any other, had been responsible for persuading the British to leave India was a familiar figure at 10, Downing Street, and at other seats of political power.

Top right: The Mahatma's petal-strewn body lies in state shortly before his cremation.

Above right: The Governor-General is escorted by his bodyguard on his way to Gandhi's funeral.

1949

Jan	7	Marshall succeeded by Acheson as US Secretary of State
	10	US introduces 45 and 33.3 rmp records
	12	Britain hangs Margaret Allen, 1st woman for 12 years
	15	Chinese Communists capture Tientsin
	21	Chiang Kai-shek resigns as Nationalist President
	22	Chinese Communists capture Peking
	25	Ben-Gurion's Mapai Party wins Israeli elections
Feb	1	Clothes rationing ends in Britain
Mar	1	US: Joe Louis retires as world heavyweight
	4	Vyshinsky replaces Molotov as Soviet Foreign Minister
	31	Newfoundland becomes Canada's 10th province
Apr	4	NATO Treaty signed in Washington, DC
	18	Ireland becomes a Republic
May	5	Council of Europe established
	11	Siam renames itself Thailand
	12	Berlin blockade lifted by Soviets
	23	German Federal Republic formed with capital at Bonn
	26	Chinese Communists capture Shanghai
Jun	2	Transjordan changes name to Kingdom of Jordan
	16	Big Communist purge in Hungary
Jul	16	Chinese Nationalists begin retreat to Taiwan

Aug	5	US stops aid to Nationalist China
	25	US: 1st experimental colour TV transmission
Sep	15	Konrad Adenauer is new Premier of West Germany
	18	UK: Pound devalued by 30%
	27	Russia denounces pact with Yugoslavia
Oct	1	Mao forms Communist People's Republic of China
	7	German Democratic Republic established in E Germany
	14	US Communist leaders convicted for conspiracy
	16	Greek Civil War ends with defeat of rebels
Nov	7	1st meeting of Council of Europe with Spaak as Chairman
	15	Nathuram Godse hanged in India for murder of Gandhi
	26	India stays inside Commonwealth as Federal Republic
Dec	15	Full membership of Marshall Plan for West Germany
	26	Einstein's new general theory of relativity announced
	27	Holland recognises independence of Indonesia
	30	Sovereignty transferred to Vietnam by France

The Arts

George Orwell's novel *1984*

Arthur Miller's play *Death of a Salesman*

Jacob Epstein's sculpture *Lazarus*

Carol Reed's film *The Third Man*

The Berlin airlift goes on . . . and on

Snow held up the Berlin airlift for a while but groups of German workers were recruited and the runways were soon cleared so that aircraft could land and take off again. Here, a DC3 aircraft waits for the runway to be cleared (below left). Women workers (below right) helped clear rubble from the ruined roads in Berlin so that food convoys were able to get through from the airport to the central distribution points in the city.

The enormous damage done to Berlin by the Allied bombing raids during the war made transport between Gatow airport and central Berlin very difficult. The work done by these old women not only helped to solve the immediate problems of the airlift, but also represented the beginning of the rebuilding of Berlin itself.

The Communists take over in China

Things went badly for the Chinese Nationalists from the very beginning and by 1949 Mao Tse-tung was on a tidal wave of victory. By January the Communists were at the gates of Peking and the Nationalists were in full retreat. As Peking fell, Chiang Kai-shek resigned and called for an armistice and an immediate ceasefire. This was rejected out of hand and the Communists took the great city of Shanghai in May. By September it was all over and Mao was elected Chairman of the People's Republic of China. On October 1st, a triumphant Mao was able to proclaim China a Communist Republic with Chou En-lai its first Prime Minster.

Above: Mute evidence of the arbitrary violence that was part and parcel of the long agony of China's civil war.

Left: A Chinese Nationalist is held at gunpoint by a Communist soldier.

Israel tidies up

Nationhood and the apparent acquiescence of her Arab neighbours meant that Israel had time to make and mend her infrastructure, to repair war damage and begin to build much-needed houses, factories and public buildings. Here (above left), soldiers have checked that the building is safe for civilian workers to clear the debris and begin to rebuild.

In Jerusalem (above right), the area between the New City and the Arab Quarter had been particularly badly hit during the fighting. In the distance is the old wall surrounding the Old City, and along the wall is the Tower of David. Jerusalem was to remain divided until 1967 when the Israelis took the whole city in the Six-Day War.

The dockers are on strike again

Old-fashioned work processes were still the norm in British docks and trouble had been brewing for some time. The London dockers had a particularly tough reputation and on June 29th some of them came out on strike. They were quickly followed by others and within a few days work on half the ships in London Docks had stopped. The Labour Prime Minister, Clement Attlee,

immediately condemned the strikes but soon 13,000 London dockers were out. On July 22nd the strike ended as suddenly as it had begun. Here, after a rousing speech by one of their leaders, the dockers decide not to go back. Few could have imagined that within a generation the London Docks – and dockers – would disappear for ever.

The young Sinatra

Frank Sinatra (1915–   ), son of immigrant Italian parents, became a singing idol in the 1940s when he was nicknamed 'Swoonlight Sinatra'. One of the most successful of his early films was *On the Town* in 1949, the story of three sailors on a shore leave spree in New York.

Wealth and beauty

The gossip columnists had a field day when one of the world's richest men married one of the world's most beautiful women. Aly Khan, heir to the enormously wealthy Aga Khan, married Rita Hayworth, one of Hollywood's most dazzling stars. They are seen here at the races, hoping for a win from one of Aly Khan's horses.

Good news for children

After seven sour years, sweets and chocolates finally came off the British ration books and children could go into a sweetshop and buy as many of their favourite sweets as they wanted.

Above: Two youngsters from Hackney, London, have their first liberated taste of lollipops and chocolates.

World's biggest telescope

Fifty miles north-east of San Diego, California, the 200-inch Hale telescope at the Mount Palomar observatory enables us to see galaxies a billion light-years away. The instrument weighs 500 tons in total. Finally installed in 1948, it was still attracting large crowds of people the following year. The telescope is named for George Ellery Hale, the American astronomer.

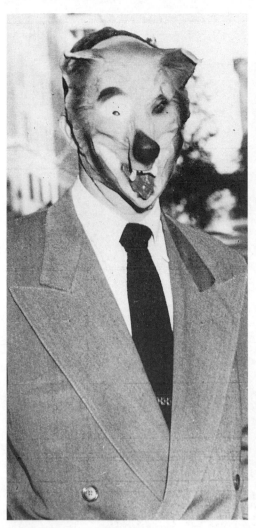

Don't be frightened!

Grotesque masks like these were popular on the cocktail party circuit. Here, a New York businessman shows off his latest acquisition outside the Rockefeller Center.

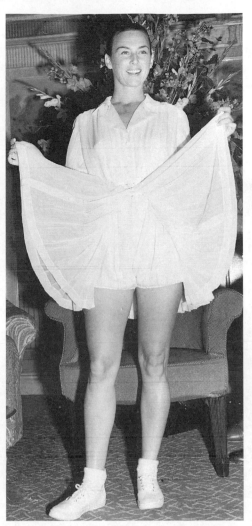

'Gorgeous Gussie'

The summer was brightened by the dazzling outfits of tennis star Gussie Moran, who arrived from America to play in the championships at Wimbledon.

Kicking Picasso's backside

The forthright words of Sir Alfred Munnings, President of the Royal Academy in London, caused a furore when he spoke out against modern art.

Comet's first flight

On July 27th, the De Havilland Comet, the world's first jet airliner, made its maiden flight from an English airfield with war hero and test pilot Group Captain John Cunningham at the controls. The Comet subsequently went into commercial service in 1952 but a series of crashes due to the previously unknown phenomenon of metal fatigue soon brought the airliner's brief career as a world leader to a close.

The strengthened and redesigned Comet went into scheduled service some years later but by then the Boeing 707 was in operation and had taken a commanding lead in the world's airliners, a lead that Boeing and a whole generation of airliners based on the 707 design were never to lose.

1950–1959

The 1950s

The Second World War was over, but despite the ever-present threat of the new atomic weapon, peace still seemed to elude the world. The 1950s were the decade of Korea and of the French war in Vietnam. They were the decade of Suez – that last flexing of British imperial muscles in the Middle East – and of the Hungarian uprising. The first stirrings of those winds of change of which the British Prime Minister Harold Macmillan was to speak so memorably in the 1960s were making themselves felt in Africa and Cyprus, and in the United States the reverberations of black consciousness gave new impetus to the civil rights movements of the deep South.

In the Soviet Union the death of Josef Stalin after years of unchallenged supremacy led to a political power struggle in the upper echelons of the Soviet hierarchy from which the mercurial Nikita Khrushchev emerged victorious. The process of de-Stalinisation began, but the cold war between East and West remained unthawed.

MacArthur and McCarthy

In 1947 President Harry S. Truman of the United States had pledged himself 'to support free peoples who are resisting attempted subjugation by armed minorities or by outside pressures'. For many in the United States and elsewhere the Korean War, which broke out with the invasion of South Korea by the Communist forces of the North in 1950, was the Truman Doctrine in action. For General Douglas MacArthur, commanding the US troops on the ground, however, it rapidly became a crusade against Communism itself. A serious rift developed between MacArthur, who favoured an all-out assault on China, and Truman, who saw the war as a limited action, designed to preserve the security of South Korea. In the end, as international tension mounted and the war threatened to develop into a major superpower confrontation, MacArthur was dismissed from his post.

The early 1950s were also the years of McCarthyism, an extraordinary witchhunt against Communists and Communist sympathisers in all walks of American life, led by Senator Joseph McCarthy of Wisconsin. Movie actors, writers and intellectuals, scientists, and even senior members of the armed forces, were summoned to appear before the Permanent Subcommittee on Investigations.

East and West

The emergence of a new leadership in the Soviet Union after the death of Stalin in 1953 produced changes both at home and in the international arena. However, the cold war continued to divide East and West, such episodes as the Burgess–Maclean–Philby espionage ring and the spying charges brought against the Rosenburgs bearing witness to the highly-charged atmosphere of uncertainty and distrust. The tensions that would lead, in the early years of the next decade, to the very brink of nuclear war pervaded the 1950s. At the same time the stakes were raised by the creation of a new generation of nuclear weapons, with America's first testing of the hydrogen bomb and the Soviet Union's development of its own nuclear capability. The arms race began in earnest, bringing in its wake the first popular campaigns for nuclear disarmament.

Colonial unrest

The independence movements which were to change the face of the less developed world in the 1960s were already challenging the assumptions of colonial rule in the 1950s. Kenya was racked with violence as the Mau Mau acted on their oath to drive the white man out of the country. In the Gold Coast Kwame Nkrumah became sub-Saharan Africa's first black prime minister and, by the end of the decade, head of the new republic of Ghana. There was serious unrest in the French colonies of Morocco and Tunisia as nationalist groups campaigned for independence. Most far-reaching of all in its effects, the situation in the French territory of Algeria erupted into violence, threatening to engulf mainland France itself and sweeping General Charles de Gaulle into power from the political wilderness of Colombey-les-Deux-Eglises. There was bloodshed too in Cyprus, where EOKA terrorists claimed many lives in support of their demands for freedom from British rule and for union with Greece. Whatever remained of British power on the international stage was dealt a severe blow by the Suez fiasco of 1956.

Civil rights in the US

Another movement which was to attain its maturity in the 1960s was born in America during the decade. A young Baptist minister and civil rights campaigner called Martin Luther King came to prominence during a black boycott of segregated bus services in Montgomery, Alabama. Demands for racial integration grew louder in the Southern states, finding their echo in the White House itself.

Science and technology

It was an exciting time in the scientific world. In Cambridge Watson and Crick unveiled their epoch-making discoveries about the structure of DNA and Sanger was awarded a Nobel Prize in Chemistry for his work on insulin. The horizons of medicine were opened up by the first human kidney transplant and the first shot of a business revolution was fired by IBM, who put on the market the first electronic computing machine. A new form of transport – the hovercraft – was put through its paces by the inventor Christopher Cockerell.

Pages 26–7: The State Coach returns to Buckingham Palace after the Coronation of Elizabeth II, 1953.

1950

The Arts

Ezra Pound's poems *Seventy Cantos*

Salvador Dali's painting *The Madonna of Port Lligat*

William Walton's *Violin Sonata*

Pablo Picasso's sculpture *The Goat*

Korean War

At the end of the Second World War Korea had been arbitrarily divided at the 38th parallel, with a Soviet-supported regime in the north and an American-supported regime in the south. Although they had originally wanted a united democratic republic, both sides remained bitterly opposed and as the USA and the Soviet Union removed their occupying forces, both declared themselves to be independent republics.

On June 25th, North Korea invaded South Korea, which was still unofficially under the auspices of the United Nations and strongly influenced by the USA. The UN called for an immediate withdrawal of North Korean forces. This call was ignored and the USA moved to support its client state of South Korea with General Douglas MacArthur as Commander-in-Chief of UN forces.

By now, North Korean forces had occupied most of the peninsula and the United Nations forces (nearly all American) were cooped up at Pusan in the south-east. The United Nations immediately initiated a powerful counter-attack aided by a bold amphibious landing at Inchon. By the end of September the North Koreans were back at the 38th parallel. Here, American Marines embark for Korea.

China joins in

General MacArthur did not stop when he reached the 38th parallel but drove on into North Korea with no objections from the United Nations. Within three weeks he had driven the North Korean forces almost back to the Manchurian border and had reached the River Yalu at several points. Here the North Koreans began their own counter-attack and soon began to drive the UN forces back south. Here too, some Chinese 'volunteers' were captured.

In November General MacArthur began another big push, this time to end the war once and for all. But at the end of the month, Chinese forces crossed the Yalu River in large numbers and had soon driven the UN forces back to the 38th parallel.

The Korean war had now polarised itself along East–West lines, with the two great ideologies which produced the Cold War facing each other. To the north were the Communist forces of China and Korea with large numbers of Soviet 'advisers'. To the south were the forces of the West, mainly American and South Korean, but with contingents from Britain and the Commonwealth and other Western States.

Top left: Mud-bespattered American troops retreat from Yongsan.

Centre left: South Korean refugees return to Inchon after the city had been recaptured by UN forces.

Bottom left: UN soldiers use metal detectors to check that refugees are not carrying concealed arms.

Below: Victims of war, this homeless brother and sister warm themselves at a small fire.

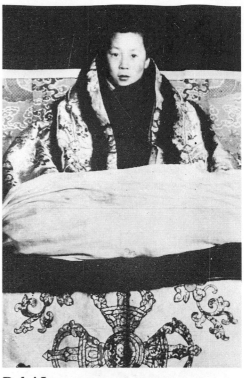

Chinese inside Tibet

On October 24th, China announced the movement of Peking forces into Tibet, penetrating as far as Lhasa, the Tibetan Holy City. On November 13th, Tibet appealed to the United Nations for aid against Chinese aggression.

Dalai Lama

His Holiness the 14th Dalai Lama, ruler of Tibet until the Chinese Communist occupation.

The Kon-Tiki Expedition

Thor Heyerdahl, the Norwegian anthropologist who sailed from Peru to Tahiti on a balsa-wood raft in 1947, published his account of the journey for the first time in English in his book *The Kon-Tiki Expedition*. Together with five men and a parrot, he made the voyage to prove that Polynesia could have been settled by South American Indians. The book was a spectacular best-seller.

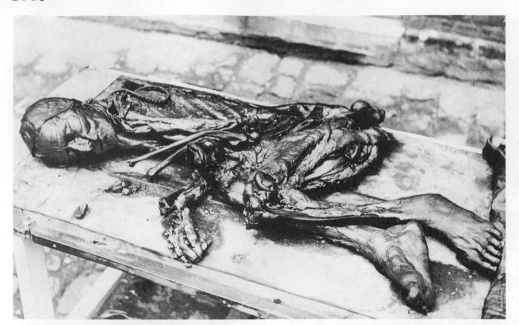

Tollund Man

In one of the most remarkable archaeological finds of recent years, the 2,000-year-old body of a man was discovered in a peat bog in Denmark. The corpse was excavated by Professor Glob from the Tollund Mose, a bog near Aarhus in Jutland. It was that of a man, wearing only a leather belt and skull-cap, who had apparently been killed by hanging or garrotting with a braided leather rope, remains of which were found around his neck, perhaps as part of a sacrificial ritual. The body was extraordinarily well preserved by the peat. Scientists were able to establish that he had had his last meal some 12 to 24 hours before he died, had eaten no meat for three days, and had lived on a thin gruel of grain and wild plant seeds. He had three days' growth of stubble on his chin.

George Orwell

The English writer George Orwell (1903–1950) died on January 21st after a long struggle with tuberculosis. Born Eric Arthur Blair in Bengal, Orwell was educated at Eton and served for some years as a policeman in Burma. He began to write in earnest after spending time as a vagrant in France and England, an experience recorded in *Down and Out in Paris and London*, published in 1933. His unorthodox socialist beliefs dictated the shape of much of his later work, including *The Road to Wigan Pier* (1937), *Homage to Catalonia* (1938), which was written after he was wounded in the Spanish Civil War, and his last novel *Nineteen Eighty-Four*, a bleak anti-Utopian view of a totalitarian future. Perhaps his most popular work was the allegorical novel *Animal Farm* (1945), which was later to be made into an animated film (left).

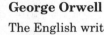

Christian Dior

The influential French fashion designer Christian Dior (1905–1957) gave his first display in London at the Savoy Hotel on April 25th (left). Dior, 45, emerged from years of obscurity to become an overnight household name in 1947 when he presented Paris with his first collection, the revolutionary 'Corolle' line. Christened the 'New Look' by the press, the fashions were a sensational success. Dior's hallmark was a return to the lines of the Edwardian age, with gathered skirts, low necklines and long flowing dresses. After the sparse fashions of the War years, his extravagant use of fabrics – one of his lines containing some 50 yards of material – was seen as representing a return to a more glamorous ideal. He was awarded the Nieman-Marcus Award in 1947.

1951

The Chinese advance in Korea

Once more the seesaw war in Korea went against the United Nations forces. In January the Chinese mounted a major offensive and the UN–American forces were again forced to retreat. The Communists soon broke through and four days after the offensive they had captured Seoul, the capital of South Korea.

General MacArthur was growing impatient with the progress of the war but President Truman was aware of the symbolic importance of this East–West conflict and made it clear that the Americans would fight on. And not everything was going according to plan for the Chinese: their lines of communication were stretched and the American Air Force was mounting massive bombing attacks. The Chinese were being pushed back towards the 38th parallel and the UN forces once more prepared to fight for Seoul.

Below: American Marines near the 38th parallel.

Korean War draws to a close

In January, the United Nations forces were able to stem the joint Chinese North Korean Army sweeping down from the north and hold them near the 38th parallel. The uneasy stalemate was abruptly broken when General Douglas MacArthur, the UN Commander in Chief, threatened to invade China. As he was already on record as having wanted to use the atom bomb against his opponent, this threat gave the war an alarming new dimension. It also infuriated President Truman who wanted to contain the conflict and had been increasingly annoyed by MacArthur's political statements. He sacked MacArthur in April. This caused an enormous outcry in America but at least focused the minds of both sides on the dangers of the situation. Soon they both began to look for ways to end the war.

Left: Korean refugees make their weary way from yet another battleground.

Below: General MacArthur inspects North Korean prisoners of war in their stockade.

The Festival of Britain

The post-war gloom in Britain was temporarily but effectively
lifted for a few months by the new Festival of Britain on the
South Bank of the Thames. It was opened by the King and Queen
at the beginning of May and was an immediate success not only
with Londoners, who flocked to it in their thousands, but with
people from all over the country and, indeed, all over the world.

The Festival's architectural style was very influential and
changed public tastes permanently. 'Skylon' was the name
suggested by poet Margaret Sheppard Fidler for the vertical
feature of the South Bank. Symbolising the spirit of new hope it
was illuminated from within at night and appeared to hang in the
sky with no visible means of support.

Trouble at Suez

In a speech the previous year, King Farouk had ordered the British to leave Egypt. The British ignored this but made a pretence of placating him. They said they were willing to leave. However they omitted to make any firm promises. This prevarication sparked off anti-British rioting and, in September, led to Egypt's decision to rescind the 1936 Anglo-Egyptian Alliance.

Britain's response was swift. At dawn on October 19th, British troops occupied the key points on the Suez Canal and abruptly stopped the peace talks. Britain also took the wise precaution of removing all civilians from the Canal Zone and in November 2,000 women and children who had been threatened by the continuous riots were evacuated.

Left: British officers and men interrogate Egyptian workers while searching for arms in the troubled Canal Zone.

Below: When Egyptian workers were threatened by the police, camels were abandoned, like this one seen outside a deserted local 'shopping parade'.

Don't cry for me

With her husband General Juan Perón (1895–1974) certain to win the presidency of Argentina, Eva Perón (1919–1952), at the height of her popularity, promised to stand as Vice-President. She was to die within the year of ovarian cancer. Eva, the one-time film and radio actress, had become a powerful though unofficial political leader. She organised women workers, secured the vote for women, pushed for government spending on welfare, and introduced compulsory religious education in schools.

Testing the H-bomb

A further series of atom bomb tests took place on Eniwetok Atoll in the Pacific Marshall islands. The H-bomb being developed by the Americans would be triggered by an atom bomb.

A familiar sign

Winston Churchill did not forget his famous wartime 'V' sign as he campaigned for the Conservative Party in the October election. He was to win by a very narrow margin.

Guy Burgess

Homosexual, drunkard, British Foreign Office favourite and Soviet spy Guy Burgess (1910–1963) caused a sensation when he defected to Moscow.

Donald MacLean

Donald MacLean (1913–1983) was linked with Burgess – he was less flamboyant and more diffident but another British traitor and spy nonetheless.

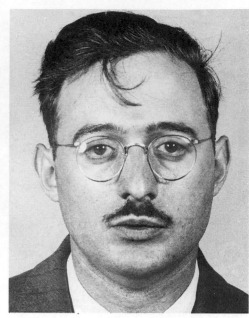

The Rosenbergs

Julius Rosenberg (1918–1953) and his wife Ethel (1915–1953) were condemned to the electric chair on April 5th for passing secrets to the Soviet Union.

Margaret Hilda Roberts

This unusual picture of the future British Prime Minister Margaret Thatcher (1925–   ) was taken when she was the youngest Conservative candidate at the 1951 election. After an uncharacteristically brief political argument she accompanied four voters on the piano in a sing-song.

The Shah of Iran marries

The Shah married the beautiful Princess Soraya.

The Cruel Sea

This screen adaptation of the famous novel by Nicholas Montsarrat (1910–1981) was among the most popular films of the year. It starred Jack Hawkins as the Captain of the *Compass Rose*, here seen sinking after a torpedo attack in one of the most dramatic scenes of the film.

1952

One of the last pictures taken of George VI.

Death of a King

In September 1951, surgeons operating at Buckingham Palace removed one of the King's lungs. He was, they said, 'as satisfactory as could be expected'. These bland words were meant to reassure people and they succeeded. But to most doctors they carried a much more ominous warning. The King had cancer. Like so many of his generation he had been a heavy cigarette smoker all his life and the connection between this and lung cancer was only just beginning to be suspected.

On February 6th, a brief bulletin on the railings of Buckingham Palace announced that the King had died peacefully in his sleep. Britain now had a new Queen.

George VI had been a good and conscientious ruler. He had accepted his fate with a good grace when his elder brother Edward VIII abandoned his throne in 1936 for the love of Wallis Simpson, an American divorcee. He had performed all his public functions admirably, and had been ably supported by a loving wife who had grown with him in popularity and public esteem.

Shortly after his reign began, he found himself monarch of a nation at war and he threw himself into an even more arduous round of public duties. When it was suggested that he and his family should live in Canada for the duration of the war, he turned down the suggestion contemptuously, preferring to share the dangers of London with his people. His house was hit and badly damaged just like theirs. His family's rations were the same as theirs and he and his family scrupulously observed all the rules and regulations imposed by a wartime government, sharing all the privations and hardships that were visited on his subjects.

Long live the Queen

The young Princess Elizabeth and her husband the Duke of Edinburgh were on a tour of the Commonwealth, including Australia, when her father died. They had to cut their tour short immediately and return to Britain. She was 25 and had inherited one of the most demanding jobs in the world.

Left: Princess Elizabeth and Prince Philip are seen off on their Commonwealth tour by King George and Queen Elizabeth.

Right: The new Queen Elizabeth returns to be greeted by the Prime Minister, Winston Churchill, and Leader of the Opposition, Clement Attlee.

Below: The funeral procession of King George VI on its way to Windsor.

Mau Mau

The struggle for freedom in British colonial Africa took many forms but in most cases the transition was peaceful. Only in Kenya did a particular freedom movement – Mau Mau – use violence, killing white settlers. The British used counter-violence and concentration camps.

Top: The British even used African magic against the freedom movements. Here, a witch doctor curses Mau Mau.
Above: Suspected Mau Mau terrorists are held in a Kenyan concentration camp.

Ending the Korean War

Although peace was very much in the offing, the Korean War went on, with each side taking advantage if a favourable situation arose. Some savage air and ground battles were fought out in Korea while world statesmen attempted to find a satisfactory solution. The end finally came in the following year, a year which also saw the beginning of conflict in Vietnam.

Top: New South Korean troops line up before embarking on a tank landing craft.
Above: American Marines bring back three prisoners of war in a jeep.

Harrow rail disaster

A horrifying British train disaster took place on October 8th at Harrow just outside London when two trains crashed and a third, travelling at high speed, hit the wreckage seconds later (above). An early-morning commuter train just leaving Harrow station was struck on the rear by an express from Scotland which had somehow got on the wrong line. An express from Euston, London, then ploughed into the other two trains and brought an overhead bridge down. A total of 112 people died, over 200 were injured and it took days to clear the tracks.

'Ike' rules OK!

Dwight Eisenhower won a resounding victory in the American presidential election, completely wiping out his Democrat opponent, Adlai Stevenson. General Eisenhower, who until a few months earlier was Supreme Commander of the Allied Forces in Europe, won the largest ever popular vote of more than 33 million. The Republican win brought California's senator Richard Nixon into the office of Vice-President.

1953

The Queen is crowned

In a ceremony seen for the first time by millions of her subjects on television, Queen Elizabeth II was crowned in Westminster Abbey by the Archbishop of Canterbury on June 2nd. It was a ritual going back centuries, with all the pomp and splendour of the greatest royal occasions. The Duke of Edinburgh was at her side and was the first of her family to pay her homage.

All the ritual implements of majesty were to be seen: the orb, the sceptre, the anointing oil and the great Crown of St Edward.

Perfectly rehearsed, the new Queen played her central role with great natural dignity, making the necessary responses during the ceremony in a cool, clear voice.

After the ceremony and the celebratory trumpet music written by Sir Arthur Bliss, Master of the Queen's Musick, she made her way to Buckingham Palace in a gold coach accompanied by the cheers of thousands of people – most of whom had waited up all night to see her.

The Coronation

At the climax of the ceremony the Archbishop of Canterbury lifts the Crown of St Edward high in the air before lowering it onto the head of 'Your undoubted Queen'. Later, a kneeling subject pays homage to the new Queen (below).

Outside, despite the cold wet weather, two million people waited. At least 30,000 spectators had camped overnight in the Mall. Tickets for seats in the stands changed hands on the black market for £40–£50, while a balcony in a choice site overlooking the route cost as much as £3,500.

Meanwhile history was also in the making – round two and a half million television sets in living rooms up and down Britain where half the nation gathered to watch the day's events. From then on, sales soared. Mass television had arrived.

Korea – the final flicker

The Korean War did not end with a bang or a final heroic gesture but fizzled out when both sides got tired of the sporadic, one-off operations which took place over the early months of the year.

Above: American 'Flying Boxcars' drop supplies to embattled US Marines.

Top right: Drums of aviation fuel wait in readiness for the first Marine Air Wing.

Centre right: Korean prisoners await the end of the war behind barbed wire.

Right: An American howitzer blasts away in the final weeks of the war.

A new war in the Far East

The guns of the Korean War were scarcely silent when the rumbles of a new conflict began. The North Vietnamese, under their charismatic leader Ho Chi Minh, were making life difficult for the French with a series of brilliant guerrilla forays. But the tough French legionnaires and paratroopers were accustomed to winning pitched battles where firepower and weapon superiority could be brought to bear. The shadowy hit-and-run tactics adopted by their opponents puzzled and irritated them.

Top: French paratroopers march to battle in enemy territory.
Left: Villagers wait behind their bamboo defences.
Above: French paratroopers watch their companions arrive for the fatal battle of Dien Bien Phu.

Revolt in East Berlin

The East German authorities and their Soviet superiors got a nasty shock in June when the workers of East Berlin rose in a spontaneous protest against the continuing Soviet presence in the city. After two days it became apparent that the uprising had got out of hand and that the East German authorities could not cope with it by themselves. More powerful and persuasive measures were needed. These were provided by Soviet tanks. The numbers killed were never disclosed but many hundreds were badly injured.

Top: Soviet tanks move into East Berlin to help put down the workers' riots.
Above: East Berliners publicly burn the Soviet flag.

Everest conquered

Everest, at 29,028 feet the world's highest mountain, was finally scaled by Sir Edmund Hillary (1919–   ) of New Zealand and Sherpa Tenzing Norgay (1914–1986) of Nepal on May 29th. The mountain, which the Tibetans call Chuomo-Lungma (Mother Goddess of the World), had defeated nine previous attempts, including the ill-fated Mallory–Irvine expedition of 1924. Working with the very latest equipment, including portable radio and closed-circuit oxygen systems, Sir John Hunt's expedition, sponsored jointly by the Royal Geographical Society and the Joint Himalayan Committee of the Alpine Club, approached the mountain from the south-west and established eight camps on the ascent. Hillary and Tenzing left the Union Jack, the Nepalese flag and the flag of the United Nations on the summit (above).

Stalin dies

Joseph Stalin dead cast about as heavy a pall of fear over his people as Stalin alive. This photograph (left) shows part of a six-mile queue of people who had come to pay their last respects to the tyrant's corpse, almost as if they were frightened he would notice if they did not. It took the Soviets many months to get used to the idea that Stalin, instigator of the Great Purge (1936–1938), had finally and irrevocably gone from their lives.

Comet crash

The revolutionary Comet jet airliners had a most encouraging debut and looked set to change the face of air transport when, after four months' scheduled service, they began to fall out of the sky. After three unexplained crashes, the Comet had to be grounded while the jets underwent a complex series of tests. The cause of the trouble was found to be the previously unknown phenomenon metal fatigue. This could easily be rectified but by then it was too late, as American rivals to the Comet were coming into commercial service. The strengthened Comets were used by BOAC with some success but the world lead established by the first jet airliner could never be regained.

Left: Indian workers examine the wreckage of a Comet that crashed outside Calcutta.

Colonel Nasser

During the year it became apparent that General Neguib was only the puppet ruler of Egypt and that the real power was held by Colonel Gamal Nasser (1918–1970).

Kennedy marries Bouvier

John Fitzgerald Kennedy (1917–1963) married the beautiful society photographer Jacqueline Lee Bouvier on September 12th. He had been elected Senator for Massachusetts the previous year.

Joseph R. McCarthy

Senator Joseph R. McCarthy (1909–1957) was at the height of his anti-Communist witch-hunt. He even accused ex-President Truman. Next year would see McCarthy's inevitable downfall.

1954

Jan	11	British Comet jet airliner falls into Mediterranean	31	Yugoslav President Tito on state visit to Greece
	24	New coalition in Israel formed by Moshe Sharett	31	State of emergency in Bugandan province of Uganda
Feb	25	Nasser takes temporary control in Egypt	Jun 18	Pierre Mendès-France becomes French Premier
Mar	1	Organization of American States holds conference	Jul 3	End of all rationing in Britain
	8	US and Japan sign mutual defence pact	15	Maiden flight of Boeing 707
	12	Kenya: British arrest 700 Mau-Mau activists	17	Theodor Heuss is new President of West Germany
	22	US H-bomb irradiates Japanese fisherman	Sep 9	Algerian earthquake kills 1,500
	23	Israel pulls out of UN Armistice Commission	15	All China People's Congress held in Peking
	31	USSR offers to join NATO	Oct 8	Hanoi taken by Communist troops
Apr	18	Nasser takes full control in Egypt	Nov 3	Outbreak of terrorism in Algiers
	27	Georgi Malenkov elected Premier in USSR	5	Burma and Japan sign peace treaty
	29	R. Oppenheimer, father of A-bomb, is 'security risk'	17	Nasser becomes official Head of State in Egypt
May	6	Roger Bannister runs mile under 4 minutes	Dec 1	US signs pact with Nationalist China
	7	Communists capture Dien Bien Phu in Vietnam	2	US Senate censures Senator McCarthy
	8	France proposes Vietnam truce	23	20,000 French troops sent to Algeria
	13	President Eisenhower signs St Lawrence Seaway Bill		*The Arts*
	15	Queen Elizabeth and Philip start Commonwealth tour		William Golding's novel *Lord of the Flies*
	17	US Supreme Court outlaws racial segregation in schools		Elia Kazan's film *On the Waterfront*
	19	US composer Charles Ives dies		J. R. R. Tolkien's fantasy *The Lord of the Rings*

Indo-China war continues

With the beginning of 1954 the French war in Indo-China entered its seventh year. It was to mark the final climax of a long and bitter conflict between the French and Vietnamese forces under General Navarre and the Viet Minh guerrillas under their commander General Vo Nguyen Giap, waged in a landscape that was to become all too familiar to television viewers throughout the world in the 1960s and 1970s. As the French dug themselves into their stronghold at Dien Bien Phu, there was intense diplomatic activity by the international powers. By the time the Geneva conference on Indo-China and Korea began in April, the French garrison was already under heavy siege.

End of the Indo-China war

The French garrison of Dien Bien Phu, a cornerstone of her Indo-Chinese defences, became the focus of the fiercest fighting of the entire war during the early months of the year. Despite some defensive successes, such as the capture of a number of Viet Minh prisoners (far left and above), the stronghold fell to the besieging Communist forces of General Giap on May 7th. The defeat was a bitter blow to French morale and proved to be the final nail in the coffin of her Indo-Chinese interests.

In June the French government fell and in July the new Prime Minister, Pierre Mendès-France (1907–1982), reached a peace agreement under which the French withdrew their forces from Indo-China and Vietnam was partitioned along the 17th parallel. As the Communist regime of Ho Chi Minh assumed control of North Vietnam, thousands of refugees fled from their villages and made for the south (left).

H-bomb tested

The nuclear arms race entered a new and more terrifying phase on March 1st with the testing of America's first true hydrogen bomb on Bikini Atoll in the Pacific. Both the Soviet Union and the United States had been working on thermonuclear devices for some years and the US Atomic Energy Commission had already tested precursors of the new device in the Pacific in 1952 and in the Nevada desert (above, insert) in 1953. However, whereas 'Mike', the 1952 bomb, used liquid deuterium, the new H-bomb used the solid lithium deuteride, making it much more practicable as a military weapon. The bomb was some 500 times more powerful than the one which destroyed Hiroshima in 1945. Above: Weather balloons used during nuclear tests.

Algeria

November saw the most serious outbreak of anti-French violence in Algeria since the end of the Second World War. Many people were killed in terrorist attacks by the nationalist Movement for the Triumph of Democratic Liberties (MTLD) before the security forces were able to restore order in the Algiers and Oran areas. There were hundreds of arrests and arms seizures (above).

The unrest followed one of the most powerful earthquakes of the century, which had devastated the Algerian city of Orléansville on September 9th. Some 1,500 people died and thousands had been left homeless (top and left).

Crowds mob Nasser

Wildly enthusiastic crowds climb up to the Presidency's balcony to embrace Prime Minister Nasser as he broadcasts to the nation. In his first major success since taking over from Naguib, Nasser managed to negotiate for the withdrawal of British troops from the Suez Canal Zone. After hard bargaining, a draft agreement was signed in July for the phased evacuation by the British over a period of 20 months. However, British 'civilian contractors' were to keep a base in the zone in case of any danger to Middle East security.

The British government honoured its agreement and evacuation was completed. But in the eyes of purist Egyptian nationalists, 'unconditional evacuation' was the only acceptable solution and Nasser and his colleagues were soon to be under attack for selling out to the British. The extremist Muslim Brotherhood made an unsuccessful assassination attempt on Nasser in October which led to the outlawing of the organization and the execution of six of its leaders.

Billy Graham

On May 22nd a mass meeting at Wembley stadium in London marked the climax of a three-month mission to the UK by the American evangelist Billy Graham (1918–   ). Born in North Carolina, he was ordained as a Southern Baptist minister, and launched a worldwide evangelical campaign. He became very influential around the world, presenting a persuasive and enthusiastic image of Christianity.

Highly charismatic in his delivery, Graham made numerous television appearances and toured widely. He wrote a number of books, including *Peace with God* (1953) and *The Seven Deadly Sins* (1955). His 1954 visit to the UK was a resounding success, with a reported attendance of some 1,300,000 and over 28,000 conversions or 'decisions for Christ', to use Graham's expression.

Bill Haley

American musician Bill Haley (1927–1981) and his Comets brought the new rock beat to country music – an exciting combination which ensured that the group achieved immense popularity. They scored some of the earliest and most resounding hits of the rock 'n' roll years – *Shake, Rattle and Roll* (1954) was followed by *Rock Around the Clock* (1955) and *See You Later, Alligator* (1956). The group continued playing and touring into the 1970s, and had considerable influence on the development of rock music.

The Flying Bedstead

August 3rd saw the first test flight at Hucknall in Nottinghamshire of the Rolls-Royce Thrust Measuring Rig (TMR) jet-lift vehicle, popularly known as the 'Flying Bedstead'. The ungainly-looking aircraft (left), more closely resembling a Heath Robinson contraption than a piece of advanced military hardware, was the first to be capable of vertical take-off from a horizontal position and created something of a sensation when pictures were released. The plane was powered by two Rolls-Royce engines set horizontally in opposition on each side of the frame and ducted so that they discharged vertically downwards. The pilot sat on a platform above the engines and controlled its movements by means of compressed air jets.

Roger Bannister

Roger Bannister (1929–   ), a medical student, a former President of Oxford University Athletics Club and the British one-mile record holder, became the first man in athletics history to run the mile in under four minutes – in three minutes 59.4 seconds to be precise. This remarkable achievement took place on May 6th 1954 during an athletics match at Oxford between the Amateur Athletics Association and the University of Oxford.

Churchill's 80th birthday

On November 30th, Sir Winston was presented with a Birthday Book of signatures and his portrait, painted by Graham Sutherland, RA. The painting was commissioned by both Houses of Parliament. Unfortunately Lady Churchill disliked the painting intensely and it was later destroyed.

Errol Flynn

The one-time Hollywood heart-throb Errol Flynn filmed *Lilacs in the Spring* with actress Anna Neagle (1908–1986).

1955

Jan	18	Government in Kenya offers terms to Mau Mau		23	Donald Campbell breaks water speed record at 202 mph
	25	USSR officially ends war with Germany		24	Bulganin and Khrushchev visit East Germany
Feb	5	Mendès-France resigns as French Premier	Aug	1	Warsaw hosts Communist Youth Congress
	8	Malenkov resigns; Bulganin becomes Soviet Premier		11	Muslim right-wing government takes over in Indonesia
	24	Turkey and Iraq sign Baghdad pact		12	German writer Thomas Mann dies
Mar	2	Egypt and Syria sign defence pact		13	UK: IRA raids training centre in Berkshire
	11	Germany, Italy and France ratify European pact		15	Indians attempt to enter Goa
	27	Pakistan declares state of emergency		20	Riots in Morocco
	28	Israel raids Gaza Strip in reprisal attack	Sep	6	Anti-Greek riots in Istanbul and Izmir
	31	Chinese Communist Party purged		19	Juan Perón resigns and leaves Argentina
Apr	5	Churchill resigns as PM; replaced by Eden		24	US President Eisenhower has minor heart attack
	18	Albert Einstein dies		25	Field Marshal Harding appointed Governor of Cyprus
May	5	Official occupation ends in West Germany		30	Young American actor James Dean killed in car crash
	6	Britain goes to International Court over Falklands	Oct	23	S Vietnam becomes a Republic under Diem
	8	Hiroshima victims arrive in US for plastic surgery		30	Abdication of Sultan of Morocco
	9	West Germany joins NATO	Nov	2	Ben-Gurion forms government in Israel
	14	Warsaw Pact signed		26	State of emergency in Cyprus
	26	Khrushchev and Bulganin visit Yugoslavia			*The Arts*
Jun	11	Le Mans car race crash kills 70			Vladimir Nabokov's novel *Lolita*
	15	US and Britain sign agreement on atomic energy			Tennessee William's play *Cat on a Hot Tin Roof*
Jul	4	British dock strike ends after a month			Nicholas Ray's film *Rebel Without a Cause*
	4	Britain will return Simonstown base to South Africa			Bill Haley's pop song 'Rock Around the Clock'
	18	Disneyland opens in Los Angeles			Michael Tippett's opera *The Midsummer Marriage*

Big Four Summit

The Geneva Summit brought together, in October, the foreign ministers of the world's four most powerful nations: the United States, England, France and the Soviet Union. They were represented by John Foster Dulles, Harold Macmillan, Antoine Pinay and Vyacheslav Molotov. The meeting opened with the three Western ministers tabling proposals for the reunification of Germany and for protecting the Soviet bloc from German aggression. The talks quickly reached deadlock however, when Molotov managed to postpone the publication of the suggestions until he could put forward the Soviet view. He ruled out German reunification, and called for the dissolution of NATO and the Warsaw Pact. Harold Macmillan said that he failed to see why in ensuring Russia's security the West had to abandon its own defences. John Foster Dulles tried to convince Molotov to recognise the significance of the US offer to underwrite European non-aggression treaties.

Riots in Cyprus

Serious rioting broke out in Nicosia on the Mediterranean island of Cyprus when the traditional parades to celebrate Oxi Day (the day when Greece entered the Second World War) were banned by the newly appointed British Governor Sir John Harding. Cyprus police were assisted by British troops in bringing the situation under control, and there were many casualties on both sides (left).

The unrest marked another stage in the deepening crisis in Cyprus. Intercommunal fighting between the majority Greek population and the Turkish minority worsened when Prime Minister Anthony Eden attempted to strengthen the British position on the island. The situation was fuelled by the terrorism of the Greek Cypriot insurrectionary movement EOKA (above) and the increasingly draconian counter-insurgency methods employed by the authorities. During 1955 EOKA, led by Colonel Grivas, stepped up its campaign of bombings, murder and civil disobedience in the cause of *enosis* or union with Greece, while Harding pursued negotiations with the leader of the Greek Cypriot community, Archbishop Makarios.

Le Mans disaster

On June 11th 1955 a very serious accident took place on the famous track at Le Mans in France during the 24-hour race. A Mercedes car crashed into the crowd of spectators, killing 70 people and injuring more than 100. This disaster caused the sport of motor racing to be curtailed for some time afterwards.

Grandma Moses

Anna Mary 'Grandma' Moses (1860–1961) emerged late in life as one of America's best-known and most prolific primitive painters. Her vivid portrayals of the farm life she knew so well such as this one, *McDonell Farm*, became very popular.

Princess Margaret

Princess Margaret announced that she had decided not to marry Group-Captain Peter Townsend, a divorcee.

London smog

Air pollution became a serious cause for concern in the early 1950s. After an exceptionally severe incidence of London smog a committee was set up under Hugh Beaver in July 1953 to investigate the problem. The Beaver Committee came up with a Clean Air Scheme, recommending that emission of industrial smoke should become an offence, that industries themselves should be responsible for removing it, and that smokeless fuel should be used in the home. On February 4th 1955, Duncan Sandys, Minister of Housing and Local Government, proposed a comprehensive Bill for the Prevention of Air Pollution, along the lines of the Beaver Report.

Disneyland

The great Walt Disney (1901–1966) founded Disneyland as a base for his television productions in 1954. Among the intensely popular television shows made there were *The Mickey Mouse Club*, *Zorro*, *Walt Disney Presents* and *Walt Disney's Wonderful World of Color*.

On July 15th 1955, Disneyland, which was based in Anaheim (California), opened to the public as the world's most elaborate amusement park. There were four main areas: Adventureland, Frontierland, Fantasyland and Tomorrowland. Equally popular with adults and children, it attracted millions of visitors each year, and in 1967 (a year after Disney's death) work began on an East Coast counterpart – Walt Disney World, at Orlando, Florida.

Albert Einstein

Albert Einstein (1879–1955), who formulated the theory of relativity, died on April 18th.

Kim Philby

British intelligence officer and diplomat, Kim Philby (1912–1988) spied for, and later defected to, the Soviet Union.

The bebop bird

Black jazz saxophonist Charlie 'Bird' Parker (1920–1955) was acknowledged as the king of bebop.

1956

Jan	1	Sudan becomes an independent Republic		31	Britain and France attack targets in Egypt
	3	USSR gives technical aid to China		31	RAF bombs Suez
Feb	11	Maltese referendum favours integration with Britain	Nov	4	Soviet troops enter Budapest
	29	Pakistan declared an Islamic Republic		6	US: Eisenhower wins 2nd term in Presidential election
Mar	9	Britain deports Archbishop Makarios to Seychelles		8	United Nations demand Soviet troops out of Hungary
	18	Khrushchev tells 20th Party Congress of Stalin's crimes		15	United Nations emergency forces arrive in Egypt
Apr	18	Bulganin and Khrushchev visit Britain		17	Kashmir votes to join India
May	14	USSR complains about overflying US aircraft		22	16th Olympic Games open in Melbourne
Jun	1	Shepilov succeeds Molotov as Soviet Foreign Minister	Dec	5	Paul Spaak appointed Secretary-General of NATO
	24	Nasser elected President of Egypt		18	Japan joins United Nations
	28	Workers' riot in Poznań, Poland, is brutally crushed		22	Last French and British troops leave Port Said
Jul	26	Egypt seizes Suez Canal		27	UN salvage fleet begins to clear Suez Canal
Aug	11	US artist Jackson Pollock dies		31	President Sukarno proclaims state of siege in Sumatra
	14	German playwright Bertolt Brecht dies			*The Arts*
Sep	10	Nasser rejects US proposals for Suez Canal			Eugene O'Neill's play *Long Day's Journey into Night*
	23	Britain and France go to Security Council about Suez			John Osborne's play *Look Back in Anger*
Oct	8	Israel leaves joint Israel-Jordan Armistice Commission			Barbara Hepworth's sculpture *Orpheus*
	23	Rioting breaks out in Hungary			Ingmar Bergman's film *Seventh Seal*

The Suez War

On July 26th, the Egyptian President Colonel Nasser responded to the Anglo-American withdrawal of funding for his Aswan Dam project by seizing all revenues from the Suez Canal, the West's commercial lifeline to the Middle East. The move effectively nationalised the Anglo-French Universal Maritime Suez Canal and closed it altogether to shipping going to or from Israel.

Britain's Prime Minister Sir Anthony Eden favoured a military response but the US was less enthusiastic and the crisis was referred to the United Nations. In October, however, talks took place in Paris between Eden and the French Premier Guy Mollet and were quickly followed by the launching of an Israeli attack against Egypt. Amid rumours of collusion with Israel, British and French naval forces were despatched to Suez in 'Operation Musketeer' (below). Despite the UN's attempt to impose a ceasefire, the Anglo-French attack, supported by bombers based in Cyprus, was launched on November 5th. However it was called off almost immediately when the Americans failed to support it.

'Operation Musketeer'

Top left: Sir Anthony Eden caricatured in the British press as a sheep in wolf's clothing. Many felt that the cartoonist was proved right by the outcome of the crisis.

Top right: A building burning as British troops take up their positions in Port Said.

Above left: Feelings ran high over the crisis in Britain, with street demonstrations and arrests. Divisions of opinion among the general public were reflected in Eden's own Cabinet.

Above right: Egyptian blockships at the mouth of the Suez Canal at Port Said. British naval salvage ships began clearing the obstructions as soon as the invasion was launched.

Left: Arab children searching through the rubble of buildings left by the British bombing raids on Port Said.

The Hungarian Rising

Nowhere did the policy of de-Stalinisation proclaimed by Khrushchev at the Party Congress in Moscow in 1956 have more dramatic effects than in the troubled Communist State of Hungary. In pursuing the 'Malenkov new course' of economic decentralisation and de-collectivisation, the Hungarian Communist Party leadership had released popular forces for change which were to prove beyond its control.

In October the people of the capital, Budapest, rose against the Soviet regime which had replaced the reforming Imre Nagy as Premier. Barricades appeared in the streets, the statue of Stalin was torn down in the city centre (above) and the revolution seemed to involve all sections of society, including women (near left), industrial workers, and intellectuals of the influential Petöfi circle (far left). The recall of Nagy only fanned the flames and in November Soviet tanks appeared on the streets of Budapest to put down the rising by force.

Makarios deported from Cyprus

There was a significant escalation in terrorist and counter-terrorist activities in Cyprus following the sudden and unexpected deportation to the Seychelles of the Greek Cypriot leader Archbishop Makarios. The deportation was ordered by the British Premier Sir Anthony Eden on the grounds that Makarios was encouraging the anti-British campaign of Colonel Grivas' EOKA movement. British troops stationed on the island sought to extirpate EOKA and its sympathisers, but arms searches in Cypriot streets and villages (above), internment and restrictions on freedom of movement only served to alienate public opinion still further from the authorities (right).

Eden drew up plans for phased self-determination and for constitutional reforms involving partition of the island, but the proposals became bogged down in disputes between the Greek and Turkish governments. While the politicians talked and failed to talk, the bloodshed and unrest continued.

Israeli reprisals in Jordan

Tension along the border between Israel and Jordan heightened significantly during the last few months of the year as sporadic Jordanian attacks were met with ever more determined reprisal raids by the Israelis. In the first major raid, on the night of September 11th, a battalion of Israeli soldiers attacked the police post at Rahwa in Jordan, killing five policemen and ten soldiers and destroying the building.

The cycle of retaliation continued with further Jordanian incursions and Israeli reprisal attacks on Gharandal and Husan. October 10th saw the largest reprisal raid, at Qalquilya, where two Israeli regiments bombarded a police barracks for three hours. King Hussein of Jordan personally directed the Jordanian forces and at least 48 Jordanians and 18 Israelis died in the fighting.

Riots in Kowloon

Fifty-one people were killed and 358 injured when serious anti-European rioting broke out in Kowloon, the mainland area of Hong Kong, in October. The disturbances took place on October 10th, the anniversary of the foundation of the Chinese Republic, and were sparked off when officials removed illegal Nationalist flags which had been put up for the celebrations of the Chinese National Day.

Mobs rampaged through the streets attacking Europeans, looting shops and setting fire to vehicles and buildings. The unrest escalated the following day with pitched battles being fought between Nationalists and Communists. Troops with tanks and armoured cars were sent into Kowloon to restore order and a curfew was imposed. Police broke up the demonstrations with teargas and baton charges and also used live ammunition on the crowd. Some 4,500 arrests were made.

Grace Kelly's wedding televised

On Thursday April 19th, the American-Irish actress Grace Kelly (1928–1982), star of such films as *Dial M for Murder* and *Rear Window*, married Prince Rainier III of Monaco in the clifftop cathedral of St Nicholas, Monaco, before a congregation which included the Aga Khan, Ava Gardner and Aristotle Onassis. The wedding was an international media event with an estimated 1,800 journalists staying in the tiny principality for the occasion. After the televised ceremony, at which the bride wore a dress presented to her by MGM studios, the couple drove to the royal palace in a cream and black open-topped Rolls-Royce for the wedding lunch. Prince Rainier and Princess Grace then left for their honeymoon on his yacht the *Deo Juvante*.

The Millers' tale

Actress and sex-symbol Marilyn Monroe married Pulitzer Prize-winning playwright Arthur Miller on June 29th.

Elvis Presley

Elvis Aron Presley, the former truck driver from the Deep South, rocketed to fame as the undisputed 'king' of rock 'n' roll. It all began for Elvis in 1956, at the age of 21, with 'Heartbreak Hotel', followed the same year by two more greats, 'Hound Dog' and 'Love Me Tender'.

Dali and Olivier

Laurence Olivier sat for the Spanish surrealist painter Salvador Dali in his latest film role as Shakespeare's Richard III at Shepperton Studios (above left). The portrait was commissioned by a Mr Robert Dowling of New York. The work (above right) was completed at Dali's Spanish home and combines profile and full-face perspectives.

1957

The Arts

Boris Pasternak's novel *Doctor Zhivago*

Leonard Bernstein's musical *West Side Story*

Francis Bacon's painting *Screaming Nurse*

David Lean's film *The Bridge on the River Kwai*

Little Rock, Arkansas

One of the ugliest confrontations between blacks and whites in the civil rights struggle in the United States took place in the southern State of Arkansas in September. A Federal district court order had decreed that nine black students should be admitted to the previously segregated Central High School in the town of Little Rock. However, the segregationist Governor of Arkansas, Orville Faubus, took every available step to prevent the students being enrolled at the school, including mobilising the National Guard to bar the doors to them (above).

At President Eisenhower's insistence, the Guard was finally withdrawn, but its place was taken by a white mob who continued to keep the black students out. In an extraordinary move, the President sent 1,000 Army paratroopers to Little Rock and removed the National Guard from Faubus' control. Only with this military escort could the nine blacks enter the school.

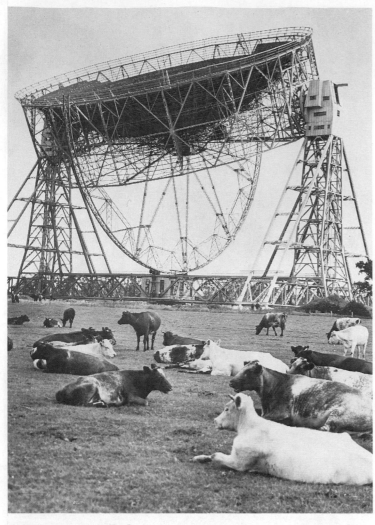

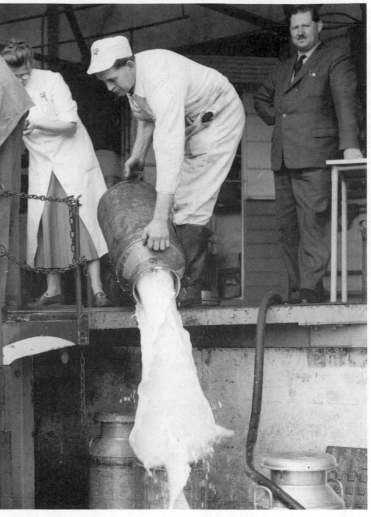

Telescope unveiled

The largest radio telescope in the world was unveiled at Jodrell Bank, England, on October 11th. It was completed ahead of schedule to track the first Soviet satellite, which had been launched the previous week.

Leak at Windscale

Thousands of gallons of contaminated milk had to be thrown away after a fire at the Windscale atomic plant in England resulted in radioactive iodine escaping over some 200 square miles of the surrounding countryside.

Lord Hailsham

The right Honourable Quintin Hogg QC, 2nd Viscount Hailsham and former Minister of Education, was elected Chairman of the British Conservative Party in September. He showed every sign of keeping his head above water in the new job. The exercise would prove useful for the future too, since he was Minister with special responsibility for sport from 1962 to 1964.

Rebellion in Cuba

During the last months of the year, the rebel '26th July' movement, operating from its base in the eastern mountains of Cuba, stepped up its campaign of guerrilla attacks on communications centres and sugar plantations throughout the country. The rebel leader Fidel Castro (above) declared 'total war' on the dictatorial regime of President Batista in the hope of precipitating economic collapse. On September 5th, the government faced a serious challenge when rebel fighters and Cuban Navy officers tried to seize the naval base of Cienfuegos, but the attempt failed and the ringleaders were executed.

Malayan independence

Widespread celebrations in Kuala Lumpur, the Federal capital, including the largest military review in the country's history (above), followed the granting of independence to Malaya by its former rulers, the British, on August 31st. The new constitution provided for a revolving presidency to be held in turn by the Malay sultans.

US ballistic missiles

Shown being lowered onto the first stage is the troublesome second stage of the US Navy's Vanguard missile at the launching pad at Cape Canaverel. The Vanguard rocket carrying the satellite exploded two seconds after take-off on December 6th. The following February the US Army successfully launched the Explorer 1 satellite into orbit around the earth with a Jupiter C rocket. Although the Explorer had a peaceful mission, it was a military rocket that made the launch possible.

First £5,000 premium bond prize

On June 1st, the fourth anniversary of his government's introduction of the first premium bond, the British Prime Minister Harold Macmillan inaugurated the improved Bond Scheme and set in motion the process of deciding who would win the first ever £5,000 prize in the monthly draw. The numbers were chosen by ERNIE (more formally, the electronic random number indicator) in Lytham St Anne's, Lancashire, which Macmillan set running by remote control from the National Savings Headquarters in London. The Prime Minister is seen writing up the number of the first lucky winner.

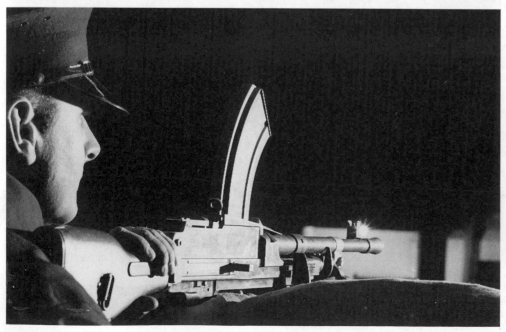

Internment in Ireland

The border between Northern Ireland and the Republic of Eire became the focus of a renewed campaign of Republican violence in the early months of the year. Operation Harvest, the IRA's third major campaign of bombing and sabotage, had as its targets a number of administrative and industrial installations, as well as the buildings and personnel of the Royal Ulster Constabulary, seen (left) patrolling the border with light machine guns. In a highly controversial move to contain the situation, the new Eire government of Eamon de Valera reintroduced internment in July. Under Part 2 of the Offences Against the State Act, terrorist suspects could be arrested and detained without trial, and by the end of the year there were some 100 people in detention in the South and 200 in the North.

1958

Jan	1	European Economic Community (EEC) formed
	1	West German forces join NATO
	3	West Indian Federation formed
	8	USSR: Bulganin proposes summit conference
Feb	1	Egypt and Sudan unite as United Arab Republic
	3	Benelux economic pact signed
	11	French warships no longer allowed to use Bizerta, Tunis
	19	Anglo-Spanish trade agreement
Mar	2	Antarctica: Vivien Fuchs completes 1st overland crossing
Mar	14	British suffragette Christabel Pankhurst dies
	21	China and Hungary sign economic treaty
	27	Khrushchev succeeds Bulganin on Council of Ministers
Apr	2	US embargoes arms shipments to Cuba
	5	Castro begins 'total war' against Cuban dictator Batista
	17	S Africa: Nationalists win big victory in elections
May	2	State of emergency declared in Aden
	3	President Eisenhower proposes demilitarised Antarctic
	13	European settlers riot in Algiers
	27	Sri Lanka: State of emergency declared
Jun	1	Iceland extends fishing limits to 12 miles
	17	Hungarian ex-PM Imre Nagy executed after secret trial
Jul	6	Alaska becomes 49th State of US
	14	King Feisal of Iraq murdered in coup
	24	First life peerage awarded in Britain
	31	Khrushchev visits Britain
Aug	9	US reaffirms refusal to recognise Red China
Sep	3	Verwoerd becomes South African Premier
	5	Martin Luther King arrested for loitering in Alabama
	14	General de Gaulle meets Chancellor Adenauer
Oct	9	Pope Pius XII dies
	9	Yankees defeat Braves to win World Series
	24	Pakistan: Ayub Khan forms Cabinet
	28	Cardinal Roncalli elected Pope John XXIII
Nov	2	Last British troops leave Jordan
Dec	3	Indonesia nationalises Dutch businesses
	12	Algiers: General Galan appointed Inspector-General
	16	NATO rejects Soviet proposals for Berlin
	21	De Gaulle elected President of France
	22	British trade pact with Egypt
	31	Amnesty declared in Lebanon

The Arts

Satyajit Ray's film *The Unvanquished*

T. H. White's novel *The Once and Future King*

Truman Capote's *Breakfast at Tiffany's*

Campaign for Nuclear Disarmament

In February a new pressure group was set up, in the words of its founders, 'to demand a British initiative to reduce the nuclear peril and to stop the armaments race, if need be by unilateral action by Great Britain'. The Campaign for Nuclear Disarmament, or CND, was launched under the presidency of the philosopher and veteran peace campaigner Bertrand Russell, with Canon L. J. Collins as the chairman of its executive committee. The Labour politician Michael Foot and the writer J. B. Priestley were also among its founder members.

One of CND's first acts was to organise a protest march from London to the Atomic Weapons Research Establishment at Aldermaston in Berkshire. A crowd of some 4,000 people gathered in London's Trafalgar Square on April 4th to hear speeches by Canon Collins and other CND leaders before setting out to walk the 50 miles to Aldermaston. Many of the marchers carried banners bearing the distinctive CND logo (left). By the time the demonstration reached the research establishment it was 5,000 strong.

First of the big jets

Before 1958 intercontinental travel by jet airliner was not the commonplace phenomenon that it is today. The introduction of the Boeing 707 changed all that forever. The 707, the first of the big jets, was larger and faster than any rivals. Described at the time as a 'giant', it weighed 311,000 pounds and its long, wide cabin could accommodate up to 189 passengers and carry them at cruising speeds of over 600 miles an hour. It rapidly transformed the image and use of international air travel.

Under the polar ice

The USS *Nautilus* was welcomed at Portland, Dorset, England, after a 6,100-mile trip that included the first voyage under the ice cap of the North Pole. The 2,980-ton *Nautilus*, built in 1954, was the world's first nuclear-powered submarine.

GI Elvis

In 1958 Elvis was drafted into the US army and served overseas in Germany, to intense media attention. His experiences formed the basis of one of his most popular movies, *GI Blues*.

Unrest in Cyprus

There was a serious escalation of violence in Cyprus during 1958.

Top left: Five people were killed when British troops opened fire on rioters in the streets of Nicosia.
Centre left: There were many women among the demonstrators who took to the streets in April to protest against detention of political prisoners.
Left: A mother weeps at the village funeral of Greek Cypriot victims of the violence.
Top right: A Greek victim of gunmen in a passing car, at a café on the outskirts of Nicosia.
Above: British paratroopers embarking from Cyprus on their way to Jordan in July.

Return of de Gaulle

On June 1st, General Charles de Gaulle, who had held no public office since 1946, took over from Pierre Pflimlin as Prime Minister of France. His emergence from the political wilderness took place amid rumours that the insurrectionary French settler administration in Algeria (the Committee of Public Safety) which was increasingly impatient of the Pflimlin regime and increasingly Gaullist in its sympathies, was planning an airborne invasion of Paris to install a military government.

One of the new Prime Minister's first acts was to visit Algeria (left), where he was greeted with enormous enthusiasm by crowds of *pieds noirs*. His message, however, was less to their taste, and some of those who had been instrumental in returning him to power felt that his commitment to the European cause was less whole-hearted than they had hoped.

Race riots in London

Police made more than 150 arrests during three days of serious rioting in the Notting Hill district of North London. The trouble flared up after five black men were beaten up by white youths on August 24th. On the night of August 30th, some 200 white and black people fought in the streets, property was damaged and one black household was petrol-bombed. The following evening saw some of the worst disturbances, with four hours of continuous running battles between 400 black and white people, during which police were attacked·and injured. On September 1st, gangs of up to 2,000 youths and children attacked black houses, breaking windows and causing extensive damage. Police suspected the involvement of extreme political groups.

US Marines in Lebanon

Holidaymakers on the beaches of Beirut helped the US Marines pull their equipment ashore from landing craft (left) when President Eisenhower responded to the pro-Western Lebanese President Chamoun's request for American assistance by sending some 3,500 troops to the Lebanon. The move came two days after an Arab Nationalist uprising in neighbouring Iraq had resulted in the murder of the Iraqi King Feisal and his Prime Minister. The arrival of the Marines was condemned by the Soviet Union and for a time the situation threatened to escalate into full-scale war.

Munich air crash

One of the greatest tragedies ever to strike the world of soccer occurred in February when eight English footballers were among the 21 passengers killed in an air crash in West Germany. The accident happened as the plane taking the Manchester United team back to the UK from Yugoslavia, where they had just drawn with Red Star Belgrade to qualify for the semi-finals of the European Cup, failed to clear a fence on take-off from Rhiem airport in Munich. Among the dead were the England regulars Roger Byrne, Duncan Edwards and Tommy Taylor. The Manchester United manager Matt Busby, after whom the team had been popularly known as the 'Busby Babes', was also seriously injured in the disaster. The plane, a BEA Ambassador, was reduced to a tangled heap of wreckage. Rescue workers (above) had to do their best in driving snow.

Manned space flight tests

In the United States a programme was launched to test the likely effects of space travel on human beings. Administered by the National Advisory Committee on Aeronautics, the US Air Force and Navy and the manufacturers of the X-15 rocket plane (whose first flight was planned for 1959), the programme involved the use of a huge centrifuge (left).

Entering the capsule, the pilot could fly the machine as it revolved on its giant arm, simulating the degree of acceleration likely to be experienced in actual space flight. The programme was used to train the X-15 pilots for their mission and to carry out medical tests on them to find out how the human body would react to the unfamiliar stresses of space travel.

Hovercraft breakthrough

The British inventor Christopher Cockerell finally succeeded in getting official funding to develop his new 'hovercraft' after submitting film of a working model to the National Research Development Corporation in April. The world's first air-cushion vehicle (AVC), the blue and silver SR-N1 (left), was built by Saunders-Roe, an Isle of Wight aircraft firm, in less than eight months and was unveiled to the public in sea-trials the following year. Its success proved that a heavy vehicle can be supported just above the ground on a cushion of air produced by a thrust much less than the vehicle's weight.

Miles Davis

Miles Davis (1926–1991), the black trumpeter and leading exponent of 'cool jazz', recorded *Porgy and Bess*, a highly original reinterpretation.

Boris Pasternak

The Soviet authorities forced Russian novelist Boris Pasternak (1890–1960) to retract his acceptance of the Nobel Prize for Literature.

Vaughan Williams

English composer and folksong collector Ralph Vaughan Williams (1872–1958) died in London at the age of 86.

1959

The Arts

Henry Moore's bronze *Two-piece Reclining Figure*

Frank Lloyd Wright's Guggenheim Art Museum

Tony Richardson's film *Look Back in Anger*

Carol Reed's film *Our Man in Havana*

Makarios elected President

After years of escalating unrest in Cyprus, the Greek and Turkish governments met in Zürich in February to discuss the future of the island and agreed that it should become independent. Under the proposed arrangements, the British government would keep its sovereign military bases on the island, but a joint Greco-Turkish administration would be set up to govern the new State. The constitution made provision for a Greek President and a Turkish Vice-President and ruled out union with Greece (*enosis*).

Even though *enosis* was the goal for which he and the EOKA movement had been fighting, Archbishop Makarios, seen (above) with EOKA's Colonel Grivas, accepted the proposed settlement, and on March 1st he returned to Nicosia after three years of exile. Elections were announced and in December Makarios became the first President of the new Republic.

Revolution in Cuba

On January 1st, the beleaguered regime of the dictator Fulgencio Batista finally collapsed and he fled to the Dominican Republic. After six years of revolutionary struggle the way was clear for the rebel guerrillas of Dr Fidel Castro, who already controlled most of the east of Cuba, to take up the reins of power. Amid general rejoicing at the fall of Batista, Dr Manuel Urrutia was declared President of the new government and named Castro his Commander in Chief. On January 8th, Castro himself, together with 5,000 of his troops, made a triumphant entry into the capital Havana along streets lined with thousands of cheering citizens.

The new regime was immediately recognised by the governments of the United States, Great Britain, France, the Soviet Union and most of Cuba's Latin American neighbours. Some doubts were expressed internationally, however, when the round-up of Batista officials was followed by swift trials and on-the-spot executions by firing squad.

Voyage of discovery

On February 21st, the British Premier Harold Macmillan made what he described as a 'voyage of discovery' to the Soviet Union. This was the first peacetime visit of a British Prime Minister, and he was met at the airport (above left) by Khrushchev and a welcoming crowd, who liked

Macmillan's gesture of wearing a white fur hat in true Soviet style. While in the Soviet Union the British team had talks with Khrushchev, attended the Bolshoi Ballet and visited Leningrad and Kiev. Arms limitation was discussed, but only limited agreement was reached.

A fortnight later Macmillan was in Washington, DC to report on his Soviet trip to President Eisenhower (above right). Talks at the presidential mountain lodge at Camp David resulted in a communiqué which spoke of 'complete agreement between our two governments'.

Riots in Durban

On June 18th, violent disturbances broke out in the South African town of Durban. Days of serious rioting were sparked off when police destroyed illicit stills during a slum clearance operation designed to resettle some 100,000 blacks. Hundreds of black women attacked beer-halls and other property in the black shanty town of Cato Manor on the outskirts of Durban. They were joined by thousands of other rioters who ran through the streets setting fire to offices, clinics, schools, shops and vehicles. Outside Durban a crowd of some 4,000 blacks blocked the main road and stoned cars as they tried to pass.

The rioting continued throughout the month, leaving buildings and vehicles smouldering (left). Four black people died in the unrest, and damage to property was estimated at some £250,000. The situation in Durban remained tense for some months afterwards and more deaths occurred in September when police opened fire on protesters.

De Gaulle in Italy

The newly inaugurated President of France, General Charles de Gaulle, made a state visit to Italy in June, where he attended a large military parade in Milan.

Indira Gandhi

In February Mrs Indira Gandhi (caricatured above), the daughter of India's Prime Minister Jawaharlal Nehru, was elected President of the ruling Congress Party, a post her father held until 1955.

Dalai Lama in India

The 14th Dalai Lama went into exile in India following the Tibetan revolt against the Chinese, who installed the Panchen Lama as ruler in his place.

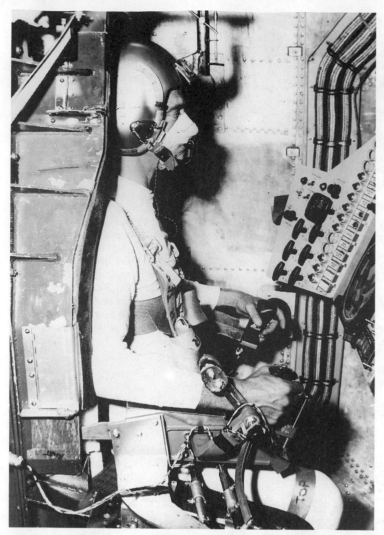

Ben Hur

One of the greatest of the Hollywood epics, famous for the technical splendour of the action scenes, such as the sea battle and the exciting chariot race. This film was to win William Wyler his third directing Oscar. Above: One of the best-known scenes from the film – the chariot race in which Ben Hur (Charlton Heston) rides against his Roman enemy Messala (Stephen Boyd).

On the way to space

Preparations for putting the first man into space continued in the United States. In 'Project Mercury' at the end of the year a monkey called Sam was launched into space to test the effects of acceleration forces and weightlessness. After a 13-minute trip he was parachuted back to Earth, and landed in the Atlantic apparently suffering no ill-effects. Top left: Astronaut Alan Shepard at the controls of a simulated space vehicle.

Classic folk opera

The lavish movie version of George Gershwin's negro folk opera *Porgy and Bess* won the Oscar for the best scoring of a musical for 1959. Set in the slums of Catfish Row in South Carolina, it tells the tragic love story of the crippled beggar Porgy (Sidney Poitier) and the beautiful, reckless Bess (Dorothy Dandridge). The stage version was first launched in New York by the Theatre Guild in 1935.

Frank Lloyd Wright

The world of architecture mourned the passing of Frank Lloyd Wright (1869–1959), who died on April 9th. One of the giants of modern architecture, his work often divided critics. Fallingwater (left), a house built over a waterfall in Bear Run, Pennsylvania, was one of his masterpieces – a living space in perfect harmony with its natural surroundings. The Guggenheim Museum art gallery (above left), opened to the public in October, was described by the *New York Times* as 'the most controversial building . . . in New York'. The pictures were displayed on the walls of a vast spiral ramp.

The Seer of Cookham

This year also saw the death of the British artist Sir Stanley Spencer (1891–1959), who had been knighted by the Queen in the Birthday Honours list in June. The son of an organist and music teacher, Spencer received little formal education before going to the Slade School of Art in 1908 at the age of 17. There he developed the techniques which formed the basis of his highly distinctive work.

A true visionary, Spencer created paintings which fused the divine and the commonplace, often transfiguring the scenes of everyday life he saw around him in the Thames-side village of Cookham, where he was born and spent most of his life. He reached the apex of his creative powers in the 1920s with his murals in Burghclere Chapel in Berkshire and paintings such as *Resurrection Cookham* (1922–1927). His last work, an altarpiece dedicated to his first wife Hilda, remained unfinished when he died.

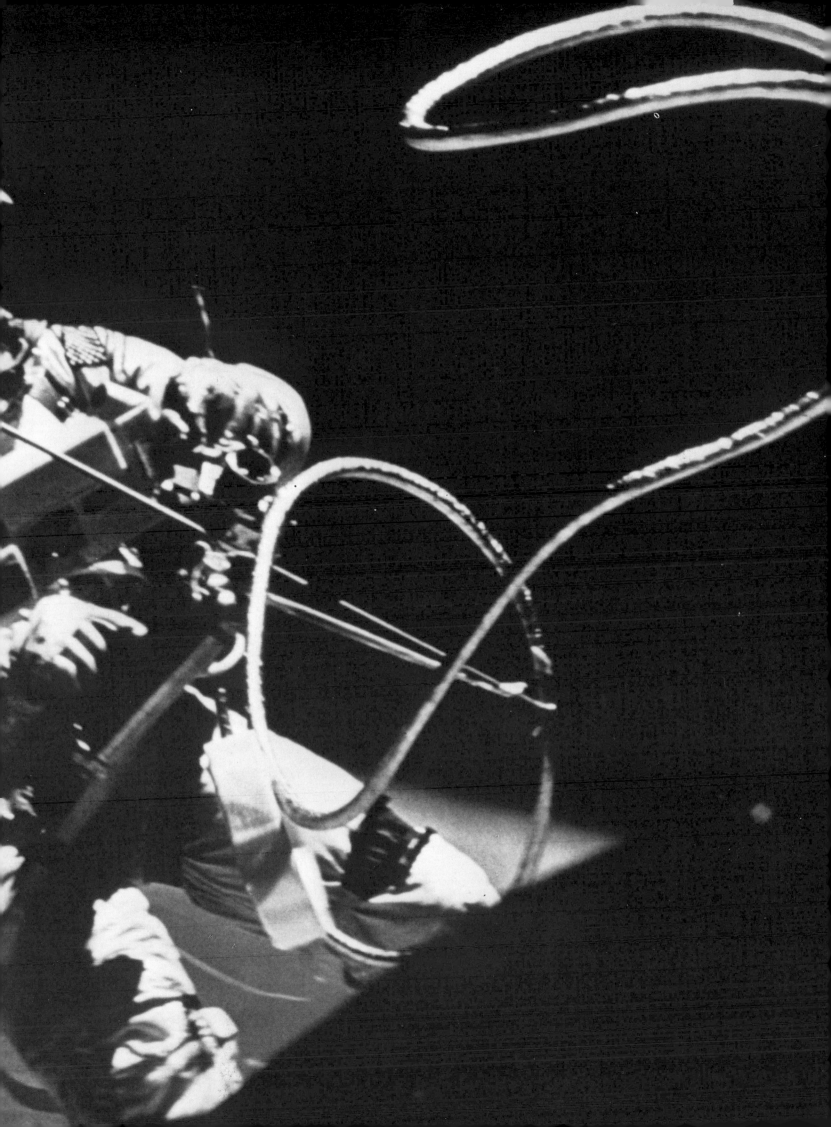

The 1960s

More than almost any decade before it, the 1960s saw the pace of change quicken in international, social and cultural affairs to the point where many of the older generation felt that the world in which they were living was becoming barely recognisable. Advances in technology that would have seemed unimaginable ten years earlier made possible such giant leaps forward as the exploration of space and the development of heart transplant surgery. The last vestiges of empire disappeared in Africa as Britain, France and Belgium relinquished their colonial interests to the seemingly unstoppable tide of black nationalism. At the same time changes in the leadership of the world's superpowers seemed unable to slow the gathering momentum of the Cold War, which in 1962 brought the human race closer to nuclear war than at any time before or since. And throughout it all, a youth culture was emerging with values that seemed to contradict all that had been assumed by the generation born between the two World Wars.

Winds of change

It was perhaps in the vast and diverse continent of Africa that the greatest changes were felt. In the opening days of the decade the British Prime Minister Harold Macmillan made his famous speech about the 'winds of change' blowing through Africa. In the years that followed, country after country was to attain independence, many after a protracted period of unrest and bloodshed. In Algeria the birth pangs of the new State threatened mainland France itself with collapse and brought the veteran General Charles de Gaulle out of the political wilderness. In the Belgian Congo the very speed with which independence had been granted created the conditions for the tragedy which ensued. In some countries what began in a spirit of hope and liberty declined into despair and totalitarianism as groups that had been united in their desire for independence fragmented into warring factions on achieving power. In Nigeria this factionalism led to the appalling human tragedy of Biafra. In South Africa and Southern Rhodesia the continuing white hold on the organs of power seemed destined to loosen under the onslaught of black unrest.

Civil rights

The black nationalism of the former colonial states found its echo in the developed world too. In the United States the black civil rights movement, under the leadership of Martin Luther King, fought for recognition against the combined forces of prejudice and inertia. Despite the passing of important civil rights legislation under President Kennedy and his successor Lyndon B Johnson, the segregationist instincts of the Governors of some Southern states still sought to maintain the old order. Nonetheless, by the time of King's untimely death at the hands of a white gunman in 1968, the black struggle for equality in the United States had made more progress in a few years than in the whole of the preceding generation.

The superpowers

The era of hope that seemed to be dawning in the United States with the youthful presidency of John F Kennedy came to an abrupt end on the streets of Dallas in 1963, but not before the relationship between the USA and the Soviet Union had been put under unprecedented strain. The attempted US invasion of Cuba and the missile crisis of 1962 left permanent scars on East–West relations and helped fuel the development of the new protest groups springing up to campaign against the proliferation of nuclear weapons. In Berlin the newly erected Wall stood as a potent symbol of confrontation and misunderstanding. In Vietnam the ugly spectacle of American involvement served daily to undermine the high moral ground claimed by the US government in the battle of democracy.

In the Middle East the uneasy stand-off between Israel and its Arab neighbours threatened the powderkeg of US–Soviet relations with the spark of military conflict. The Arab–Israeli war in 1967 changed the map of the region in just six days and established its political contours for the next 20 years. The Palestinian cause also gave impetus to the growing phenomenon of international terrorism which was to dominate the 1970s.

The space race

Even the startling achievements of the space programme derived their momentum from the East–West divide. The world watched in astonishment as the American and Soviet programmes vied to outdo each other in the very public arena of the space race. The decade began with the first man in space and ended with the first men setting foot on the moon. By the time the 'giant leap for mankind' fulfilled President Kennedy's determination to put a man on the moon by 1970 the American space programme alone had cost some $24,000 million. It had also allowed a television audience of 600 million people to watch one of the greatest scientific achievements in the history of mankind.

Beatles and barricades

A revolution in fashion, music, literature and the arts took place as the opening up of mass communications helped create and sustain a worldwide youth market. Mini-skirts and caftans made their appearance on the streets of London and San Francisco. The music of bands such as the Rolling Stones and the Doors came to symbolise their young audiences' rejection of parental values, while the 'pop art' of Andy Warhol and his bizarre entourage drew a cult following for its parodies of the images of mass-production. The word 'permissive' entered the household vocabulary as sexual and social taboos were eroded by the contraceptive pill and the marijuana joint.

Pages 80–1: Edward White's spacewalk outside Gemini 4, June 3rd 1965.

1960

Jan	1	Independent Republic of Cameroons proclaimed
	9	Egypt: Work begins on Aswan Dam
Feb	2	Blacks begin lunch counters sit-in campaign in US
	17	Martin Luther King is arrested in US
	21	Castro nationalises private business in Cuba
Mar	1	Morocco: Agadir is devastated by earthquake
	5	President Sukarno suspends Indonesian Parliament
	13	British government scraps Blue Streak missile project
	30	State of emergency in S Africa after Sharpeville
Apr	1	S African govt bans ANC and Pan-African Congress
	21	Brasilia inaugurated as new capital of Brazil
	27	Synghman Rhee resigns from Presidency of S Korea
May	1	US U-2 aircraft shot down by USSR
	7	Brezhnev replaces Voroshilov as USSR President
	16	Summit meeting in Paris
	23	Israelis arrest former Gestapo chief Eichmann
	27	Turkey: Premier A. Menderes ousted in military coup
	30	Soviet writer Boris Pasternak dies
Jun	9	Hong Kong struck by typhoon
	30	Lumumba becomes first Prime Minister of Congo
Jul	1	USSR shoots down US aircraft

	7	Belgium sends troops to Congo
	8	U-2 pilot Gary Powers indicted as spy by USSR
	11	Congo: Tshombe proclaims Katanga independent
	18	Malcolm Campbell's *Bluebird* car has first UK test
Aug	7	Castro nationalises all US-owned property in Cuba
	16	Cyprus gains independence under Archbishop Makarios
	22	Two dogs return to Earth from Soviet space trip
	25	Olympic Games open in Rome
	31	East Germans close border with West Berlin
Sept	1	Nyerere becomes Tanganyika's first Prime Minister
Oct	5	S African referendum favours Republic
	19	US imposes embargo on shipments to Cuba
Nov	7	Moscow: missiles first appear in Red Square parade
	9	John F. Kennedy is elected US President
Dec	2	Britain refuses independence for Bugunda
	21	King Saud takes over Saudi Arabian government
		The Arts
		Hitchcock's film *Psycho*
		Ionesco's play *Rhinoceros*
		Fellini's film *La Dolce Vita*
		Robert Bolt's play *A Man for All Seasons*

Kennedy elected to White House

On November 9th, a new period of American history, and a new era in international relations, was ushered in with the election of the Democrat John F. Kennedy (1917–1963) as the 34th President of the United States of America.

Kennedy, a 43-year-old Senator from Massachusetts, had been groomed for the presidency since childhood by his ambitious father (a one-time US Ambassador to Britain) and stood for many people as the living embodiment of the 'new generation of Americans'. His youth, his charismatic style, his harnessing of the Black vote and to some extent his Catholicism sustained his popularity through a vigorous campaign against the Republican Richard Nixon, which also saw the introduction of the first televised debates between candidates.

The vote itself was a cliff-hanger. Despite carrying 23 states with 303 electoral votes, as against Nixon's 219 votes from 26 states, Kennedy in fact gained only 0.1 per cent more of the popular vote for his dream of a 'New Frontier'.

The Sharpeville massacre

On March 21st, what began as a peaceful protest ended in tragedy in the South African township of Sharpeville when police opened fire on a black crowd, killing 67 people and wounding 186.

The shootings happened on a day of mass demonstrations against the white government's hated pass laws. In a campaign organised by the Pan-African Congress, a breakaway group from the African National Congress, black people all over the country left their passes at home and gave themselves up at their nearest police station to be arrested. Thousands took part in the protests, which were peaceful in the majority of places.

However, at Sharpeville, a township five miles north of Vereeniging, police officers confronted the crowd outside the police station and opened fire, apparently without warning. Official statements claimed that the shootings took place in self-defence, when a crowd of 20,000 tried to storm the station. Black witnesses at the subsequent inquiry said that only 5,000 people were involved and that they had gone peacefully to the police station to discuss the pass laws. A medical expert testified that some 70 per cent of the victims had been shot from behind.

Revolt in Algeria

Among the European community in Algeria, simmering unease with General de Gaulle's Algerian policy, which seemed destined to lead to Muslim rule of the country, boiled over into open revolt on January 24th, after de Gaulle dismissed the *pieds noirs'* hero General Massu. Crowds of demonstrators took to the streets of Algiers to protest against Massu's dismissal and the lack of protection they felt had led to the deaths of increasing numbers of French settlers in FLN terrorist outrages. People who only two years before had cheered de Gaulle's return to power in France now chanted anti-de Gaulle slogans, distributed insurrectionary propaganda from their cars (near right), and dug up roads to make barricades against the police (far right and above). A general strike was declared.

De Gaulle ordered the Commander in Chief in Algeria, General Challe, to restore order, and paratroopers surrounded the barricaded insurgents. The atmosphere became extremely tense as the government in Paris debated whether or not to order the paratroopers to open fire against their fellow Frenchmen. The order was never given and by the beginning of February the stalemate ended with the collapse of the revolt, and the surrender and arrest of many of the insurgents.

Chaos in the Congo

Within days of the hasty transfer of power from Brussels to the independent government of Patrice Lumumba in Léopoldville on June 30th, conflict between the Congo's many political groupings, seen (left) on the eve of independence, plunged the country into lawlessness. A mutiny of the Congolese Army led to attacks on Europeans, and many reports of beatings and rape resulted in Belgians being sent in to restore order.

The most widespread violence ensued when the provinces of Katanga and South Kasai declared themselves independent States. United Nations troops were sent to the Congo and, to US horror, Lumumba sought Soviet military aid. As the bloodshed and chaos mounted, an Army colonel, Joseph Mobutu, staged a military coup on September 14th and by the end of the year the country was torn between four separate regimes.

Macmillan's African tour

In January the recently elected British Premier Harold Macmillan, seen (left) in Basutoland, became the first serving British Prime Minister to set foot in Africa when he began a six-week tour of the continent. The visit – during which he visited Ghana, Nigeria, the Central African Federation and South Africa – marked British recognition of the growth of nationalism in Africa and the need for moves towards independence from colonial rule. In the Ghanaian capital, Accra, Macmillan spoke memorably of 'the winds of change blowing through Africa', a theme to which he returned in Cape Town in February, where he also spoke of the British government's disapproval of apartheid in South Africa.

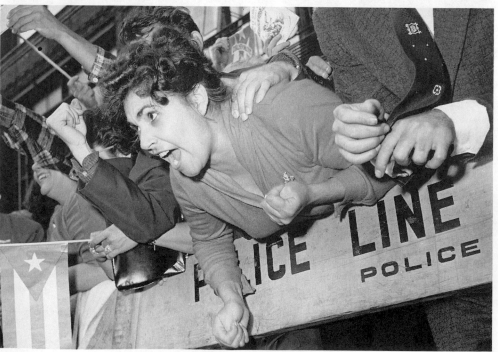

Cuba and the United States

Relations between the Eisenhower administration and the new revolutionary regime of Fidel Castro in Cuba deteriorated badly after initial US recognition of the Castro government in 1959. Despite having disclaimed all personal presidential ambitions when his movement first took power, Castro had declared himself President in July 1959.

During the course of 1960 he began buying oil and arms from the Soviet Union and when the US exerted economic pressure by stopping its purchases of Cuban sugar, he responded by nationalising American businesses in Cuba. Tension increased still further when Cuba set about 'exporting revolution' to its Latin American neighbours, conducting clandestine operations in the Dominican Republic, Nicaragua and Panama.

However, despite the US government's growing distrust of the Cuban regime, Castro and his right-hand man 'Che' Guevara aroused enthusiastic support among many young Americans (left).

The Royal Family

1960 was marked by three major royal events: on February 19th, the Queen (left) gave birth to Prince Andrew – the first time a child had been born to a reigning British sovereign since the birth of Princess Beatrice, Queen Victoria's youngest child, in 1857. A week later, Princess Margaret took the world by surprise with her engagement to Antony Armstrong-Jones (top left), whom she married in Westminster Abbey on May 6th (top right). Finally, in August Queen Elizabeth the Queen Mother celebrated her 60th birthday and is seen (above) with her grandchildren in the gardens of Clarence House.

U-2 incident

On May 1st, an American U-2 reconnaissance plane piloted by Francis Gary Powers (above) was shot down over the Soviet Union.

Death of Camus

The French existentialist novelist Albert Camus (1913–1960), author of *La Peste* (*The Plague*) and *L'Étranger* (*The Outsider*), was killed in a car crash near Villeneuve-la-Guyard on May 4th. The car in which he was travelling as a passenger, was written off when it collided with a tree.

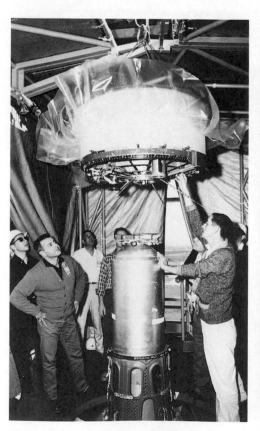

A weather eye

The world's first weather satellite, Tiros, was launched by the United States from Cape Canaveral on April 2nd.

Lasers demonstrated

The first laser, a device which can generate and focus a highly intense beam of light, was demonstrated by scientists working in California. Laser is an acronym for **L**ight **A**mplification by **S**timulated **E**mission of **R**adiation.

1961

Jan	3	US severs diplomatic and consular relations with Cuba
	17	Congo: Former PM Lumumba murdered
	20	Queen Elizabeth tours India, Pakistan, Iran and Cyprus
	20	John F. Kennedy becomes President of the US
	30	Riots in Sri Lanka
Feb	4	Civil war begins in Angola
	16	Cyprus will apply to join Commonwealth
	22	W German Chancellor Konrad Adenauer visits London
	26	Morocco: Hassan II becomes King
Mar	1	US President Kennedy sets up Peace Corps
	26	British PM Macmillan meets Kennedy in Florida
Apr	12	Soviet Cosmonaut Yuri Gagarin is 1st man in space
	17	Failed 'Bay of Pigs' invasion of Cuba
	22	Right-wing rebellion in Algeria threatens France
	27	Sierra Leone is independent member of Commonwealth
May	1	Tanganyika independent with Nyerere as leader
	8	British spy George Blake sentenced to 42 years
	24	Cyprus becomes member of the Council of Europe
	28	Last journey of Paris–Bucharest Orient Express train
	31	Kennedys welcomed in Paris
	31	S Africa becomes a Republic
Jun	16	Soviet ballet dancer Rudolf Nureyev defects to West
Jul	2	Author Ernest Hemingway commits suicide
Aug	10	Britain applies to join European Economic Community
	13	E Germany closes frontier between E and W Berlin
	17	E Germany erects Berlin Wall
	31	Morocco: Last Spanish troops withdraw
Sep	18	Head of UN, Dag Hammarskjöld, is killed in air crash
	28	Syria: Army coup in Damascus
	29	Syria secedes from United Arab Republic
Oct	9	NY Yankees win World Series for 26th time
	15	Turkey: General Gürsel is elected President
	24	Malta becomes independent from Britain
Nov	2	Israel: Ben Gurion forms new coalition govt
	3	U Thant becomes interim Secretary-General of UN
	16	UK: Commonwealth Immigration Bill is introduced
Dec	9	USSR severs relations with Albania
	13	US painter Grandma Moses dies
	19	India takes Goa from Portuguese after 400 years

The Arts

Benjamin Britten's opera *A Midsummer Night's Dream*

Jean Anouilh's play *Becket, Or the Honour of God*

Lionel Bart's musical *Oliver*

Joseph Heller's novel *Catch-22*

Film of *West Side Story*

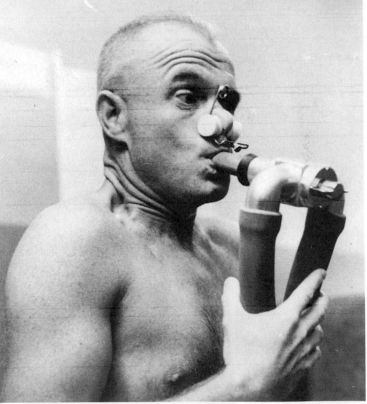

First man in space

On April 12th, the Soviet Union won the race to put the first man in space. That man was Major Yuri Alexeyevich Gagarin (1934–1968) (top), who instantly became a household name throughout the world. The spacecraft in which he was launched from the Baikonur Cosmodrome in Kazakhstan, the 4.7-tonne Vostok 1, orbited the Earth once at an altitude of 327 kilometres before re-entering the atmosphere and landing 108 minutes after take-off. Five weeks later President Kennedy inaugurated the Apollo programme, but it was another nine months before John Glenn (training above) became the first American in orbit.

The Bay of Pigs

A mere three months after the inauguration of the new President, the Kennedy administration was plunged into crisis by an unsuccessful attempt to invade the island of Cuba. On his election in November 1960, Kennedy discovered that the Central Intelligence Agency (CIA) had been training a small army of Cuban exiles in Guatemala with a view to invading Cuba and overthrowing the revolutionary regime of Fidel Castro. Despite his doubts about the plan Kennedy allowed it to proceed, but the outcome was to be one of the greatest humiliations of his presidency.

On the night of April 14th, American B56 bombers took off from bases in Nicaragua to provide air support for the invasion, and 48 hours later a force of some 1,400 men, the majority of them partly trained civilians, landed at the Bay of Pigs. They were met by a stronger Cuban defence than had been anticipated (above left) and fierce fighting ensued. Further American military support was not forthcoming and to make matters worse, the expected risings in Cuba itself failed to materialise. The invasion was a complete failure and within 72 hours had been roundly defeated, leaving the Bay of Pigs littered with the debris of battle (above right). Despite the façade of friendship preserved at the Vienna summit in June (left), relations between America and the Soviet Union were severely strained by the incident.

The Generals' revolt in Algeria

The Algerian War moved into its final phase in January when de Gaulle held a referendum on the future of Algeria, in which French and Algerian people voted overwhelmingly in favour of talks on self-determination. Negotiations were proceeding towards talks at Evian-les-Bains between the French government and the FLN's so-called provisional government of Algeria when suddenly, on the morning of April 22nd, a division of paratroopers (below left) surrounded Government House in Algiers and arrested the French Delegate-General. The Generals' revolt had begun.

Troops took over the major civil and military installations in the city and announced over the radio that the Army was now in control of the country. The four leaders of the military coup, Generals Challe, Jouhaud, Zeller and Salan, declared that they had saved Algeria for France and imposed a state of emergency. By the evening, as rumours circulated of an airborne invasion of Paris by the rebels, General de Gaulle assumed special powers and the capital prepared to repel any attack (top).

In Algeria itself, however, support for the revolt proved to be limited and on April 26th it collapsed. Police set about recovering arms that had been handed out to the paramilitary OAS during the coup (above left) and ringleaders were arrested and tried, with Challe and Zeller being sentenced to imprisonment and Salan and Jouhaud to death.

The Berlin Wall

The political map of Europe was changed literally overnight on August 13th. At 2.30 a.m. the East German government sealed the border between East and West Berlin. and began the building of the wall that has divided the city ever since.

As steel-helmeted border guards and People's Police rolled out the barbed wire and the prefabricated concrete blocks that were to form the basis of the wall (bottom, far left), many East Germans made desperate last-ditch attempts to reach the West. In all some 1,500 people, taking only the bare minimum of possessions with them (above right), escaped during the day across back yards or through the city's many bomb sites. Others swam canals or the River Havel, or ran the gauntlet of border guards in their cars (above left). But these were to be virtually the last of the 2,600,000 refugees who had fled to the West since 1949, an exodus that had left East Germany dangerously short of professional people to staff its hospitals and industries.

Over the following days the wall was reinforced (left), and on August 22nd a 100-metre no-man's-land was created on both sides (top, far left), with warnings being given to West Berliners not to approach 'in the interests of their own safety'. There was a chorus of Western condemnation at this violation of freedom of movement, but no action was taken to reopen the border.

The banality of evil

In April the trial began in Jersualem of the Nazi war criminal Adolf Eichmann (1906–1962). Eichmann stood accused of crimes against the Jewish people and crimes against humanity for his part in the extermination of the Jews in Hitler's 'Final Solution'. During the trial, which took place amid unprecedented security, Eichmann, whose appearance of sheer ordinariness surprised and unsettled many people, listened impassively to the evidence against him from behind a bullet-proof glass screen. He pleaded 'not guilty' to the indictment, claiming only to have been following orders. Despite the mounting evidence of his involvement in the organisation of the Holocaust, he insisted that there was 'no blood on my hands'. On December 12th, however, the three judges delivered a unanimous verdict of guilty and Eichmann was sentenced to death.

Kenyatta released

Following the Lancaster House conference on the future of Kenya in January 1960, black demands for the release of the Kenya African National Union (KANU) leader Jomo Kenyatta (top) mounted both in Kenya and elsewhere. Kenyatta had been sentenced to seven years' hard labour in 1953 for his part in the activities of the Mau Mau movement but had not been allowed to return to Nairobi at the end of his term. His continued detention became increasingly embarrassing for the authorities after KANU won a clear majority in the first elections to be held under the new Kenyan constitution in February 1961. Eventually, despite strong opposition from the white community, Kenyatta was allowed to return to his home near Nairobi on August 14th, to be greeted by an enthusiastic crowd of more than 3,000 people (above).

The pill

Despite opposition from religious groups, conservatives and others, the female oral contraceptive pill was launched on to the market after extensive trials.

Adenauer meets Kennedy

Konrad Adenauer, Chancellor of the German Federal Republic, held talks with President Kennedy at the White House in November. They discussed East-West tensions since the Berlin Wall.

Ban the Bomb

1961 was a year of demonstrations in London against the nuclear arms race. Many members of CND were arrested, including the 89-year-old philosopher Bertrand Russell.

Dag Hammarskjöld

A year of intense diplomatic activity in Africa was tragically cut short for the United Nations Secretary-General Dag Hammarskjöld (1905–1961) in September when he was killed in a plane crash while flying to Northern Rhodesia for talks with the Katangan leader Moise Tshombe. Earlier in the year he had met the South African Premier H. F. Verwoerd to discuss apartheid.

1961

Rudolf Nureyev

Nureyev (1938–   ), a leading dancer with Leningrad's Kirov Ballet, caused a sensation by defecting to the West just before the opening of the company's season at Covent Garden in June.

From stage to screen

The smash hit Broadway musical *West Side Story*, the modern-day *Romeo and Juliet*, was translated into a spectacular movie in 1961. Bitter gang rivalries mean that love between Natalie Wood and Richard Beymer is doomed.

Bridget Riley

Bridget Riley (1931–   ), the most exciting young British artist of the 1960s, is seen here with an example of her highly distinctive 'op art'. After her first one-woman exhibition in 1962 she exhibited in 1964 in the New Generation show at the Whitechapel Gallery, in London, and Painting and Sculpture of a Decade at the Tate, then in the Responsive Eye at New York's Museum of Modern Art the following year. In 1969 she won the international prize for painting at the 34th Venice Biennale.

1962

Jan	1	W Samoa becomes an independent Polynesian state
	9	Soviet-Cuban trade treaty signed
	14	EEC agrees on Common Agricultural Policy
Feb	10	US exchanges Soviet spy for captured pilot Gary Powers
Mar	2	UK applies to join European Coal and Steel Community
	2	Burma: Ne Win overturns U Nu in coup
	5	UK applies to join European Atomic Energy Community
Apr	18	W Indian Federation dissolved
May	13	Indonesia: Assassination attempt on President Sukarno
	31	Nazi war criminal Adolf Eichmann hanged in Israel
Jun	14	European Space Research Organisation formed in Paris
Jul	1	Ruanda and Burundi become independent states
	3	Independence of Algeria proclaimed by France
Aug	6	Jamaica independent within Commonwealth
	6	US writer William Faulkner dies
	13	Ghana expels Archbishop of W Africa
	15	Holland and Indonesia agree over West New Guinea
	22	President de Gaulle escapes assassination attempt
	31	Trinidad and Tobago independent in Commonwealth
Sep	1	Earthquake disaster in Iran
	2	USSR to supply Cuba with weapons
	8	China steps up border dispute with India

Oct	9	Uganda an independent state within Commonwealth
	10	Ceasefire in Congo civil war
	20	China attacks Indian border positions
	22	Kennedy says USSR has missile bases in Cuba
	28	US pledges to send arms to India
Nov	2	Tanganyika: Nyerere elected President
	2	Kennedy announces dismantling of Cuban missile bases
	5	Saudi Arabia breaks with United Arab Republic
	10	Eleanor Roosevelt dies
	14	Negotiations with EEC resumed by UK
	21	Sino-Indian ceasefire declared
	30	U Thant to be UN Secretary-General
Dec	5	Dean Acheson, US diplomat, says Britain is 'played out'
	8	Revolt in Brunei ends as British intervene
	9	Tanganyika an independent state in Commonwealth
	10	Crick and Watson win Nobel Prize in DNA work
		The Arts
		Solzhenitsyn's *One Day in the Life of Ivan Denisovich*
		Orson Welles' film *The Trial*
		David Lean's film *Lawrence of Arabia*
		Edward Albee's play *Who's Afraid of Virginia Woolf?*
		Arnold Wesker's play *Chips with Everything*

MISSILE READY TENT FOUNDATIONS (TENTS REMOVED)

ABANDONED LAUNCH POSITION

The Cuban missile crisis

In October the world seemed closer to nuclear war than at any time before or since. Following the previous year's Bay of Pigs fiasco, the Kennedy administration obtained conclusive proof that the Soviet Union was building offensive missile bases in Cuba (left) which could have doubled the number of American cities and bases threatened by Soviet attack. After rejecting the option of an immediate military strike against the installations, Kennedy ordered a naval blockade against Soviet ships bringing military equipment to the island, with the threat of retaliation if the blockade was broken.

The situation threatened to escalate into full-scale conflict between the superpowers as Khrushchev considered whether to accept the challenge thrown down by the Americans. In the end, six days after the US ships moved into the path of the Soviet vessels, Khrushchev ordered his convoy to turn back and agreed to dismantle the Cuban bases.

Independence for Algeria

Despite the intensification of terrorist activity in Algeria in the early months of 1962, with OAS bombs killing many police and civilians and Muslim terrorist organisations staging bloody reprisals, talks on the future of the country continued between the French government and the FLN's provisional government of Algeria, now headed by Ben Khedda, at Evian-les-Bains. They ended on March 18th with the declaration of a ceasefire which came into effect at noon the following day. Plans were also announced for a referendum on the question of independence, under the terms of which France agreed to withdraw its troops over the next three years except from its bases in Mers-el-Kebir and in the Sahara, where it had already begun a nuclear testing programme.

The OAS, which had come to prominence during the Generals' revolt of 1961, responded by stepping up its campaign of propaganda (left) and terrorism still further. The prospect of a Muslim state drew closer, and a mass exodus of Europeans began, as the bombings and murders continued (above left). On April 8th, a referendum in metropolitan France came out strongly in favour of the Evian proposals for independence and large numbers of Muslims began to return to Algeria for the referendum there on July 1st (above right).

The result was an almost unanimous vote for President de Gaulle's independence plan and on July 3rd the French High Commissioner officially handed over the reins of power to the provisional government of Ben Khedda, who became the new Prime Minister. With the raising of the Algerian flag over the capital, eight years of war and 132 years of French rule came to an end. Algeria became an independent sovereign state for the first time in its history.

East–West tension in Berlin

Tension remained high throughout 1962 in the divided city of Berlin, where the recently built Wall had become a potent symbol of East–West confrontation. The sound of gunfire at night bore witness to the continuing attempts of East Germans to escape to the West. Meanwhile, West Berliners were leaving for West Germany at an alarming rate. Propaganda patrols paraded on both sides of the Wall (left) in a 'loudspeaker war' of words.

In February the crisis moved into a new and potentially more dangerous phase when the Soviet Union announced that it was reserving the air corridors between West Germany and West Berlin for use by its own military aircraft at specific times. A campaign of harassment began. Soviet jets buzzed commercial aircraft in the corridors and dropped tin foil to interfere with their radar equipment. Searchlights were trained on Western airliners as they came into land at Berlin's Tempelhof airport, blinding the pilots and seriously increasing the risk of crashing. Western fighter aircraft in West Germany were put on alert but no military action was taken.

In August the first anniversary of the building of the Wall was marked by violent demonstrations in West Berlin.

Bomb attacks in Ghana

On August 1st a hand grenade was thrown at Ghana's President Nkrumah, who narrowly escaped injury: further bomb attacks followed in September, when a curfew was imposed in the capital, Accra.

Here, coffins with the effigies of Nkrumah's three former associates who were charged with the assassination attempt are burnt by loyal supporters in Accra's Black Star Square.

Danish physicist dies

Professor Niels Bohr (1885–1962), the Danish atomic scientist regarded as the greatest physicist since Einstein, died in November this year. Here Bohr is inspecting the atomic plant at Roskilde.

A spy at the Admiralty

On October 22nd a British Admiralty clerk, William Vassall, was sentenced to 18 years' imprisonment for spying for the Soviet Union.

Racism in the Deep South

Racial violence erupted in America's Deep South when attempts were made in September to block Negro James Meredith's registration at the University of Mississippi.

Eleanor Roosevelt

Eleanor Roosevelt (1884–1962) died on November 10th. Besides supporting her husband in politics, she was a writer, journalist, delegate to the United Nations and human rights activist.

1963

Jan	14	Britain's entry to EEC blocked by de Gaulle of France
	29	US poet Robert Frost dies
	30	French composer Francis Poulenc dies
Feb	1	Autonomy for Nyasaland under Hastings Banda
	19	USSR agrees to pull troops out of Cuba
	20	UK: Lord Beveridge, founder of the Welfare State, dies
Mar	17	Volcano erupts in Bali, killing 11,000
Apr	2	Black civil rights campaign begins in US
	6	Anglo/US Polaris weapons agreement signed
	9	Winston Churchill given honorary US citizenship
	17	Canada: Diefenbaker's Prog. Con. govt resigns
	22	Canada: Lester Pearson forms Liberal Govt
	28	Cuban President Fidel Castro visits USSR
May	22	Formation of Organisation for African Unity
Jun	3	Pope John XXIII dies
	20	US and USSR agree on 'hotline' link
	21	France pulls her navy out of NATO
	29	President Kennedy visits British PM Macmillan
Jul	1	Kim Philby, British spy, revealed as 'third man'
	26	Big earthquake at Skopje in Yugoslavia
Aug	8	UK: Armed gang rob train, netting over £1 million
	22	Lord Nuffield, founder of Morris Motors, dies
	28	200,000 US blacks demonstrate for civil rights
	31	French Cubist painter Georges Braque dies
Sep	4	US: Desegregation riots in Birmingham, Alabama
	4	Death of French statesman Robert Schumann
	16	Malaysia is formed as a new nation
	19	Channel Tunnel agreed in Anglo-French report
Oct	1	Nigeria becomes a Republic within the Commonwealth
	3	Army takes control in Honduras
	6	Los Angeles Dodgers win World Series
	7	Kennedy signs treaty to limit nuclear tests
	9	Kabaka is 1st President of Uganda; Dr Obote is PM
	11	French writer and poet Jean Cocteau dies
	11	French singer Edith Piaf dies
	15	Ludwig Erhardt becomes German Chancellor
Nov	22	President Kennedy is assassinated
	24	L. H. Oswald, accused of killing Kennedy, is shot
Dec	10	Linus Pauling wins Nobel Peace Prize
	12	Kenya becomes a Republic; Kenyatta as President

The Arts

British National Theatre opens

Thomas Pynchon's novel *V*

Tony Richardson's film *Tom Jones*

Mankiewicz's film *Cleopatra*

The Profumo affair

On June 5th, John Profumo (1915–) (top) resigned from his parliamentary seat and post as British Secretary of State for War, admitting that he had misled the House of Commons following an investigation into his relationship with model Christine Keeler (above), whose favours he was alleged to have shared with the former Russian naval attaché Captain Ivanov. The Profumo affair, with its grave implications for national security, rocked the country and the scandal almost brought down the government.

Poet of nature

It was only in the second half of his life that Robert Frost (1874–1963) was able to win recognition for his poetry and in his later years he established himself as a major literary figure. He had worked as a New England shoemaker, teacher and farmer and his poetry, based on themes drawn from that rural life, had more in common with 19th century poets than with the modern drive towards realism.

He won the Pulitzer Prize four times: for *New Hampshire* in 1924, *Collected Poems* in 1931, *A Further Range* in 1937 and *A Witness Tree* in 1943. On his 75th and 85th birthdays he was honoured in the US Senate and he played a prominent role at the inauguration of John F. Kennedy in 1961, reciting the poem 'The Gift Outright', specially written for the occasion.

Protests in Saigon

Saigon's two faces of protest. (Left), given the day off for the occasion 50,000 people demonstrate their support for President Diem's crackdown on the Buddhists.

A young Buddhist priest (right), burned himself to death in Saigon's market square neither moving nor uttering a sound during his ordeal. He was the fifth to commit ritual suicide since May when Vietnamese government soliders fired on a Buddhist demonstration killing nine. The United States government, believing in the Buddhist cause, feared Saigon's chances of beating the Viet Cong without first gaining Buddhist support.

'I have a dream'

1963 was a climactic year in the black struggle for civil rights in America. Black rights workers were murdered in Alabama and Mississippi and in June President Kennedy had to federalise the Alabama National Guard when George Wallace, the segregationist Governor of Alabama, tried to prevent two black students from taking up their places at the University of Alabama in Tuscaloosa. Peaceful protest marches in Birmingham were met by force, and weeks of violent rioting ensued on the city's streets (top left) with police using teargas and fire hoses to contain the situation (bottom left). In September a bomb killed four black schoolgirls in the city.

On August 28th, the wave of black protest crested in an enormous peaceful demonstration, when some 200,000 black and white civil rights supporters marched on Washington, DC from all over the United States. The climax to the march came when the crowd gathered at the Lincoln Memorial. There they were addressed by Martin Luther King (above) who told them, in a powerful and moving speech, of his continuing dream of an equal and united America.

President Kennedy assassinated

In one of the greatest political tragedies of the century, US President John Fitzgerald Kennedy was gunned down in Dallas, Texas, on Friday November 22nd. The shooting took place as the presidential motorcade drove through the city's main business centre. Three shots were fired from the sixth floor of a building near the junction of Elm Street and Houston Street, below, and the President slumped forward, hit in the head and neck. With Mrs Kennedy cradling her husband in her arms, the car sped to the Parkland Hospital where the President died half an hour later without regaining consciousness.

Within two hours (far right) Vice-President Lyndon Baines Johnson, who had been travelling in the car behind the President's, was sworn in as the 35th President of the United States at Dallas airfield. Also within hours of the killing, police had arrested Lee Harvey Oswald, a 24-year-old former Marine, and charged him with the President's murder. Two days later, below right, television viewers throughout the world saw Oswald himself gunned down at point blank range as he was being transferred to the county jail from the basement of Dallas police headquarters. The gunman, a 42-year-old Dallas nightclub owner called Jack Ruby, was immediately arrested.

Kennedy's funeral was held in Washington, DC on November 25th, right, in the presence of the greatest gathering of heads of state in the history of the USA. More than a million mourners lined the route as the coffin, draped in the American flag, was taken to St Matthew's Roman Catholic Cathedral.

Above: Only five months earlier Kennedy had seemed to signal new hopes for Western unity when he visited Berlin and made his famous 'Ich bin ein Berliner' speech at the Berlin Wall.

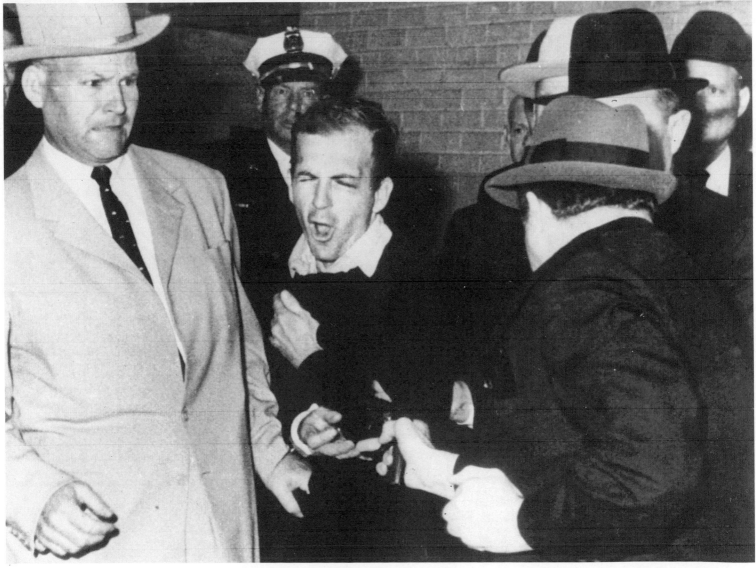

Kenyan independence

Colourful tribal dancing (above) and
widespread celebrations followed the end
of 68 years of British rule in Kenya with
the granting of independence at midnight
on December 12th. The following day, on
behalf of the Queen, Prince Philip handed
the Kenyan Prime Minister Jomo
Kenyatta the constitutional instruments of
power in a ceremony attended by
thousands of people at the Uhuru Stadium
in Nairobi (left). In a moving speech
Kenyatta described it as 'Kenya's greatest
day' and spoke of the 'British principles
and justice' on which the new state would
be built.

The Great Train Robbery

One man was badly injured and mailbags worth more than £2½ million were stolen on August 8th in what became known in Britain as the Great Train Robbery. The crime took place in the early hours of the morning near Linslade in Buckinghamshire when an armed gang held up an overnight Royal Mail train travelling from Glasgow to London. In a meticulously planned operation, the 15 raiders used four six-volt batteries to simulate a red stop signal. When the train stopped, they coshed the driver, Jack Mills, decoupled the engine and some of the carriages and drove them to Bridego Bridge further along the line. Here, the mailbags were loaded into a waiting lorry. Police quickly found the gang's hideout in a nearby farm and Charlie Wilson, the first of the Great Train Robbers to stand trial, was arrested and charged later the same month.

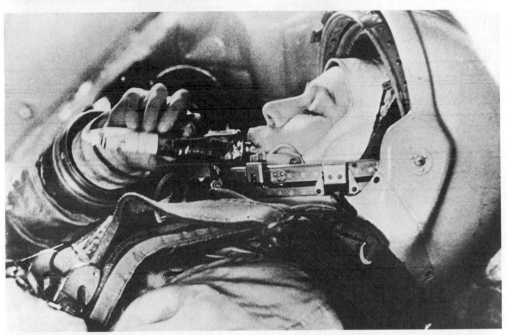

First woman in space

Two years and two months after Yuri Gagarin became the first man in space, the Soviet space programme scored another coup when it put the first woman cosmonaut into orbit. Twenty-six-year-old Lieutenant Valentina Tereshkova (left) achieved this distinction on June 16th when the spacecraft Vostok 6 joined its immediate predecessor Vostok 5 in orbit around the Earth. Feminist groups in the United States claimed that the Soviet Union was demonstrating a more enlightened attitude to women than the United States, but NASA showed less immediate enthusiasm for this new challenge than they had when Gagarin pipped them to the post in 1961.

Regrets for Edith Piaf

The death was announced of the French singer Edith Piaf (1915–1963). Piaf, known as 'The Little Sparrow', was born Edith Giovanna Gassion in Paris. She began her singing career in the bars, cafés and streets of the French capital at the age of 15 and was soon discovered and transferred to the cabaret circuit by her first husband. After the Second World War she went on to international stardom with her deeply emotional performances of such songs as 'Milord', 'La Vie en Rose' and 'Je Ne Regrette Rien'. She also appeared in films, including *Le Bel Indifférent* (1940) which was written for her by her close friend Jean Cocteau.

1964

The Arts

Saul Bellow's novel *Herzog*

Eric Berne's book *Games People Play*

Cacoyannis's film *Zorba the Greek*

Stanley Kubrick's film *Dr Strangelove*

The Beatles's film *A Hard Day's Night*

US support for Vietnam

Throughout 1964 President Lyndon Johnson's administration debated how best to support their allies in the Republic of Vietnam. The Republic was on the verge of collapse, with mounting support for the Communist revolution and a succession of unstable civil and military governments. For the US, failure to maintain a pro-western government in Saigon would destroy their credibility as a dependable ally and possibly represent the first 'domino' in a chain of losses feared in the area.

Johnson (above) continued the policy of the 'pacification' of the south. Millions of peasants were moved into 'strategic hamlets', the defences of one of which are shown (right), in order to deny the PLAFSVN (the southern Communist forces) their sources of supply. Top right: A Viet Cong ambush victim is carried away.

In August American involvement was increased in controversial circumstances. On August 2nd, the USS *Maddox* was attacked by North Vietnamese vessels in the Gulf of Tonkin close to the Democratic Republic's coast. Two days later it was involved in another incident which some have suggested was staged to justify an escalation in the war. In retaliation the US bombed targets inside North Vietnam and Johnson secured the authority to use American troops to aid any State in S. E. Asia.

Although there were only 23,000 US military personnel in Vietnam at year's end, most in an advisory capacity, the Resolution provided the basis for the subsequent escalation of American involvement in Vietnam. Far right: One of the Haiphong 'Amazons'.

Death of Nehru

Jawaharlal Nehru (top left), the elder statesman of the Commonwealth, died suddenly in New Delhi on May 27th. He was 74 and had been Prime Minister of India since the country became independent from Britain in 1947. An estimated three million people lined the route of the funeral cortège on May 28th. In a moving ceremony attended by many world leaders, Nehru's grandson Sanjay lit the funeral pyre near the Gandhi Mausoleum. Nehru was succeeded as Prime Minister by L. B. Shastri.

Changing course

Khrushchev visited Egypt in May for the ceremonial opening of the Aswan High Dam on the River Nile (above). Together the Soviet Premier and President Nasser detonated an explosion in the dam, diverting the water into a new channel. It was one of Khrushchev's last international visits. In October he was sacked as Soviet leader for reasons including 'undignified personal behaviour' and foreign policy failures. He was replaced as First Secretary of the Communist Party by Leonid Brezhnev and as Chairman of the Council of Ministers by Alexei Kosygin.

Wilson elected

Harold Wilson became Prime Minister after the British general election of October 15th. His Labour government, which ended 13 years of Conservative rule, had a parliamentary majority of only four.

Bob Hayes is fastest man

Bob Hayes (1942–   ), from Jacksonville, Florida, won himself the title of the 'world's fastest human' by gaining two gold medals at the Tokyo Olympics. He set world records in both the 100 yard and 100 metre dashes. He won the 100 metre semi-final in an amazing 9.9 seconds but this was disallowed because of winds. In the final he tied the world record of 10 seconds.

Kenya becomes a Republic

On December 12th, the first anniversary of Kenya's independence, the country officially became a Republic within the Commonwealth. The Queen sent President Kenyatta a message of goodwill and the change in the constitution was marked by days of celebrations throughout the country. In Nairobi's Jamhuri Stadium (above) President Kenyatta and the departing Governor-General Malcolm MacDonald watched colourful displays of tribal dancing.

Conflict in the Congo

The trauma of decolonisation ravaged the former Belgian Congo (now Zaire) in the 1960s. After Belgium's swift withdrawal in 1960 a series of provincial revolts broke out, with UN forces aiding the government in Léopoldville as it struggled to control the situation. In 1964 Prime Minister Tshombe faced opposition from the Chinese-trained former Cabinet Minister Pierre Mulele, some of whose followers, armed with bows and arrows, are seen above right. The capital, Léopoldville, was bitterly fought over, and only recaptured from the rebels after a counter-attack in which no prisoners were taken (above left). Many Europeans were kidnapped during the conflict. The American Protestant missionaries of Kintshua (above), were held for four days.

Greville Wynne is freed

On April 22nd, the British businessman Greville Wynne arrived back in Britain after his release from prison in the Soviet Union on spying charges.

Jean-Paul Sartre

The 59-year-old existentialist philosopher, novelist and playwright Jean-Paul Sartre (1905–1980) declined the Nobel Prize for Literature on the grounds that it gave undue weight to a writer's influence.

Ian Smith in Britain

The Prime Minister of Southern Rhodesia, Ian Smith (above), visited Britain in September for talks on Rhodesian independence with the British Premier Sir Alec Douglas-Home.

Nobel Peace Prize for King

The American black civil rights leader Martin Luther King was awarded the Nobel Peace Prize for 1964 in Oslo, Norway. The award was made in recognition of his work towards racial integration in the United States.

Independence for N. Rhodesia

The former colony of Northern Rhodesia achieved independence in October. Kenneth Kaunda (1924–   ), leader of the United Nationalist Independence Party, became the first President of the new State of Zambia.

Mandela imprisoned

In June the black nationalist leader Nelson Mandela (1918–   ) was sentenced to life imprisonment by a South African court, having been found guilty of conspiring to overthrow the white government.

1965

Jan	4	T.S. Eliot, US poet, dies
	7	Indonesia pulls out of United Nations
	20	US: Lyndon Johnson inaugurated as President
	24	Winston Churchill (British PM 1940-45, 1951-55) dies
	30	State funeral for Churchill
Feb	7	US aircraft bomb N Vietnam
	15	American signer Nat 'King' Cole dies
	18	Independence for Gambia
	21	Black Muslim leader Malcolm X shot dead in the US
Mar	3	Seretse Khama becomes 1st President of Bechuanaland
	8	US steps up military involvement in Vietnam
	18	Soviet cosmonaut makes 1st ever space walk
	28	Big earthquake in Chile
Apr	4	US jets shot down by N Vietnamese
	9	Indian and Pakistani soldiers clash on border
	17	US students protest against bombings of N Vietnam
	23	Heavy US air raids on N Vietnam
	30	Dominican President Cabral deposed in coup
May	12	W Germany establishes relations with Israel
	13	Franz Jonas elected President of Austria
Jun	19	Bloodless coup in Algeria

	19	Nguyen Cao Ky becomes President of S Vietnam
	24	S Vietnam severs relations with France
	30	India and Pakistan sign ceasefire
Jul	14	US statesman Adlai Stevenson dies
Aug	2	UK: White Paper limits Commonwealth immigrants
	7	Singapore leaves Malaysian Federation
	11	Race riots in Los Angeles, US
	27	Swiss architect Le Corbusier dies
Oct	17	Anti-Vietnam War demonstration in US and UK
	25	Harold Wilson goes to Rhodesia for talks with Ian Smith
Nov	9	Death penalty abolished in Britain
	11	Rhodesian unilateral declaration of independence (UDI)
Dec	16	British novelist Somerset Maugham dies
	19	France: General de Gaulle is re-elected President
	29	N Vietnam leader Ho Chi Minh rejects US peace talks
	30	Philippines: Ferdinand E. Marcos becomes President

The Arts

UK: MBE for Beatles in Queen's Birthday Honours

Norman Mailer's novel *An American Dream*

The Sound of Music film musical

David Lean's film *Dr Zhivago*

Vietnam escalates

1965 marked the first massive deployment of US forces in Vietnam. To try to force a negotiated settlement a bombing campaign known as 'Rolling Thunder' was begun in February. Because air bases were vulnerable to guerrilla infiltration and sabotage, large numbers of marines were deployed in March to protect them. Below: Marines are shown landing 10 miles north of the vast airfield at Da Nang.

By July 1965, 175,000 US troops were in Vietnam, most assigned to base protection. The Americans relied upon their technological superiority and immense amounts of firepower (right, a village thought to harbour Communist troops is bombed). The helicopter was vital to the notion of 'airmobility'. Below, South Vietnamese soldiers are shown disembarking for an attack.

The helicopter was, however, difficult to maintain and vulnerable to ground fire, while the influx of supplies presented the Americans with immense logistical problems.

The NLFPAVN (northern Communist forces) harried and chased the South Vietnamese forces and their US allies, ensuring that firm control was never established over the Republic of Vietnam. Opposite: Victims of a terrorist bomb outside the US embassy in Saigon.

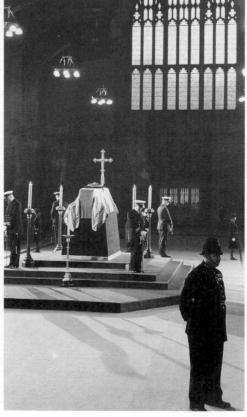

Churchill's funeral

Sir Winston Churchill's state funeral took place in London on Saturday January 30th. The British elder statesman had died, aged 90, on January 24th. His coffin, draped with a Union Jack, was borne by gun carriage from Westminster Hall, where some 300,000 people had paid their last respects during the lying-in-state, to St Paul's Cathedral, where the funeral service was held. Three thousand people attended, including Queen Elizabeth, who broke with royal precedent by awaiting the arrival of the body in the cathedral.

After the service, the coffin was carried through streets lined with mourning crowds to Tower Pier on the River Thames. From there, to the sound of massed pipe bands and a 17-gun salute, it was taken by river to Waterloo Station for the last leg of its journey to Oxfordshire, where Sir Winston Churchill was laid to rest in Bladon churchyard next to his parents and within sight of Blenheim Palace, the home of the Churchill family for more than two centuries.

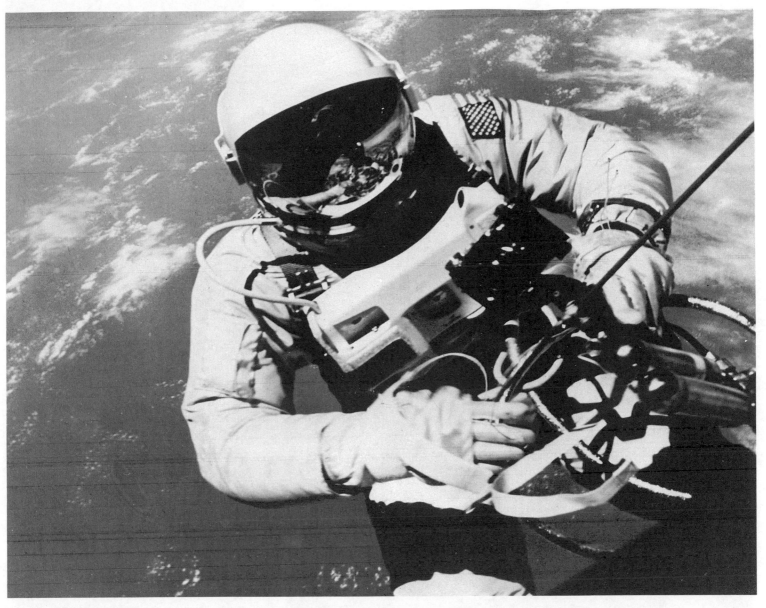

First walks in space

Another milestone in the ever-quickening East–West space race was passed on March 18th when the Russian cosmonaut Alexei Leonov became the first man to walk in space. Three months later, astronaut Edward H. White (left) became the first American to walk in space. On June 3rd, he left the Gemini 4 spacecraft and floated outside the ship for a record 21 minutes.

The moors murders

A full-scale search was launched on Saddleworth Moor near Manchester, England (above), after the body of a ten-year-old girl was found buried there in October. The discovery, and the resulting charges of murder against Ian Brady and Myra Hindley (above), opened perhaps the most notorious murder case of the century.

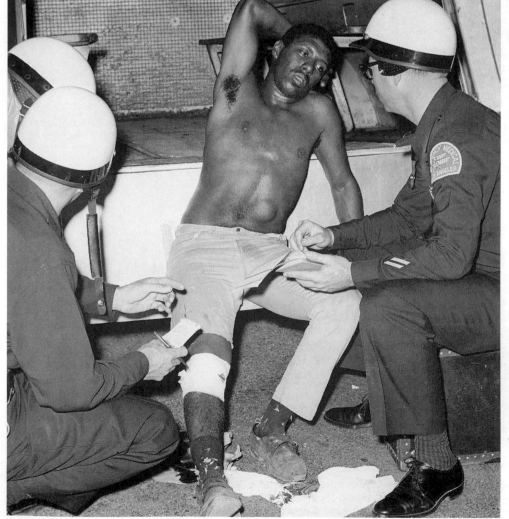

Black civil rights

In the United States the black civil rights
struggle moved into a new phase. In the
wake of President Johnson's Civil Rights
Act of 1964, Martin Luther King
concentrated his campaign for black voter
registration on the town of Selma in
Alabama. Only 335 of the black population
of about 14,000 were registered to vote
here and attempts to increase this number
had been resisted by the local authorities.

On March 7th, a black protest march to
the State capital, Montgomery, was
violently broken up by State troopers
acting on the orders of the State Governor
George Wallace, and one of the
demonstrators was killed. Two weeks later
Johnson federalised the National Guard to
give protection to a peaceful march led by
King himself. Twenty-five thousand people
gathered in Selma in the morning drizzle
(above, left and right) to walk the 52 miles
to Montgomery, where King addressed the
crowd.

Despite the passing of the 1965 Civil
Rights Act, which removed further
obstacles to black voting, unrest continued
and spread to cities outside the South. In
August the worst riots in living memory
took place in the Watts district of Los
Angeles, where 34 people were killed and
35 million dollars worth of property was
destroyed in violent disturbances (left).

Rhodesian unilateral declaration of independence

On November 11th, a few days after the British Prime Minister Harold Wilson was greeted by demonstrators while visiting the Rhodesian Premier for talks in Salisbury (above) Ian Smith unilaterally declared Rhodesia an independent State. The minority white government ignored its technical dismissal by the Governor Sir Humphrey Gibbs and the British Labour government rushed legislation through Parliament to impose economic sanctions on the rebel regime.

Kennedy memorial

Queen Elizabeth unveiled a memorial to John F. Kennedy at Runnymede, the meadow by the Thames where the Magna Carta was signed in 1215. The former President's widow Jacqueline and his son John (above) were present at the ceremony.

MBEs for The Beatles

Controversy erupted in Britain when the Queen's Birthday Honours List included MBEs for The Beatles. John, Paul, George and Ringo received their awards at an investiture held at Buckingham Palace in October.

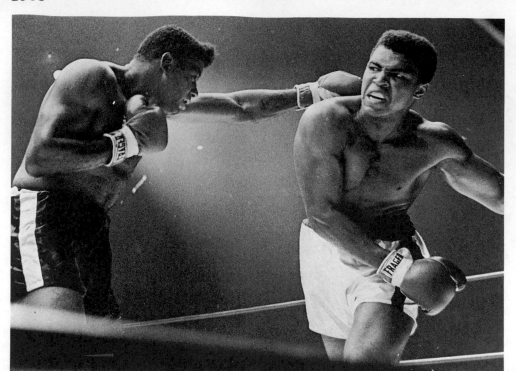

Muhammed Ali

On November 23rd the controversial boxer Muhammed Ali (left) defeated Floyd Patterson in Las Vegas to retain his title as Heavyweight Champion of the World. Ali, who changed his name from Cassius Clay the previous year after his conversion to Islam, retained his heavyweight title after a technical knockout in the 12th round.

Brigitte Bardot

The French actress and sex-symbol Brigitte Bardot (above) became the focus of enormous media attention when she visited the United States in December to publicise her new film *Viva Maria!*, in which she played a gun-toting South American revolutionary. The journalists who followed her everywhere during her stay compared her to Marilyn Monroe.

Le Corbusier

The Swiss-born architect, born in 1887, died on August 27th. A legend in his time, he was a major pioneer of the modern movement in architecture. His major achievements include the Unité d'Habitation at Marseilles, which housed 1,600 people under a single roof. He is seen with the magnificent enamelled door he designed for the Punjab Parliament.

The Spy Who Came in from the Cold

John le Carré's third novel, *The Spy Who Came in from the Cold*, clinched his reputation as the grand master of spy fiction with its complex, gripping plot exposing hypocrisy and betrayal within the intelligence services. It was also made into a memorable film, released in 1965 and starring Richard Burton who gave a remarkable performance in the title role.

1966

US sends more troops to Vietnam

The Republic of Vietnam and their American allies increased their efforts to isolate the southern revolutionaries by stopping the flow of troops and supplies from North Vietnam. Communist leaders were hoping for a mass rising in the towns of the south to topple the fragile government. By now they had infiltrated most rural areas, where government forces were weak. Here (below),

North Vietnamese regulars and southern National Liberation Front guerrillas patrol the Saigon River in South Vietnam.

Meanwhile, US bombing of the north escalated and petrol dumps were attacked to prevent fuel reaching the supply convoys, leading to evacuation of the northern capital Hanoi. The US then flooded South Vietnam with troops and supplies.

Aberfan

At 9.30 on the morning of October 21st tragedy struck the small Welsh mining village of Aberfan, near Merthyr Tydfil, when a slag heap collapsed, engulfing the village school. The disaster left 147 dead, and virtually wiped out an entire generation of schoolchildren.

The children were gathering for morning assembly when the landslide began, and in a matter of seconds both Pantglas Infants' and Junior School, together with surrounding buildings, were buried under two million tons of mine waste, rocks and sludge. From midday the school would have been empty for the half-term holiday.

Rescue work went on all day and throughout the night as more than 2,000 police, firemen, civil defence workers and volunteers tunnelled through 45 feet of slag to recover bodies and search for survivors. Hardened reporters and policemen broke down in tears as the first bodies were carried out of the mud and the full extent of the tragedy began to become clear. Mothers and grandmothers scrabbled at the rubble with their bare hands and miners from nearby pits left their work to help with the rescue operations. The Prime Minister and the Duke of Edinburgh flew to the scene to offer their condolences to the bereaved.

A hundred thousand people were present on October 27th when the first funerals took place. Eighty-one small coffins were lowered into two long trenches in the hillside cemetery. A 100-foot cross of floral wreaths was laid across the graves and throughout Britain flags were flown at half-mast as the burial service was read.

Reagan elected Governor

Former Hollywood actor, Ronald Wilson Reagan (1911–   ), was elected Governor of California on November 8th. Reagan had only joined the Republican Party in 1962.

Truman Capote

The American writer (1924–1984) had a phenomenal success with his best-selling documentary, *In Cold Blood*, an account of the mass killing of a Kansas family.

Dr Martin Luther King

Civil rights leader Dr Martin Luther King sits with his wife in their four-room slum apartment in Chicago after moving in on January 26th. Dr King decided to experience the problems of slum life first-hand as part of his massive anti-slum campaign.

Dylan and Baez

Bob Dylan (born Robert Zimmerman, 1941–   ), and Joan Baez became two of the great cult figures of the 1960s, enthralling huge audiences with their compelling folk music and songs of protest. Baez first introduced Dylan at one of her own concerts.

Verwoerd assassinated

On September 6th Dr Hendrik Verwoerd (above), Prime Minister of South Africa and leader of the Nationalist Party, was stabbed to death by a white extremist in the House of Assembly.

Top: Forced labour for Africans in Johannesburg.

The Cultural Revolution

In August, Chairman Mao Tse-tung launched the Great Proletarian Cultural Revolution to release the revolutionary fervour of Chinese youth. Millions of young Chinese, brandishing copies of the *Little Red Book*, formed themselves into Red Guards and set about extirpating all revisionism and Westernism.

1967

The *Torrey Canyon* disaster

On March 18th, a giant oil tanker, the *Torrey Canyon*, ran aground on the Seven Stones Reef between the Scilly Isles and Land's End, causing the greatest oil pollution threat to the coasts of Britain this century. The 975-foot tanker, laden with some 117,000 tons of Kuwaiti oil, was bound for Milford Haven when struck the reef. Within six days some 30,000 tons of oil had escaped into the sea, producing a slick covering 260 square miles. Thousands of gallons of detergent were dumped on it, but two days later the tanker broke her back during a salvage attempt (above), releasing a further 30,000 tons of oil.

Emergency measures were taken on March 28th and 29th when Royal Air Force bombers dropped aviation fuel, high-explosive bombs, rockets and napalm on the tanker to sink it and burn off the remaining oil. The six hours' continuous bombardment was a success, but by then 100 miles of Cornish beaches were polluted and irreparable damage had been done to wildlife.

The Six-Day War

In one of the most efficient military operations of modern times, Israeli forces routed the armies of three Arab States and occupied an area larger than the entire State of Israel in just six days.

The Six-Day War began after Colonel Nasser, who had entered a pact with Jordan and Syria, moved his troops into Sinai and closed the Straits of Tiran to Israeli shipping. On June 5th, the Israeli Air Force launched a lightning attack against Arab airbases, and the air forces of Egypt, Jordan and Syria were left in ruins. At the same time three Israeli tank divisions moved into the Sinai desert. They took the Sinai capital of El Arish and by June 6th the Egyptian Army was in total disarray (above).

By June 7th, King Hussein's Jordanian forces had also been routed and most of the West Bank, including the Old City of Jerusalem (top left), was in Israeli hands. On June 9th, amid calls for a ceasefire, Israeli forces pressed on to the Suez Canal (centre and bottom right). At the same time an attack was launched on the Syrian-held Golan Heights and by June 10th, when the war ended, these too had fallen to Israel. Right: Some of the casualties of the war. Top: El Quantowa, on the Suez Canal.

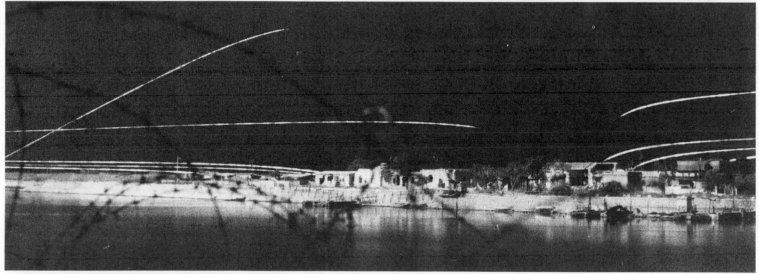

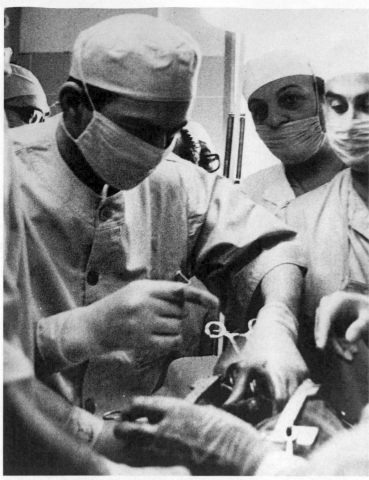

First heart transplant

The first ever human heart transplant was carried out successfully at a Cape Town hospital by surgeon Dr Christiaan Barnard. Fifty-three-year-old Louis Washansky received a new lease of life in the pioneering operation.

Trouble in Aden

Housewives took to carrying sub-machine guns in the colony of Aden (above) as the pace of nationalist terrorism increased. The death toll rose sharply as the struggle for independence moved into its final phase.

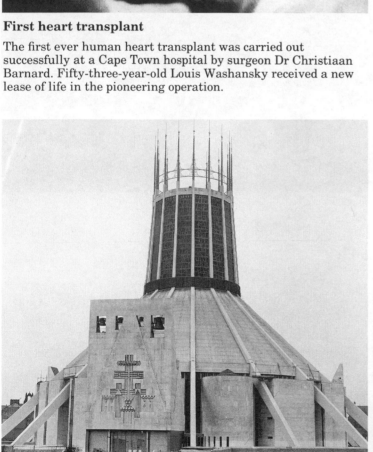

Liverpool Catholic Cathedral consecrated

In May a new Catholic cathedral was consecrated in Liverpool. The work of Sir Frederick Gibberd (1908–1984), it was constructed around a circle 194 feet in diameter and incorporated the crypt of an earlier unfinished cathedral.

Anti-Vietnam war rally

New York's First Avenue is filled with demonstrators during an anti-war rally on April 15th. The 100,000 marchers started their rally at Central Park and made their way through the streets of Manhattan to the United Nations.

Pressure on South Vietnam

Throughout the year Communist forces maintained pressure on the South Vietnamese government and their American allies. Above: An American success – a North Vietnamese soldier is captured just south of the de-militarised zone (the 'DMZ') separating North and South Vietnam.

Death of Donald Campbell

Millions of people watched their television sets in horror as Donald Campbell's attempt to break his own world water speed record of 276.33 miles per hour ended in tragedy on Coniston Water in England's Lake District. At 300 miles per hour on his return run, his boat *Bluebird* suddenly somersaulted backwards and sank. Campbell's body was never found.

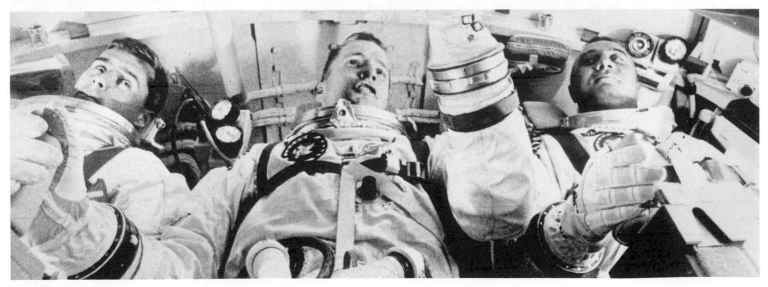

Apollo tragedy

The American space programme claimed its first lives on January 27th when disaster struck the first manned Apollo spacecraft during ground testing at Cape Kennedy. Fire engulfed the command module after an electrical fault on the launchpad and the three astronauts inside – Roger Chaffee, Virgil Grissom and Ed White (who had made the first American spacewalk 18 months earlier) – were killed before they could escape. They are shown during training for the mission.

Svetlana Stalin defects

Svetlana Stalin, daughter of the discredited Soviet dictator, gave a press conference in New York after her defection to the West in April.

QE2 launched

The £25½-million liner, the *Queen Elizabeth II*, seen during preparations at John Brown's yard, was launched by her namesake on September 20th.

Harold Holt

Australia's Prime Minister, Harold Holt (1908–1967), disappeared and was presumed drowned while swimming in the sea on December 16th.

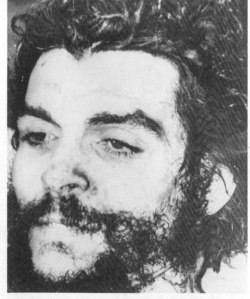

Death of Jayne Mansfield

The Hollywood actress Jayne Mansfield was killed at the age of 35 when the car in which she was travelling collided with a lorry near New Orleans on June 29th (above). She was best known as a blonde sex symbol in such films as *The Girl Can't Help It* and *Kiss Them for Me*. Despite success in publicity, her film career was in a decline by the mid-60s. She never broke out of the sexpot mould.

Che Guevara killed

Bolivian troops displayed the body of Ernesto 'Che' Guevara (above), the guerrilla revolutionary and former lieutenant to Fidel Castro, after shooting him dead in the jungle.

1968

Martin Luther King assassinated

The leading voice of black America was brutally silenced on the night of April 4th when Martin Luther King, the civil rights leader and Baptist minister (top), was gunned down in Memphis, Tennessee, by James Earl Ray, an escaped convict. King, whose campaign for civil rights extended beyond the black community to all the poor of America, was in Memphis to support a strike of the city's dustmen. He had walked out on to the balcony of his motel room for some air when shots were fired from a neighbouring boarding house. His funeral in Atlanta, Georgia (above), was attended by some 150,000 people, including representatives of the US government.

Unrest on the streets of Paris

The worst rioting ever to hit mainland France took place in Paris, leaving scenes of devastation not seen since the Second World War. There was turmoil on May 6th when some 10,000 left-wing students fought CRS riot police, armed with teargas, fire hoses and batons, in the streets of the Latin Quarter. Cars and buses were overturned and burned. There were 600 injuries and 422 arrests. On May 10th, further pitched battles took place between police and students, who dug up paving stones for barricades. The rioting was followed by a five-week student occupation of the Sorbonne University (left) and a general strike, during which rubbish piled up in the streets (above).

Robert Kennedy assassinated

Victory turned to tragedy on June 5th when Senator Robert Kennedy (above) was gunned down after celebrating his success in the California primary election for the Democratic presidential nomination. Kennedy, 42, the brother of the assassinated President, was shot in the head and shoulder by a Jordanian Arab, Sirhan Bishara Sirhan, who was immediately arrested. The shooting happened just after midnight at the Ambassador Hotel, Los Angeles, where the Senator had been making a victory speech to a packed meeting of his supporters. He was rushed to hospital where doctors fought to save him, but he died 24 hours later without regaining consciousness.

Moon orbit by US astronauts

Another milestone in man's journey into space was passed on Christmas Eve when the United States put the first manned spacecraft into orbit around the moon. The ship, Apollo 8, had taken off from Cape Kennedy on December 21st (above) and orbited the moon ten times before returning to Earth. The astronauts – Colonel Frank Borman, Captain James Lovell and Major William Anders – sent photographs and television pictures back to Earth, but the emotional climax of the mission came on Christmas morning with Borman's voice reading from space the opening verses of the Book of Genesis.

The Ronan Point disaster

Three people were killed and others were trapped when part of a block of flats collapsed in the East End of London. The disaster happened on March 16th in Butcher's Road, Plaistow, when a gas explosion brought down all the corner flats in the 22-storey tower block Ronan Point (above). Police and firemen were joined by dock workers and other volunteers as the rescue work began. An inquiry was set up to investigate the construction of the block, which was built to a design common in London and elsewhere in the UK.

The invasion of Czechoslovakia

August saw the end of the 'Prague Spring', a period of liberalisation and reform in Czechoslovakia in which a new leadership, headed by Communist Party chief Alexander Dubček and State President Svoboda, had begun a 'socialist democratic revolution' including a relaxation of censorship and constitutionally guaranteed popular freedoms. The Kremlin, aware of the possible impact of such changes on their position in eastern Europe, sent in Warsaw Pact armies to prevent what they termed a 'counter-revolution'.

In Prague, crowds milled around the Soviet tanks (left and above left). Sporadic fighting broke out but, with over 600,000 troops occupying the country, resistance was futile. The majority could only keep a melancholy vigil like this one (above) in Wenceslas Square on August 28th.

Spring turned to winter as Czechoslovakia underwent a process of 'normalisation'. A new leadership reintroduced curbs on the press, banned the formation of new parties and brought the government back into line with the rest of the Warsaw Pact nations.

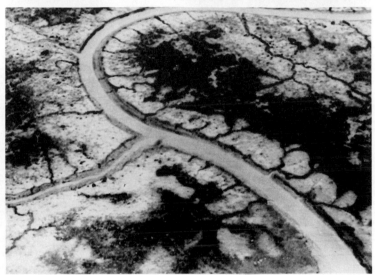

The 'Tet' Offensive

On January 31st, the National Liberation Front (NLF) and North Vietnamese troops launched the 'Tet' Offensive on the major urban areas of South Vietnam. Fierce street fighting continued during February, notably in Saigon where landmarks like the US Embassy and the Presidential Palace were stormed, and in the town of Hue (left) where 113,000 of the 145,000 inhabitants were left homeless. The strength with which the offensive was resisted, seen by millions worldwide on television, cast doubt on the ability of the US and South Vietnamese troops to defeat their enemies. Above left: South Vietnamese casualties in Saigon.

President Johnson initiated the first peace talks by halting the bombing of North Vietnam, the North's precondition for negotiation.

Defoliation

The systematic defoliation of South Vietnam was increasingly being questioned as a military tactic. Designed to deny the NLF food and shelter, South Vietnamese President Thieu concluded in 1968 that its effects on the populace as a whole made it counterproductive. Two areas of mangrove forest are shown (above), before and after defoliation.

Biafran tragedy

While politicians argued and the civil war dragged on in Nigeria, a worldwide relief operation was mounted for the starving people of Biafra.

Hair

The American rock musical *Hair*, now under Tom O'Horgan's direction, opened on Broadway in April. The new, shocking, version was a huge success.

Hancock suicide

The British comedian Tony Hancock (1924–1968), who became a household name with his radio show *Hancock's Half Hour*, committed suicide in a hotel room in Sydney, Australia.

Bridge crosses the Atlantic

London Bridge was sold to an American oil millionaire for £1 million. Every stone was numbered for reassembly before the bridge was dismantled and reassembled in Arizona.

1969

Biafra

The civil war in Nigeria, which had dragged on for 18 months since the secession of Biafra, entered its final phase in 1969. The new State was surrounded by a Federal Nigerian Army of some 250,000 men. Its remaining territory was home to eight million people, a third of them refugees, many of whom were dying of starvation in squalid temporary camps. Thousands of people were dying every day by the middle of the year, and a vast international relief operation was sending 40 flights a night into the country. Despite worldwide sympathy for the plight of the Biafran people, it was fast becoming clear that the forces of their leader Odumwega Ojukwu would not be able to hold out indefinitely against such overwhelming odds.

Man on the moon

A great milestone in human history was passed when man first set foot on the surface of the moon. The moment was broadcast live to an estimated 600 million people, or one in five of the world's population. The lunar landing was the successful culmination of the Apollo space project and fulfilled President Kennedy's ambition to put a man on the moon by the end of the decade.

Apollo 11's historic mission began at Cape Kennedy on July 16th at 9.32 a.m. Three days and 240,000 miles later, the three astronauts (Neil Armstrong, Edwin 'Buzz' Aldrin and Michael Collins) went into orbit around the moon, and at 1.47 p.m. on July 20th Armstrong and Aldrin began their descent in the lunar module 'Eagle'. (Inset: The lunar module photographed from the window of the command module.) The module's three landing probes touched down in the Sea of Tranquillity at 4.17 p.m. and just over six and a half hours later Neil Armstrong became the first human being to set foot on the moon, with the words 'That's one small step for a man, one giant leap for mankind.'

Aldrin joined him shortly afterwards and together the two men set up a television camera to film themselves as they planted the American flag, unveiled a plaque, collected samples from the lunar surface and conducted scientific experiments. During their eight and a half hour moonwalk they received a congratulatory telephone call from President Nixon and demonstrated the effects of one-sixth gravity by jumping in their 16-layer moonsuits.

'Eagle' rejoined the orbiting command module after 21 hours and 37 minutes on the moon. The return to Earth, below, went almost exactly according to schedule and splashdown took place in the Pacific on July 24th.

Jan Palach's funeral

Flowers are heaped upon the grave of Jan Palach, the 21-year-old Prague philosophy student who burned himself to death in protest at the Soviet invasion of Czechoslovakia. Over half a million people paid their respects to the funeral cortège on January 25th. Wenceslas Square's newly painted signs reading *Red Army Square* were replaced by *Jan Palach Square*.

Rioting in Londonderry

Sectarian strife flared up once more in Northern Ireland. After Unionist Orange Day parades on July 12th, rioting broke out in many of the main towns. Above: A burning shop in the predominantly Catholic Bogside area of Londonderry later in the summer of 1969. British troops were brought in at the request of the Ulster cabinet to 'prevent a breakdown of law and order'.

Chappaquiddick

In July Senator Edward Kennedy was given a two-month suspended prison sentence for leaving the scene of an accident in which a woman passenger in his car was drowned. Mary Jo Kopechne died when the car, driven by the Senator, plunged over a bridge on Chappaquiddick Island, Massachusetts. Hours elapsed before Kennedy reported the accident.

Charles Manson

Charles Manson, head of a Californian commune of hippies and drifters, brutally murdered Sharon Tate, pregnant wife of film director Roman Polanski, at their Hollywood home on August 9th, along with four other victims. The trial revealed the power he exerted over his followers. He was sentenced to death – commuted to life imprisonment – along with three others.

Trudeau in London

The flamboyant Canadian Prime Minister Pierre Trudeau (above), whose Liberal Party won a landslide victory in 1968, arrived in London for talks with the British Premier Harold Wilson.

Ho Chi Minh dies

Ho Chi Minh, founder and ideological leader of the Vietnamese Communist Party, died on September 3rd. To commemorate his contribution to the Revolution, Saigon was renamed Ho Chi Minh City.

Judy Garland dies

The singer and actress Judy Garland (1922–1969) died in London a few days after her 47th birthday. Born Frances Ethel Gumm, she was best known for her portrayal of Dorothy in the film *The Wizard of Oz*.

Concorde's first flights

The controversial supersonic jet airliner Concorde 001 had its maiden flight at Toulouse on March 2nd. The flight, which had originally been scheduled for February 1968, began at 3.30 p.m. and lasted about half an hour. At the controls was the chief test pilot of Sud Aviation, André Turcat, who took the plane to a speed of 300 miles per hour.

The British-built Concorde 002 (above) flew for the first time at Filton airfield in Bristol the following month. Brian Trubshaw, the test pilot, attained a speed of around 200 miles per hour and landed the plane at the RAF airfield at Fairford, Gloucestershire, some 20 minutes after take-off. It was a 'wizard flight' he said.

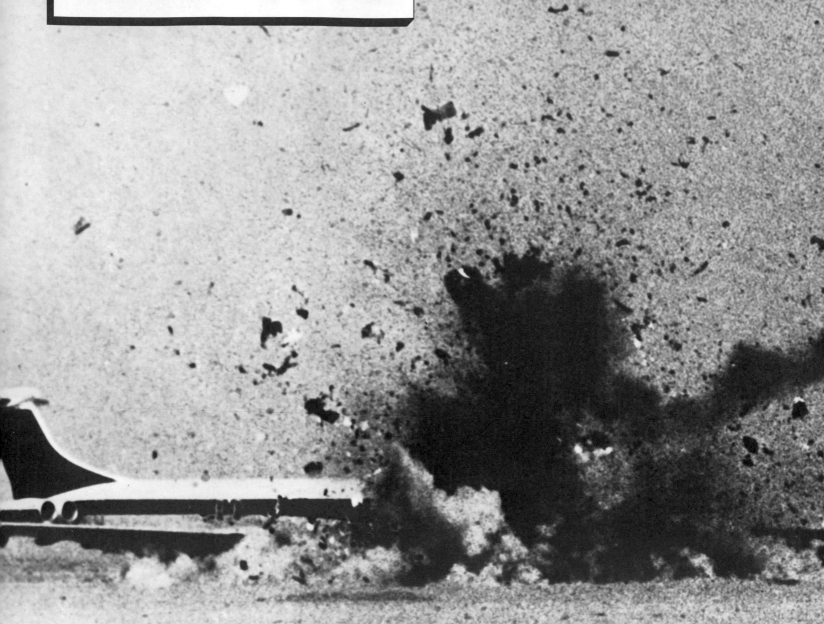

1970-1979

The 1970s

For many people it was the decade of disillusionment, the years in which the heady idealism of the 1960s, the belief of millions of young people that they could really change the world, collapsed into cynicism and bitterness. From the ashes of revolutionary fervour arose the ugly phoenix of terrorism.

In the United States the American dream changed into the reality of Vietnam and Watergate. On the international stage the first overtures of East–West détente were abruptly silenced by the Soviet invasion of Afghanistan. War flared again in the Middle East, where revolutionary changes in Iran and chaos in Lebanon undermined the promise of stability held out by the Egypt–Israel peace settlement. The seemingly insoluble Palestinian problem fuelled international terrorism on an unprecedented scale. Hijacks and hostages became the headlines of the 1970s.

Meanwhile the economies of the Western nations slid inexorably towards recession. As oil prices rose, inflation and unemployment moved towards the top of the political agenda. The scene was set for far-reaching social changes.

International terrorism

Perhaps the most disturbing development of the decade was the spread of international terrorism. Political violence was nothing new. Its history was as long as the history of mankind. What distinguished the terrorist movements of the 1970s from their predecessors was the international scale of their operations. The terrible roll-call of deaths and kidnappings paid eloquent testimony to the failure of governments to find an answer to the problem, as ordinary citizens joined the front-line casualties of an insidious undeclared war. Hijackings brought terror to the airways, with outrages such as those at Dawson's Field in Jordan and Entebbe in Uganda making headline news. In West Germany the Red Army Faction, generally known as the Baader–Meinhof gang, brought chaos to the streets with their campaign of bombings in major cities. In Munich Palestinian guerrillas shocked the world with their murder of Israeli athletes competing in the Olympic Games and in Northern Ireland and mainland Britain the IRA stepped up its nationalistic campaign of terror after the 'Bloody Sunday' shootings. In Italy the Red Brigades proved able to kidnap and murder a former premier at will. Even the relative tranquillity of Canada was not immune: in 1970 the Quebec Liberation Front abducted and killed the Minister of Labour.

Vietnam and Watergate

The decade began with the United States still firmly entrenched in Vietnam, as the war that had provided a focus for so much protest in the 1960s dragged on with no conclusion in sight. Unprecedented television coverage beamed the stark realities of war into millions of homes throughout the world. Its nightly images, showing as they did the effects of military action on the civilian population of Vietnam, helped to turn public opinion against the war in America and elsewhere. The US withdrawal, when it finally came, was soon to be followed by Communist occupation of Saigon and the creation of a worldwide refugee problem as the first Vietnamese boat people fled the new régime. The damage to morale was compounded by the breaking of the Watergate scandal, which swept Richard Nixon from the White House in America's first ever presidential resignation. The disillusionment went very deep. With its apparent helplessness in the face of the Iranian hostage crisis at the end of the decade, America's guardianship of the free world seemed threatened.

The Middle East

The Arab–Israeli conflict continued to make the Middle East the focus of international tension. The powderkeg of Middle Eastern politics was further primed during the 1970s by the outbreak of the Yom Kippur War and the descent of Lebanon into political anarchy as civil war began to turn the city of Beirut from the playground of the Arab rich to the burned-out ruin familiar from so many television pictures. Despite the award of the Nobel Peace Prize to Egypt's Anwar Sadat and Israel's Menachem Begin for their 1978 peace treaty, stability in the region seemed as elusive as ever. In 1979 a new and unpredictable element entered the picture as the Shah's régime was swept from power in Iran on a tide of Islamic fundamentalism and popular dissent. By the end of the decade the Ayatollah Khomeini had returned to Tehran after years of exile and the American hostage crisis had begun.

Economic affairs

It was a decade of economic decline and industrial unrest in the Western democracies. The swingeing OPEC oil price rises that followed in the wake of the Yom Kippur War sent shock waves through the industrial world. In Britain governments of right and left seemed equally unable to arrest the descent into economic chaos, of which the three-day working week and the 'winter of discontent' became potent symbols. Inflation rose inexorably. A wave of strikes paralysed the country in an outbreak of what Britain's European neighbours – whom she joined in the Common Market in 1973 – were to call the 'British disease'. But this was not a British problem alone. By 1977 there were some 15 million people registered as unemployed in the seven countries – the UK, the US, France, West Germany, Italy, Japan and Canada – whose leaders met in London for urgent talks on the economic outlook. Controversial remedies were already being discussed. Many people looked to the 1980s with apprehension.

Pages 142–3: Three hijacked aircraft blown up by the PFLP at Dawson's Field, 1970.

1970

Jan	1	Age of majority reduced from 21 to 18 in UK
	12	Biafra capitulates to Nigerian forces
Feb	9	PLO leader Yasser Arafat visits Moscow for talks
	25	US painter Mark Rothko commits suicide
Mar	2	Israel and Syria in biggest clash since Six-Day War
Apr	16	Ian Paisley wins Bannside by-election in N Ireland
	30	US troops sent to Cambodia to attack communist bases
May	4	4 US students shot dead at Kent State University, Ohio
	12	6 blacks die in racist riots in Georgia, US
Jun	4	Tonga becomes independent from Britain
	11	Former Russian statesman Alexander Kerensky dies
	18	Conservatives win election in Britain
	26	Dubček is expelled from Czech Communist Party
	29	Last US troops withdraw from Cambodia
Jul	8	UK: Roy Jenkins elected Deputy Leader of Labour Party
	20	British Conservative politician Iain Macleod dies
	21	Aswan Dam in Egypt is completed
	27	Portuguese Fascist dictator Antonio Salazar dies
Aug	2	British army in Belfast uses rubber bullets for first time
	9	Police and blacks clash in Notting Hill, London
	24	Radioactivity leaked at Windscale power station, UK
Sep	4	Salvador Allende is elected President of Chile
	12	Palestinians blow up 3 hijacked jets in Jordan

	18	US rock musician Jimi Hendrix dies of drug overdose
	28	Egyptian leader Gamal Abdel Nasser dies
Oct	5	Anwar Sadat succeeds Nasser as President of Egypt
	9	Cambodia declared a Republic
	10	Fiji becomes independent of Britain
	10	Quebec minister Pierre Laporte kidnapped and killed
	16	Sadat of Egypt is President of United Arab Republic
Nov	3	Allende becomes President of Chile
	9	De Gaulle (French President 1944–5, 1959–69) dies
	12	US: Court martial of Lt Calley for My Lai massacre
	13	Syria: General Hafez el-Assad seizes power
	27	Gay Liberation Front marches in London for first time
Dec	3	Publication of Industrial Relations Bill in UK
	16	Six killed in Polish riots at Gdansk shipyard
	17	*Pravda* attacks Soviet writer Solzhenitsyn as 'hostile'
	20	Polish leader Gomulka resigns after rioting

The Arts

Ted Hughes's poem *Crow*

Dmitry Shostakovitch's *Symphony No 14*

Butch Cassidy and the Sundance Kid film

Young Vic Theatre Company formed in London

Robert Bolt's play *Vivat! Vivat Regina!*

Henri Charrière's book *Papillon*

Shootings at US anti-war demonstration

Four students were killed and nine others injured when National Guardsmen opened fire on a student demonstration at Kent State University, Ohio. The shootings occurred during a wave of campus protests against the entry of American troops into Cambodia on May 1st. On May 4th, between 1,500 and 3,000 students gathered on the college campus at Kent State University, contravening an order by the State Governor banning all meetings, whether peaceful or otherwise. At about midday tear gas was used to break up the demonstration. When some students threw back the canisters and started to hurl stones, the National Guard opened fire without warning. The four students killed – two women and two men, aged 19 and 20 – were not involved in the demonstration itself.

US bombs Cambodia

Both sides in the Vietnam War used the small neighbouring states of Laos and Cambodia in their operations. Bases and supply-lines were established (most notably the Ho Chi Minh trail linking southern Communists with North Vietnam) while the United States tried to destroy these facilities by secret bombing.

Once the pro-American General Lon Nol had seized power in Cambodia, US and South Vietnamese forces searched the country for the Communist headquarters directing operations in South Vietnam. The operation failed to remove the insurgents. Their presence, and the continued bombing and covert operations in Cambodia and Laos, only served to destabilise further these already fragile nations. Left: Cambodian villagers await transport from a US helicopter out of the new battle zone.

Riots in Northern Ireland

In the summer, attempts were made to quell widespread civil disobedience in Northern Ireland. Major Chichester Clark, Northern Ireland's Prime Minister, announced the deployment of 3,500 additional troops in the province at the end of June.

And on the night of July 3rd, the reinforced Army made a comprehensive search for arms in the Falls Road area. They encountered fierce resistance, including barricades and gunfire. Over 200 arrests were made and a curfew was established in 50 streets around the Falls Road. Two rioters were reported to have been shot dead by the Army, and a third was killed by an armoured car, leading to complaints that excessive force had been used in the search. Left: Soldiers on alert the day after the most serious disturbances.

Premiership for Heath

In a surprise result, the Conservative Party won the British general election with an overall majority of 31 seats. Their victory, which confounded most of the opinion pollsters, brought to an end almost six years of Labour rule. The election took place on June 18th and was the first one in which 18-year-olds were allowed to vote.

The following day the outgoing Prime Minister, Harold Wilson, tendered his resignation and was succeeded by Edward Heath, a 53-year-old bachelor. He is seen (left) meeting Conservative women MPs, including Mrs Margaret Thatcher (far left), the only woman member of Mr Heath's Cabinet, who was appointed Secretary of State for Education and Science.

Airliners blown up in Jordan

Three airliners were blown up by Arab guerrillas on September 12th after a triple hijack. The British, Swiss and American planes were seized by members of the Popular Front for the Liberation of Palestine (PFLP) who had been holding about 300 passengers hostage at Dawson's Field, a desert airstrip near Amman. After days of negotiation, the hostages were finally released in exchange for seven Arab detainees.

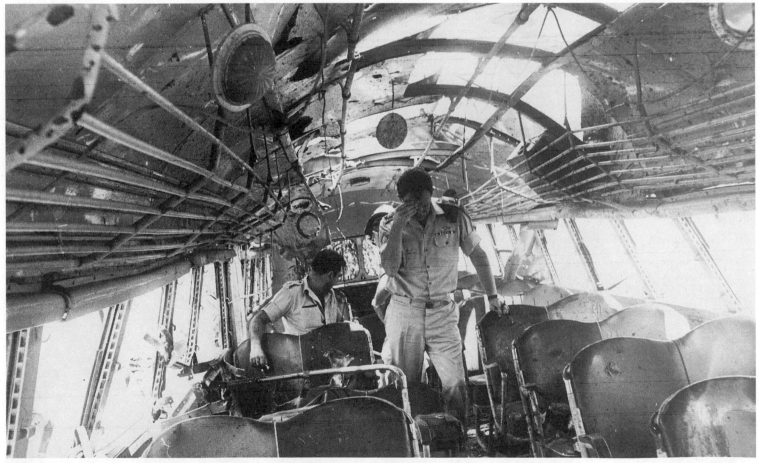

Israeli school bus attacked

There was outrage in Israel when a bus carrying children from school was shelled by Arab guerrillas on the Israel–Lebanon border. Eight children and three adults were killed and 21 were injured (many of them seriously) when the guerrillas fired bazookas at the vehicle from a distance of 20 yards. The PFLP claimed responsibility, and within hours Israeli forces had shelled four Lebanese villages in reprisal.

Victory for Lester Piggott

Champion jockey Lester Piggott (1935–) rode Nijinsky to victory in the 2,000 Guineas at Newmarket, England, on April 29th. He is shown being led in after the race.

Jimi Hendrix

Pop star Jimi Hendrix arrives at London's Heathrow Airport on his way to the Isle of Wight Pop Festival. He died in September of a drug overdose.

US Open Championship

In June, 26-year-old Tony Jacklin (1944–) became the first British golfer for half a century to win the US Open Championship.

Dirty jobs strike

As plastic bags full of rubbish piled up in the streets and squares of London in October, troops were sent into some areas to break the strike called by the city's refuse collectors. The government action followed growing concern among local councils about the risk to public health from the rotting piles of rubbish.

Mishima commits suicide

Yukio Mishima (1925–1970), the internationally acclaimed Japanese author, killed himself by ritual disembowelment after occupying the Army Headquarters in Tokyo.

Allende becomes President of Chile

Caricatured here, Dr Salvador Allende (1908–1973), the left-wing candidate of the Popular Unity coalition, was elected President of Chile on September 4th.

Death of Nasser

Egyptians throughout the world mourned the death of President Gamal Abdel Nasser on September 28th. He was 52 and had ruled for 14 years when he died of a heart attack.

Funeral of de Gaulle

'France is widowed,' said President Pompidou in his broadcast on the death of Charles de Gaulle on November 9th. Tributes were paid by leaders worldwide as the former President of the French Fifth Republic was buried in his home village of Colombey-les-Deux-Eglises. Some 40,000 French men and women arrived at Colombey to pay their last respects.

Janis Joplin takes drug overdose

The American rock singer Janis Joplin (1943–1970), who was once described as a white woman with a black woman's voice, died of a drugs overdose in Los Angeles on October 4th. She was 27.

Bertrand Russell dies

On February 2nd, Bertrand Russell died at his home in North Wales at the age of 97. His distinguished career as mathematician, philosopher and peace campaigner had a profound influence on the development of Western thought.

Mrs Bandaranaike

On May 27th, ten years after becoming the world's first woman Prime Minister, Mrs Sirimavo Bandaranaike, left-wing leader of the Sri Lanka Freedom Party, was elected Premier of Ceylon (now Sri Lanka) for the second time.

Love, light and peace

Leading figures from the world of popular music were among those seeking spiritual renewal at the feet of the Maharishi in the Himalayas. The Maharishi, leader of the Spiritual Regeneration Movement which practised transcendental meditation, became the guru of Beatles John Lennon, Paul McCartney and George Harrison after they were introduced to him by the latter's wife Patti in 1967. Also learning from the Maharishi's blend of Eastern mysticism and Western materialism were the Scottish singer Donovan (far left) and the young American actress Mia Farrow (third from left).

1971

Jan	10	400 Palestinian guerrillas deported by Jordan
	17	US: Baltimore Colts win Super Bowl
	25	Coup in Uganda puts Idi Amin in power
Feb	1	Israeli troops cross Lebanese border to defend frontier
	4	Rolls-Royce declared bankrupt in UK
	5	US spacecraft *Apollo 14* lands on moon
	15	UK: Introduction of decimal currency
	24	UK: Bill to limit Commonwealth immigrants
Mar	8	US comedian Harold Lloyd dies
	16	US politician Thomas Dewey dies
	25	Civil war breaks out in Pakistan
	31	US: Lt Calley convicted in My Lai massacre case
Apr	6	Soviet composer Igor Stravinsky dies
	15	UK: Barbican Arts Centre to be built in City of London
	21	Haitian dictator 'Papa Doc' Duvalier dies
May	19	US humorous poet Ogden Nash dies
	21	Pompidou says way is clear for UK to join EEC
Jun	4	Hungarian philosopher and critic Georg Lukács dies
	7	Soviet spacecraft docks with space station
	21	Japan: Student riots in Tokyo
	30	US: Supreme Court upholds print of 'Pentagon Papers'
	30	USSR: 3 cosmonauts die on return trip
Jul	6	US jazz trumpeter Louis Armstrong dies
	29	Tito re-elected as President in Yugoslavia
Aug	12	Syria and Jordan sever relations
Sep	11	Nikita Khrushchev, Soviet statesman, dies
	14	Duke Ellington gets rapturous reception on Soviet tour
Oct	7	Israel refuses entry to 21 Jewish black Americans
	17	US: Pittsburgh Pirates win World Series
	27	Congo changes name to Zaire
	28	President Nixon meets President Tito of Yugoslavia
Nov	15	Chinese delegates take UN seats for first time
Dec	3	Pakistan and India go to war over Bangladesh
	20	Zulfikar Bhutto succeeds Yahya Khan in Pakistan
	21	Kurt Waldheim elected UN Secretary General
	26	US resumes bombing of N Vietnam
		The Arts
		Andy Warhol Exhibition at Tate Gallery, London
		Stanley Kubrick's film *A Clockwork Orange*
		Visconti's film *Death in Venice*

Civil war breaks out in Pakistan

In March a bitter and bloody civil war broke out in Pakistan after talks on the autonomy of East Pakistan collapsed between Zulfikar Ali Bhutto and Sheikh Mujibur Rahman, leader of the Awami League. On March 26th, Mujibur declared East Pakistan an independent Republic under the name of Bangla Desh (or the Bengal Nation). And there was heavy fighting as General Yahya Khan's Army moved into the province to deal with the rebels. By the end of April it was all over, with Pakistani forces in control of most areas. Amid widespread reports of civilian massacres (below), thousands of refugees began to flee to India.

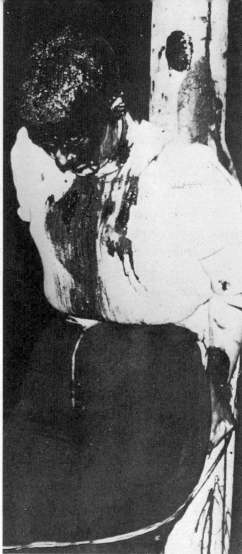

Internment in Northern Ireland

In August 1971 'internment' was introduced in Northern Ireland. Individuals who represented, in the words of Northern Ireland Prime Minister Brian Faulkner, 'a serious and continuing threat to public order and safety' could be held without trial for up to two weeks under the terms of Special Powers Acts dating from the 1920s. The first 300 people were detained on August 9th on the morning of the announcement, and riots broke out in Republican areas of Belfast, Londonderry and Newry. Here (left), British troops survey the aftermath of Belfast street battles in August 1971. On September 7th, the Troubles claimed their 100th civilian fatality when a teenage girl was shot during a gun battle.

Tarring and feathering

In November three women from the Republican Bogside area of Londonderry were 'tarred and feathered' for 'fraternising' with British soldiers. One of them, with head shorn and daubed with red paint and tar, is shown (above). The IRA admitted responsibility at first but the almost universal revulsion expressed at the mutilations caused them to disassociate themselves. One of the women went on to marry her soldier fiancé soon afterwards.

Driving on the moon

In July David Scott and James Irwin became the first astronauts to drive on the surface of the moon. Using a lightweight battery-controlled Lunar Roving Vehicle, the Apollo 15 team were able to explore a wider area than had been possible before. The men spent two hours covering a five mile area, managing to manoeuvre their vehicle on rear wheels only since the front pair failed to work. Wonderfully clear colour pictures of the astronauts were transmitted back to Earth.

Hirohito in Britain

Emperor Hirohito, the first Japanese sovereign to leave Japan in more than 2,000 years, visited seven Western countries. From October 5th to 7th he was in the UK, where he and the Empress Nagako attended a state banquet at Buckingham Palace.

Tragedy in East Pakistan

Serious flooding in September added to the misery of East Pakistan, which had been devastated by a cyclone towards the end of 1970. As many as half a million people may have died in the disaster, which also left a million people homeless.

Chay Blyth sails round the world

Chay Blyth, (1940–   ) the lone yachtsman, returned to England on August 6th after sailing round the world in 293 days in his 59-foot ketch the *British Steel*. He was greeted by the Prime Minister and members of the Royal Family.

Death of Stravinsky

The musical world was robbed of one of its leading figures with the death in April of the Russian-born composer Igor Stravinsky (1883–1971). His operas, ballets and orchestral works are among the great legacies of modern music.

Etna erupts

As Mount Etna erupted after years of sporadic activity, the people of the Italian village of Sant'Alfio carried relics of saints to the very edge of the river of lava that threatened their homes.

Mother Teresa visits the USA

In the autumn Mother Teresa of Calcutta, who had been active in caring for the refugees from East Pakistan, visited the United States where she set up a mission in the Bronx area of New York City.

Idi Amin gains control in Uganda

On January 25th, Major-General Idi Amin (1925–   ) took power in Uganda after overthrowing the government in a military coup. The President, Milton Obote, was at a conference in Singapore at the time.

'Coco' Chanel

The French fashion designer Gabrielle 'Coco' Chanel (1884–1971) died in Paris at the age of 87. After coming to prominence in the 1920s, she exerted a continuing and powerful influence in matters of style.

1972

Jan	1	French singer and actor Maurice Chevalier dies
	9	Liner *Queen Elizabeth* destroyed by fire in Hong Kong
	12	Sheikh Mujibur Rahman sworn in as PM of Bangladesh
	16	US: Dallas Cowboys rout Miami in Super Bowl
	17	350 Soviet Jews arrive in Israel
	30	Pakistan quits Commonwealth over Bangladesh
	30	N Ireland: British troops fire on civil rights march
Feb	4	Britain recognises Bangladesh
	17	UK: Parliament passes Bill on entry to EEC
	22	US President Nixon visits China for summit
	24	British PM Heath announces direct rule for Ulster
	28	UK: Miners' strike ends after 7 weeks
Mar	30	North Vietnam launches heavy attack on South
Apr	15	US bombers in heavy raids on N Vietnam
	20	American spacecraft *Apollo 16* lands on moon
May	2	US: FBI Director J. Edgar Hoover dies
	9	Israeli commandos rescue 92 hijack victims at Entebbe
	21	Rome: Michelangelo's *Pietà* damaged by maniac
	22	US President Nixon on state visit to USSR
	22	UK: Poet Cecil Day Lewis dies
	28	Duke of Windsor, former British monarch, dies in Paris
Jun	17	US: Attempted bugging of Democrats' Watergate HQ

	27	French Socialist Mitterand and Communists make pact
	29	Supreme Court abolishes death penalty in US
Jul	6	UK: Poulson corruption inquiry set up
	6	Kakuei Tanaka is new PM of Japan
	28	UK: National dock strike
Aug	6	Uganda: President Amin plans to expel 50,000 Asians
	26	20th Olympic Games open in Munich
	28	UK: Air crash kills Prince William of Gloucester
Sep	1	Bobby Fischer becomes World Chess Champion
	5	Arab terrorists kill 11 Israeli athletes at Olympics
	8	Israeli planes raid Lebanon in retaliatory attack
Oct	17	S Korea: President declares martial law
	25	Iceland boycotts British goods as part of cod war
Nov	17	Ex-President Perón back in Argentina after 17 years
	19	SDP govt under Willy Brandt wins German elections
	22	First US B52 bomber shot down over Vietnam
Dec	18	Heavy bombing of Hanoi by American B52s
	24	Huge earthquake in Nicaragua: 10,000 dead
	26	Harry S. Truman (US President 1945–53) dies

The Arts

Lloyd Webber's musical *Jesus Christ, Superstar*

Francis Ford Coppola's film *The Godfather*

Vietnam War nears its end

In March, North Vietnamese forces launched their biggest offensive to date, making inroads on three fronts in South Vietnam. The United States came to the aid of their beleaguered southern allies but, having greatly reduced their troop contingent, they could only resume their bombing of the north and mining of Vietnamese ports. American bombing culminated in a massive Christmas campaign using B52s. The heavy losses suffered by the USAF and the selection of civilian targets drew much domestic and international criticism.

In Paris the lengthy peace negotiations finally began to achieve results. Despite the opposition of South Vietnamese President Thieu, American and Communist negotiators worked on a solution which would leave the North and South Vietnamese to finalise a political settlement after a ceasefire.

The most famous of all Vietnamese war photographs was taken this year. The picture of children (left) fleeing from a napalm raid came to represent the whole conflict in the eyes of the western world.

Munich Olympics

The stunning performances of the young Soviet gymnast Olga Korbut (far left) and the gold medals of American swimmer Mark Spitz (above) and British athlete Mary Peters (left) could not dispel the horror in Munich when the 20th Olympic Games became the setting for an unprecedented terrorist outrage which left 11 Israeli athletes dead.

The tragedy began just before dawn on September 5th when eight hooded terrorists scaled the fence around the Olympic Village. Bursting into the dormitory where the 11 Israeli athletes were sleeping, they shot two dead and took the other nine hostage, threatening to kill them unless 200 Arab guerrillas were released. The German authorities agreed to take the terrorists to Fürstenfeldbruck military airfield where a Lufthansa airliner was waiting on the tarmac to fly them out of the country. There they were ambushed by German marksmen, but in the ensuing gun battle all nine hostages were killed by their captors.

George Wallace

During his campaign in the Maryland primary elections, George Wallace, the Governor of Alabama, was shot by a would-be assassin and left paralysed from the waist down. In the mid-60s Wallace had consistently defied US integration laws by ordering the arrests of thousands of both black and white civil rights protestors.

Shootings in Northern Ireland

In the bloodiest incident of the Ulster 'Troubles' 13 men were shot dead by British paratroopers in Londonderry's Bogside area. After being stoned by some members of a civil rights march the British troops vaulted over barricades (above) and attacked. Allegations of indiscriminate shooting were rejected, and they claimed that individually identified snipers had been fired upon.

Spaghetti Junction

On May 24th, Peter Walker, British Secretary of State for the Environment, opened the Midlands Links Motorways, thus completing the continuous motorway route from London to the Scottish border, a distance of some 300 miles. This final connecting seven-mile stretch – between Great Barr and Castle Bromwich near Birmingham – included the Gravelly Hill Interchange, familiarly known as 'Spaghetti Junction', a very apt name as this aerial photograph shows.

Britain in Europe

In what the British Prime Minister Edward Heath described as 'another great step forward towards the removal of divisions in Western Europe', Britain finally joined the European Community on January 22nd, together with Ireland, Denmark and Norway. In a televised ceremony, delayed by almost an hour when a young German woman threw a bottle of ink at him, Mr Heath signed the Treaty of Accession in the Palais d'Egremont in Brussels.

SALT Treaty signed

The US President Richard Nixon spoke of 'a new age in the relationship between our two great and powerful nations' when he visited the Soviet Union in May. During his visit he and the Soviet leader Leonid Brezhnev signed two treaties limiting and freezing nuclear missile systems in both countries. The leaders shook hands and toasted each other with champagne at the signing ceremony in the St Vladimir Hall in the Kremlin.

Death of the Duke of Windsor

His Royal Highness the Duke of Windsor died at his home in the Bois de Boulogne on May 28th at the age of 77. As King Edward VIII, the Duke had been the only British monarch to abdicate of his own free will and had lived in self-imposed exile since giving up his throne in 1936 to marry the American divorcee Mrs Wallis Simpson.

The body of the man once described by Lloyd George as Britain's greatest ambassador was flown to Oxfordshire on May 31st and lay in state for two days at St George's Chapel in Windsor, where thousands of people filed past the coffin in silence to pay their last respects. In accordance with the Duke's wish not to be given a state funeral, a simple private service was held in the chapel on June 5th in the presence of the Duchess of Windsor and the Queen (left). After the ceremony the Duke's body was interred in the Royal Family's burial ground at Frogmore in Windsor Great Park, near his great-grandparents Queen Victoria and Prince Albert.

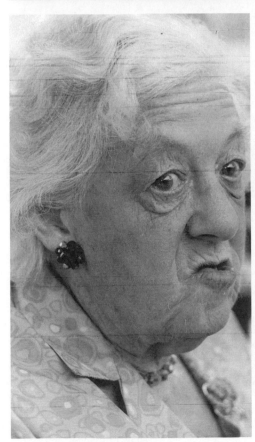

Death of Margaret Rutherford

The British actress Dame Margaret Rutherford (1892–1972) died in May shortly after her 80th birthday. In her latter years she specialised in playing eccentric spinsters and was much loved for her portrayals of Miss Marple.

John Betjeman is Poet Laureate

In October the poet and architectural critic John Betjeman (1906–1984), was appointed British Poet Laureate, a post held before him by Dryden, Wordsworth and Tennyson among others. He succeeded Cecil Day Lewis, who died in May.

First Prime Minister of Bangladesh

Sheikh Mujibur Rahman, leader of the Awami League, was released from detention by President Bhutto of Pakistan in January to become the first Prime Minister of the new state of Bangladesh.

1973

Jan	1	Britain, Denmark and Eire now full members of EEC
	14	US: Miami Dolphins win Super Bowl
	15	Bombing of N Vietnam halted by Nixon
	17	Filipino President Marcos extends his term indefinitely
	22	US: Ex-President Lyndon B. Johnson dies
	23	5,000 evacuated in Iceland as volcano erupts
	27	Vietnam peace treaty signed in Paris
Feb	5	20,000 black workers go on strike in South Africa
	8	Makarios re-elected as President of Cyprus
	27	US: American Indians take hostages at Wounded Knee
Mar	29	Last US troops leave Vietnam
Apr	1	Value Added Tax (VAT) introduced into UK
	8	Indian troops annex Sikkim in Himalayas
	16	US resumes bombing raids on Laos
	30	US: 4 of President Nixon's aides resign over Watergate
May	14	US: Skylab launched and put into orbit
	17	US Senate hearings begin on Watergate
Jun	1	Greece: Republic proclaimed with President Papadopoulos
	3	Israel frees 96 Arabs in return for 3 pilots
	4	Soviet version of Concorde crashes at Paris Air Show
	7	W German Chancellor Willy Brandt visits Israel
	16	US: Visit of Soviet leader Brezhnev
	24	President de Valera of Eire resigns at 90
Jul	15	US oil billionaire Paul Getty's grandson kidnapped
	21	French test H-bomb in Pacific
Aug	28	500 feared dead in Mexican earthquake
Sep	2	British fantasy author J. R. R. Tolkien dies
	3	UK: 20 trade unions expelled from TUC
	11	Chilean President Allende killed by rebels
	23	Juan Perón elected President of Argentina
Oct	5	UK: Dan Smith arrested on Poulson corruption charges
	6	Egypt and Syria attack Israel on two fronts
	12	US Vice-President Spiro Agnew resigns over tax evasion
	17	Oil prices rise by 70 per cent.
	19	Severe floods in Spain drown 500
	21	US: Oakland Athletics win World Series
Nov	9	Six Watergate burglars jailed in the US
Dec	6	Gerald Ford sworn in as US Vice-President
	17	Arab terrorists hijack US jet killing 31
	20	Spain: PM Admiral Carrero Blanco assassinated
		The Arts
		Thomas Pynchon's novel *Gravity's Rainbow*
		Pulitzer Prize for Watergate journalists
		Peter Schaffer's play *Equus*
		Robert Redford and Paul Newman star in *The Sting* film

Yom Kippur War

On the religious holiday of the Day of Atonement (Yom Kippur), Israel was invaded by Egypt and Syria in a surprise attack. The first assaults, on October 6th, were soon strengthened by forces supplied by Iraq, Morocco, Saudi Arabia and Jordan. Each side was heavily armed by a superpower patron. Israel suffered substantial losses in the air from Soviet-supplied SAM missiles but American and British-supplied tanks proved to be superior in the decisive confrontations in the desert.

Despite the substantial forces ranged against her, Israel absorbed the attacks and advanced into Egypt and Syria. Israeli troops are shown (above) on the road to Damascus. And a Syrian prisoner is escorted (top) by Israeli soldiers.

This war seriously damaged the détente that had developed between the USA and the Soviet Union. International tension increased when Brezhnev threatened 'unilateral action' if the USA did not help to enforce a United Nations-sponsored ceasefire. This prompted the United States to place its forces on full alert but in the event the ceasefire of October 24th did hold.

London car bombings

One person was killed and nearly 200 injured on March 8th when two car bombs exploded in central London. The IRA claimed responsibility for the bombs, which had been left outside the Old Bailey and in Whitehall (above).

Spanish Premier assassinated

The Spanish Prime Minister Luis Carrero Blanca was killed in Madrid on December 20th when a bomb planted by the Basque separatist organisation ETA destroyed the car in which he was travelling. The blast threw the car 60 feet into the air.

Peace in Vietnam

In Paris a Peace Agreement was signed providing for a ceasefire in Vietnam and the withdrawal of US troops.

Left to right: Xuan Thuy and Le Duc Tho of the North Vietnamese delegation and US Secretary of State Henry Kissinger.

The Watergate hearings

In Washington the 'Watergate Seven' – including Howard Hunt (above right), a security consultant at the White House – were tried on charges arising from the break-in at the Democratic Party National Committee Headquarters.

Noel Coward dies

On March 26th, the gifted writer and musical entertainer Noel Coward (1899–1973) died in Jamaica at the age of 74. His diverse compositions included stage plays, musicals, films and numerous popular songs.

Space station launched

The American space station Skylab 4 was launched into orbit from Cape Kennedy on May 14th. One of the solar shields was damaged shortly after lift-off, but was dramatically repaired in space when a mission manned by Charles Conrad, Joseph Kerwin and Paul Weitz docked with Skylab some ten days later.

Royal wedding

On November 14th, Princess Anne and Captain Mark Phillips were married at Westminster Abbey in London. Thousands of well-wishers, some of whom had camped in the city overnight, lined the streets to wave and cheer as the couple returned to Buckingham Palace after the ceremony.

Ministers in scandal

The British government was rocked by scandal in May following the resignations of two ministers. In apparently unrelated incidents Lord Lambton (left), the Under-Secretary of State for Defence for the Royal Air Force, and Earl Jellicoe, the Lord Privy Seal and Conservative Leader of the House of Lords, resigned after admitting to a 'casual acquaintance' with prostitutes in London.

The affairs had come to light when compromising photographs and tape-recordings of Lord Lambton were sold to a Sunday newspaper by the husband of one of the call-girls involved. Both ministers denied that their activities had caused any risk to national security, a view upheld by the Security Commission set up to investigate the case.

J. Paul Getty kidnapped

On December 14th, J. Paul Getty III, grandson of the American oil billionaire, was released by his kidnappers after being held for five months in hideouts in the mountains of southern Italy. The 17-year-old playboy had been snatched from a street in Rome on the morning of July 15th. Police were initially sceptical about the kidnapping. But there could be no doubt about the authenticity of the ransom demands sent to his mother, Gail Harris, seen here with Getty after his release, when she received a grisly package containing her son's severed ear. The boy was finally released after his estranged grandfather was prevailed upon to pay a ransom of one million dollars.

Brezhnev visit to West Germany

The Soviet leader Leonid Brezhnev made history in May when he became the first General Secretary of the Communist Party of the Soviet Union to visit the Federal Republic of Germany. He was greeted at Cologne airport by the Federal Chancellor Willy Brandt and his wife before beginning four days of talks with West German ministers. The two countries signed a ten-year agreement on economic, industrial and technological co-operation. A joint statement issued by the two leaders at the end of the talks described Brezhnev's visit as 'an historic landmark in relations between the Federal Republic of Germany and the USSR and in European evolution as a whole'. Earlier in the month the Soviet leader had visited Poland and East Germany.

1974

Jan	1	Golda Meir re-elected in Israel		15	Makarios ousted by military in Cyprus
Feb	22	Pakistan recognises Bangladesh		24	Greece: Colonels ousted; Karamanlis new PM
	28	US and Egypt resume diplomatic relations after 7 years	Aug	8	Nixon resigns as US President; Gerald Ford takes over
Mar	24	US spacecraft *Mariner* photographs planet Mercury	Sep	1	General Somoza elected as President of Nicaragua
Apr	2	French President Georges Pompidou dies		12	Emperor Haile Selassie is deposed in Ethiopia
	10	Golda Meir resigns as Israeli Premier		20	Cyclone Fifi kills 10,000 in Honduras
	22	Yitzhak Rabin new Leader of Israeli Labour Party	Oct	5	UK: Guildford pub bombing by IRA
May	6	W German Chancellor Brandt resigns over spy scandal		11	UK: Labour win second election of the year
	11	Big earthquake in Sichuan, China, kills 20,000		29	Mohammed Ali regains world heavyweight title
	14	New Archbishop of Canterbury to be Dr Donald Coggan	Nov	21	UK: IRA bomb two Birmingham pubs
	16	W Germany: Helmut Schmidt becomes Chancellor		29	W German terrorist leader Ulrike Meinhof is jailed
	18	India tests a nuclear bomb		29	IRA is outlawed in UK
	19	Valéry Giscard D'Estaing wins French presidency	Dec	8	Greece votes to abolish the monarchy
	24	US: jazz musician Duke Ellington dies		12	US: Jimmy Carter says he will run for President
	31	Israel signs truce with Syria		19	Nelson Rockefeller sworn in as US Vice-President
Jun	3	Yitzhak Rabin is new Israeli Premier		25	Cyclone wrecks northern Australian city of Darwin
	6	Jimmy Connors and Chris Evert win Wimbledon singles			*The Arts*
	26	UK: Labour govt and TUC agree on 'Social Contract'			Tom Stoppard's play *Travesties*
Jul	1	President Perón dies in Argentina			David Hockney exhibition in Paris

IRA bombing campaign

One person was killed and 48 were injured when two bombs exploded in central London on June 17th. The first explosion occurred just before 8.30 a.m. at the Houses of Parliament, causing a serious fire which damaged parts of the 800-year-old Westminster Hall (below). A second and larger bomb went off at the Tower of London later in the day – the Tower was crowded with tourists at the time and the casualties were much more serious. No group immediately claimed responsibility for the bombings, but police said they had all the hallmarks of the IRA.

Watergate

The long running Watergate scandal claimed its most senior victim on August 8th, when President Richard Nixon became the first ever President of the United States to resign his office. The announcement came after a series of damaging revelations about the role of the President and his advisors in the break-in at the Democratic Party's National Headquarters, the Watergate Building in Washington, DC on June 17th 1972, and in the cover-up which followed.

The sensational story, which came to light partly as a result of a sustained press campaign by the *Washington Post* journalists Carl Bernstein and Bob Woodward (top left), moved into its final phase in March when a federal grand jury indicted seven former Nixon aides on charges of conspiracy and obstruction of justice. The accused men included the President's former domestic affairs advisor John Ehrlichmann (left) and former chief of staff H. R. Haldeman. Much speculation centred on the contents of tape recordings made at the White House in the weeks following the Watergate break-in, in which the President discussed the implications of the affair with his advisors. When these were finally surrendered to the investigators they were found to have been wiped in parts.

On August 5th, amidst growing demands for his impeachment, Nixon admitted that he had withheld information on the scandal and had made misleading statements. Three days later, with his support in Congress almost evaporated, he announced his resignation in a televised address to the nation (above). Vice President Gerald Ford was sworn in on August 9th as Richard Nixon bade farewell to his White House staff (top right).

Ford is sworn in

Gerald Ford, former Vice-President, is sworn in as the 38th President of the United States, watched by his wife Betty who holds the family bible. Following Nixon's downfall over the Watergate investigations, and his resignation, Ford's accession was greeted with relief and euphoria.

His informal inaugural address was summed up when he said: '. . . I expect to follow my instincts of openness and candour with full confidence that honesty is always the best policy in the end'.

The Flixborough disaster

Twenty-eight people were killed and hundreds were injured when an explosion ripped through a chemical plant at Flixborough in Lincolnshire, UK. The factory was reduced to a mass of tangled wreckage by the force of the blast on Saturday June 1st.

The explosion devastated acres of surrounding farmland, some 2,000 houses were damaged and the village of Flixborough was evacuated as a vast cloud of poisonous cyclohexane gas escaped.

Britain's general election

In an atmosphere of almost unprecedented industrial tension the British premier Edward Heath announced a general election, to be held on February 28th. The results of the poll were inconclusive, with no party winning an overall majority. However, after coalition talks broke down between the Liberal and Conservative Parties, Edward Heath resigned and Harold Wilson (above) became Prime Minister on March 4th.

Turkish invasion of Cyprus

Tension ran high in the eastern Mediterranean following the overthrow of President Makarios of Cyprus in a military coup led by Nicos Sampson, the extreme Greek-Cypriot leader of the Progressive Party. The Turkish Premier Bülent Ecevit claimed that Greek forces were reinforcing the new regime in Cyprus, and a major international crisis threatened as Turkish troops invaded the island at dawn on July 20th. Two days of fierce fighting, involving some 30,000 Turkish troops, left a triangle of land between the coast and the capital Nicosia under Turkish control. Thousands of residents were evacuated by the Royal Air Force and Royal Navy. After only a few days Sampson resigned and was replaced by the moderate Glafkos Clerides, and peace talks began in Geneva.

Angola moves towards independence

The Portuguese colony of Angola contained three major groups fighting for independence: the MPLA (Popular Movement for the Liberation of Angola), the FNLA (National Liberation Front) and UNITA (National Union for the Total Independence of Angola). Each had a different vision for their country, the MPLA's being the most radical. Dr Agostinho Neto's Marxist MPLA was supported by the Soviet Union and included revolutionary ideology in the training of its troops. An Instruction Centre for recruits in the Cabinda Enclave, north of Angola, is shown (left).

In April the Portuguese right-wing government of Marcello Caetano was toppled by a military coup. Successive changes moved the government to the left, raising hopes of independence in the Portuguese colonies of Angola, Mozambique and Guinea-Bissau.

Air crash in France

In one of the world's worst air crashes, all 346 passengers and crew on a Turkish Airlines jet were killed when the plane fell out of the sky shortly after taking off from Orly airport in France. The wide-bodied DC10 was on the last leg of its journey from Ankara to London when the accident happened.

Eye witnesses said that the jet appeared to explode in mid-air before plummeting to the ground in the Forest of Ermenonville, 30 miles north-east of Paris. Rescue workers and accident investigators found wreckage and the remains of bodies strewn over some eight miles of countryside (left). Among the dead were at least 200 Britons, 40 Turks and 49 Japanese.

Patty Hearst in bank raid

The American newspaper heiress Patty Hearst (1954–   ) was seen taking part in an armed raid in April. Hearst's whereabouts had been unknown since a revolutionary group had kidnapped her in February.

Coup in Ethiopia

After months of instability Emperor Haile Selassie of Ethiopia was deposed by a group of radical Army officers. The Emperor, known as 'The Lion of Judah', was 82.

Solzhenitsyn exiled

On February 13th, Alexander Solzhenitsyn (1918–   ), the Russian dissident author and winner of the 1970 Nobel Prize for literature, became the first Soviet citizen to be expelled from the Soviet Union since Leon Trotsky went into exile in 1929.

Cyclone in Australia

In Australia a cyclone devastated the city of Darwin on Christmas Day, leaving 49 dead. More than half the city's inhabitants were evacuated and the Prime Minister, Gough Whitlam, interrupted a European tour to visit the scene of the disaster.

1975

Jan	10	Portuguese government agrees Angolan independence
	20	Channel Tunnel abandoned by British govt
Feb	11	UK: Margaret Thatcher is new Tory leader at 49
	19	West Indian cricket hero Garfield Sobers knighted
	28	US: 3 Nixon aides sentenced for Watergate cover-up
	28	London: Tube train crash at Moorgate station kills 35
Mar	14	US film actress Susan Hayward dies
	21	Monarchy abolished in Ethiopia
	21	British MP John Stonehouse arrested in Australia
	25	King Faisal of Saudi Arabia killed by mad nephew
Apr	5	Nationalist Chinese statesman Chiang Kai-shek dies
	13	Jack Nicklaus wins 5th Masters golf championship
	16	USSR: Ex-KGB Chief Shelepin expelled from Politburo
	17	Cambodia: Khmer Rouge take Phnom Penh
	30	Vietnam: Saigon falls to N Vietnamese
May	16	Japanese is first woman to climb Everest
	21	Trial starts of Baader-Meinhof gang in Stuttgart
Jun	5	Suez Canal reopens after 8 years
	6	UK: Referendum votes to stay in EEC
	12	Greece applies for membership of the EEC
	13	UK: Ex-Minister John Profumo is awarded CBE
Jul	8	Yitzhak Rabin first Israeli Minister to visit W Germany
Aug	27	Ethiopian ex-Emperor Haile Selassie dies
	29	Irish statesman de Valera dies
Sep	1	Kissinger arranges Israel-Egypt accord on Sinai
	15	Papua New Guinea becomes independent from Australia
	18	Patty Hearst found after 1½ years with Symbionese
Oct	3	UK: Ulster Volunteer Force banned
	22	US: Cincinnati Reds win World Series
Nov	10	Portugal to leave Angola after 320 years
	20	General Franco of Spain dies (Head of State since 1939)
Dec	4	Moluccans seize Indonesian Consulate in Amsterdam
		The Arts
		Antony Powell's novel *A Dance to the Music of Time*
		Anatoly Karpov becomes World Chess Champion
		Steven Spielberg's film *Jaws*
		Saul Bellow's novel *Humboldt's Gift*
		James Clavell's novel *Shogun*

Famine in Ethiopia

Every year areas of Ethiopia were stricken with drought and famine. Haile Selassie had consistently neglected the rural economy and criticism of his failure to acknowledge the existence of famine had contributed to his downfall in 1974. The new regime nationalised land and attempted to remove rural landlords who had exacted onerous dues from their tenants. However the populace still remained at the mercy of the weather.

The desperate plight of the rural poor was worsened by the outbreak of fighting in many areas. Eritrean and Tigrean independence movements were joined by dispossessed landlords and local potentates in challenging the government. This scene of a woman begging for food was reproduced all over the world.

South Vietnam falls

The long war in Vietnam had a swift dénouement. The towns and cities of South Vietnam fell to Communist forces as they swept towards their main objective – Saigon. As each town was approached, a chaotic evacuation of military personnel and civilian refugees took place. The coastal town of Nha Trang fell on April 1st. Here (below left), an American official punches a man away from the door of a plane leaving Nha Trang. On April 21st, Xuan Loc (38 miles east of Saigon) was taken. Refugees are seen (above left), waiting on Highway One for a helicopter to take them to the already crowded capital.

In Saigon US officials and desperate South Vietnamese sympathisers scrambled to leave. By late April it had become impossible to use transport planes to get them out because of the crowds swarming over the runways at Saigon's Ton Son Nhut Airport. Helicopters were therefore used to ferry Americans and what President Ford described as 'high-risk South Vietnamese' out of Saigon. Marines used rifle-butts and tear gas to keep crowds back as evacuation flights took off from the roof of the US Embassy. The last helicopter left at 8 a.m. on April 30th, the day President Duong van Minh surrendered to the provisional revolutionary government of the National Liberation Front (the 'Viet Cong').

The new regime in Saigon entered negotiations with the Hanoi government on the reunification of Vietnam. By the end of 1975 the three states of South-East Asia had Communist governments, a process completed with the victory of the Pathet Lao and the formation of the People's Democratic Republic of Laos in December.

Khmer Rouge overruns Cambodia

On April 17th, Phnom Penh was overrun by the Khmer Rouge, toppling the US-sponsored leader Lon Nol and beginning the most horrific period in Cambodia's history. The Khmer Rouge consisted of dissident Communists who had begun mounting armed opposition to the government from the countryside in the 1950s. With Chinese aid they took over a country weakened by years of fighting which had spilled over from the conflict in neighbouring Vietnam.

When Phnom Penh fell it had already suffered greatly – swollen by over one million refugees and frequently shelled by the Khmer Rouge. Here (left), a man lies dead beside his burning motorcycle after a rocket attack. Under the new régime the population was immediately forced into the fields. For four years virtually every Cambodian worked on the soil in constant danger from suspicious and violent Khmer Rouge soldiers.

The Balcombe Street siege

Police surrounded a London house where four IRA gunmen held two people hostage for six days.

Armed attack

The siege began on December 6th after Martin O'Connell, Edward Butler, Harry Duggan and Hugh Doherty mounted an armed attack on a restaurant in the West End of London. The authorities had been expecting the raid and there was a gun battle with police as the four men made a run for it. They took refuge in a flat in Balcombe Street in the Marylebone area, holding the flat's occupants hostage – Mr John Matthews, a Post Office employee, and his wife Sheila. Hundreds of armed police surrounded the building as the terrorists demanded safe passage to the Republic of Ireland. And a tense waiting game began, with the authorities refusing to give in to the kidnappers' demands.

Surrender

On December 12th, the siege moved into its final phase. A huge screen was erected around the area of operations and it became known that a Special Air Service assault team was about to arrive. At that point the kidnappers released Mr and Mrs Matthews, who emerged on to the balcony and edged their way to a neighbouring flat under cover of police marksmen. Shortly afterwards the four IRA men gave themselves up. Here (left), one of the terrorists surrenders to police.

Kissinger meets Gromyko

US Secretary of State Henry Kissinger meets Soviet Foreign Minister Andrei Gromyko in Geneva. Kissinger's famous shuttle diplomacy culminated in 1974 with a marathon 32-day flying stint, negotiating between Israel and Syria, which resulted in the first signed accord between the two hostile states since 1948. He also mediated in an interim agreement between Israel and Egypt that provided for Israel's further withdrawal from the Sinai Peninsula.

Kissinger's secret missions to China and Russia, during the Nixon administration, paved the way for Presidential visits and a general detente. But by 1975 US–Soviet relations were somewhat strained and strategic arms limitation talks were bogged down with accusations of Soviet violations of the agreements.

In 1973 Kissinger won the Nobel Peace Prize – shared with Le Duc Tho, the North Vietnamese Politburo member. This was largely for his negotiation of the American withdrawal of its troops from Vietnam, and his involvement with the ending of the 1973 Arab–Israeli War.

Reopening of the Suez Canal

During the early months of the year work continued to clear the Suez Canal in time for its reopening on June 5th, eight years after it had been closed during the Six-Day War. By April some ten sunken warships, 120 smaller wrecks (including tanks and aircraft) and 42,000 live explosive devices had been dredged out of the waterway. An additional 750,000 mines were removed from its banks.

Fighting in Angola

As Portugal hurriedly pulled out of Angola, the rival independence movements began fighting. The FNLA and UNITA, backed by South African troops, challenged the MPLA who had declared themselves the government of the new People's Republic of Angola, until Cuban troops were airlifted in to halt the advance. The conflict had repercussions in Portugal, and Angola House in Lisbon was sacked and daubed with pro-FNLA slogans.

King Hassan of Morocco

King Hassan organised 350,000 Moroccans to march into the Spanish Sahara to back his claims on the Spanish colony. Here, women wait at Marrakesh station to join the march.

Hurricane Gladys

Hurricane Gladys threatened the coast of the United States with wind speeds of up to 140 miles per hour, before veering north-east and dissipating over the Atlantic.

Civil war in Lebanon

Fighting between Druze-Palestinian groups and Maronite Christians escalated into full-scale civil war in Lebanon. Barricades in the capital Beirut testified to the failure of numerous peace initiatives.

Starvation in Bangladesh

Thousands of people were dying of hunger in Bangladesh. And Sheikh Mujibur Rahman, founder and President of Bangladesh, was murdered in April – another victim of the political chaos.

Return of Spanish monarchy

Following the death of Generalissimo Francisco Franco on November 20th, Prince Juan Carlos I was sworn in as King of Spain.

Barbara Hepworth

The celebrated sculptor Barbara Hepworth (1903–1975), died on May 21st in a fire at her home in the Cornish village of St Ives. She was 72.

Charlie Chaplin is knighted

The much-loved silent-screen tramp took on a new role as Sir Charles Chaplin when he was knighted by Queen Elizabeth in March.

Streaking

Streaking came to Great Britain in the summer. And streakers, such as this famous one at Lord's cricket ground, gave a whole new meaning to 'getting media exposure'.

John Stonehouse arrested

John Stonehouse, the British Labour Member of Parliament who disappeared after faking his suicide on a Miami beach in 1974, was arrested in Australia on charges of theft and forgery.

Heath replaced by Thatcher

On February 11th, Mrs Margaret Thatcher succeeded the former British Prime Minister Edward Heath as leader of the Conservative Party. She was the first woman ever to hold the post.

1976

Jan	8	Chinese Premier Chou En-lai dies
	12	British writer Agatha Christie dies
	18	US: Pittsburgh Steelers defeat Cowboys in Super Bowl
	23	US singer and actor Paul Robeson dies
Feb	2	US: Daniel Moynihan resigns from UN
	4	US: Trial of Patty Hearst begins
	6	Lockheed says it bribed Dutch Prince Bernhardt
	7	China: Hua Kuo-keng becomes Premier
Mar	14	US musical film director Busby Berkeley dies
	16	UK: PM Harold Wilson announced retirement
	20	US: Patty Hearst found guilty of armed robbery
	24	Argentina: President Isabel Perón is deposed
	24	UK: Ex-Commander Lord Montgomery of Alamein dies
Apr	1	German-born French artist Max Ernst dies
	5	UK: James Callaghan becomes new Labour PM
	5	US: Tycoon Howard Hughes dies
	25	Portugal: Socialist Mario Soares wins free elections
May	6	Earthquake in northern Italy kills 2000
	9	W Germany: Jailed terrorist Ulrike Meinhoff found dead
	24	*Concorde* makes first commercial transatlantic flights
Jun	1	Britain and Iceland end Cod War
	6	US oil tycoon J. Paul Getty dies
	18	S Africa: Over 100 killed after 3 days of rioting

	28	Seychelles become independent Republic
Jul	7	British Queen Elizabeth II starts official visit to US
	4	Israeli commandos storm hijacked plane at Entebbe
	10	Italy: Chemical plant at Seveso leaks toxic dioxin cloud
	13	UK: Roy Jenkins is President of European Commission
	17	Canada: 21st Olympic Games open in Montreal
	21	Eire: British Ambassador to Dublin killed by car bomb
	27	Soviet chess champion Korchnoi defects to West
Sep	9	Chinese leader Mao Tse-tung dies
Oct	11	China: Gang of four arrested, accused of plotting coup
	11	China: Hua Kuo-feng confirmed as Mao's successor
	21	Americans win 5 Nobel Prizes
	25	S Africa: Transkie black 'homeland' given independence
	28	Switzerland: Rhodesia conference opens in Geneva
Nov	2	US: Jimmy Carter is elected President
Dec	3	US: Vance replaces Kissinger as Secretary of State
	4	British composer Benjamin Britten dies

The Arts

UK: National Theatre opens

Marquez's novel *The Autumn of the Patriarch*

Alex Haley's novel *Roots*

Alan Pakula's film *All The President's Men*

Martin Scorcese's film *Taxi Driver*

Riots in South Africa

At least 176 people were killed and 1,228 injured in the worst outbreak of violence between blacks and police in South Africa since the Union was formed in 1910.

Trouble in Soweto

The trouble began in the township of Soweto near Johannesburg which housed more than a million black people. In June some 2,000 secondary school pupils went on strike in protest against the compulsory use of the Afrikaans language in Bantu schools. On June 16th, a procession of demonstrators was broken up by police and one 13-year-old boy was shot dead, sparking off violence in other parts of Soweto, in which a black policeman and a white official were killed. As the unrest escalated police dropped teargas from helicopters in an attempt to disperse angry crowds. Buildings were set alight and vehicles damaged; shops were looted and vigilante groups roamed the streets. A cordon of 1,000 armed police was thrown around Soweto to seal off the township.

Unrest spreads

From Soweto the lawlessness spread to other areas. Rioting broke out in Alexandra Township, Natalspruit, Boksburg and other townships around Johannesburg and Pretoria. There were serious disturbances at black universities in Zululand and in Northern Transvaal, with buildings and cars being burnt. Rioters with rocks, staves and knives clashed in the black homelands and by the time the bloodshed died down, towards the end of June, there had been some 1,298 arrests. The damage to property in Soweto alone was estimated at more than 20 million pounds, with almost every municipal building destroyed. Of the hundreds of dead and wounded only eight were white.

International condemnation

In July M. C. Botha, Minister of Bantu Education, withdrew the Afrikaans language ruling that had sparked off the troubles. But there was international condemnation of the South African government, and the United Nations Security Council passed a resolution describing apartheid as 'a crime against the conscience and dignity of mankind' and upholding the 'legitimacy of the struggle of the South African people'.

Carter wins

Jimmy Carter, one-time peanut farmer from Plains, Georgia, won the November Presidential election bringing back the Democrats to the White House after an eight-year absence. He was the first President from the South since the Civil War.

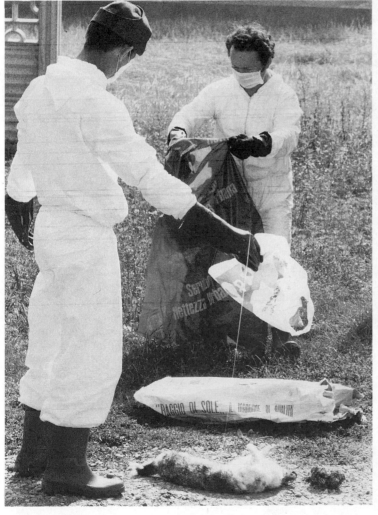

Seveso

One of Italy's worst ever environmental accidents occurred on July 10th, when highly toxic dioxin escaped from a chemical plant in the northern Italian town of Meda near Seveso. The accident, which was caused by a faulty pressure valve, sprayed some two tons of chemicals over the surrounding area, causing burning rashes, headaches, diarrhoea and vomiting in the local population. Many birds and animals died in the contamination (above) and the people of Seveso were not evacuated until more than two weeks after the leak. There were protests at the slowness of the official reaction to the disaster (top).

Drought in the UK

Emergency legislation was rushed through Parliament because of an increasingly serious problem of water supply during the driest summer since records began in 1727. In Gloucestershire the source of the River Thames dried up (top) and in London it reached its lowest level in living memory as week after week passed without rain. As reservoirs turned into arid plains, local authorities were given powers to control many types of water use, from carwashes to hosepipes; and water rationing was introduced in South Wales, south-west England and parts of Yorkshire.

Changes at the top

In a move that came as a complete surprise to his Cabinet colleagues, the British Prime Minister Harold Wilson (far left) announced his resignation as leader of the parliamentary Labour Party, and therefore as Premier, on March 16th. He had apparently made the decision in March 1974 when the Labour Party returned to power, and had told the Queen of his intentions in December 1975.

The ensuing elections for the leadership of the Labour Party were won by James Callaghan (left), the Foreign and Commonwealth Secretary, who defeated Michael Foot by 176 votes to 137 in a ballot of all Labour Members of Parliament. Callaghan, 64, had been Chancellor of the Exchequer and Home Secretary in Wilson's first administration. By the evening of April 5th, when the ballot results became known, he was installed at Number 10 Downing Street as the new Prime Minister.

Death of Mao Tse-tung

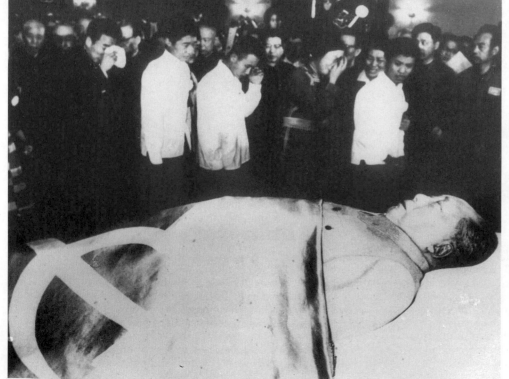

On September 9th, Mao Tse-tung, Chairman of the People's Republic of China, died at the age of 82. Here, selected 'workers, peasants and soldiers' are seen filing past his body as it lies in state in the Great Hall of the People in Beijing.

The death of the founding father of Communist China sparked a bitter successional crisis. Initially the ultra-radical 'Gang of Four', including Mao's widow, the former film star Chiang Ching, seemed to be gaining control. They promoted a continuation of Mao's 'Cultural Revolution', attacking moderate elements in government as 'capitalist-roaders'. But in October Hua Kuo-feng was appointed Chairman of the Party and the Gang of Four were arrested, accused of plotting to seize power.

By mid-1977, Deng Xiaoping, Mao's Vice-Chairman who had been ousted by the Gang of Four, was restored and Chairman Hua announced eight 'musts' for the economic and political reform of China.

Madame Mao

Chiang Ching, the 62-year-old widow of the former Chinese leader Mao Tse-tung, was arrested in October. She was a member of the notorious Gang of Four who tried to seize power after Mao's death.

Paul Robeson

Paul Robeson (1898–1976) the US bass singer, actor and black rights activist died. His association with left-wing movements brought him before the Un-American Activities Committee in 1950.

Agatha Christie

The doyenne of crime fiction writers, Dame Agatha Christie (1891–1976) died at her home in Wallingford, England, on January 12th at the age of 85. She had some 80 books to her name.

The Entebbe raid

The hijack of a French airliner was brought to a dramatic end when a team of Israeli commandos carried out a daring night raid on Entebbe airport in Uganda. The Air France A 300-B airbus was hijacked shortly after take-off from Athens airport on June 27th by a Palestinian group. They forced it to fly to Entebbe where 98 Israeli and other passengers were detained. Just before midnight on July 4th, three Israeli Hercules C-130 transport planes landed at the airfield. In just 53 minutes, 200 commandos overpowered the Ugandan guards, killed seven terrorists and snatched all but three of the hostages, who were flown back to Israel.

Above: Relatives of one of the terrorists bewail his death in the raid.

Death of a tycoon

J. Paul Getty (1892–1976) the American oil tycoon, died near London on June 6th. A billionaire by the age of 21, he amassed a vast fortune estimated at between 2 and 4 billion dollars – from oil investments and interests in some 200 other concerns. Getty, something of a recluse, married five times and lived the last 25 years of his life outside the United States.

Frank Sinatra

On July 12th, Frank Sinatra, seen with Sammy Davis Jnr in *Robin and the Seven Hoods* (1964), married Barbara Marx, former wife of Marx Brother, Zeppo.

Pictures of Mars

The US spacecraft *Viking* landed on Mars on July 20th and began to send back the first photographs of the surface of the red planet.

Earthquake in Italy

An earthquake left at least 925 dead and as many as 150,000 homeless in the mountains of north-east Italy on May 6th. Above: One of the refugees waits for food.

Scandal in the Netherlands

The Royal Family of the Netherlands was rocked by a scandal connecting Prince Bernhard, the husband of Queen Juliana (above), with irregular payments by the Lockheed Corporation.

1977

Death of Biko

A storm of international protest greeted the announcement that the black consciousness leader Steve Biko had died in police detention in South Africa in September. Biko, 30, was one of a number of black leaders arrested under the 1977 security legislation. A post-mortem revealed brain damage and severe bruising. Denounced by the South African authorities as a violent revolutionary, Biko was described by the liberal journalist Donald Woods as 'quite simply the greatest man I have ever had the privilege to know'. His funeral in King William's Town on September 5th was attended by 15,000 people, including diplomats from 12 Western countries.

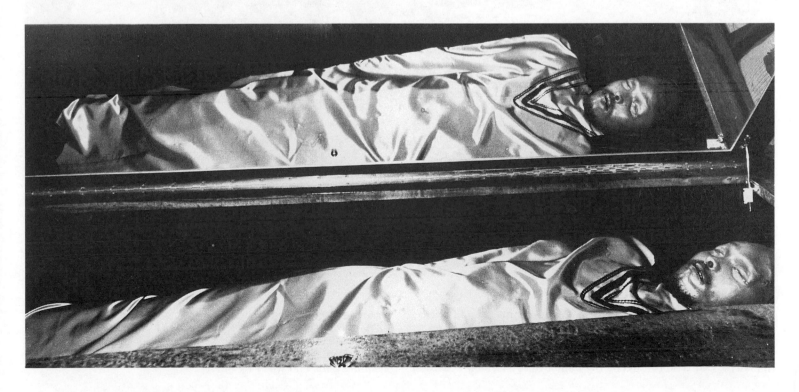

War in Rhodesia

The Rhodesian government had been at war with the Zimbabwean independence movements: ZANU (the Zimbabwe African National Union) and ZAPU (Zimbabwe African People's Union). And the conflict spilled over into neighbouring Mozambique and Zambia in 1977. Rhodesian forces raided Mozambique in search of ZANU fighters (led by Robert Mugabe). They also went into Zambia looking for supporters of Joshua Nkomo's ZAPU and causing widespread destruction.
Above: Refugees rebuild their homes destroyed during a Rhodesian raid on Mozambique.

Fighting continues in Angola

The Angolan civil war continued as the government and their Cuban allies sought to quell opposition outside their only relatively secure stronghold, the capital Luanda. The FNLA (supported by Zaire) claimed to control a third of the country in the north, and UNITA (led by the flamboyant Dr Jonas Savimbi) recovered from a government offensive launched at the end of 1976. By September 1977 they announced that ten of Angola's 16 provinces were in their hands.
Above: Domestic chores in a UNITA camp in southern Angola – cleaning guns and washing babies.

Idi Amin

The oppressive regime of Idi Amin, President of Uganda, came under increasing pressure. Amid accusations of mass murder, including that of the Anglican Archbishop of Uganda, Amin was not invited to the meeting of the Commonwealth Heads of State in 1977.

Bokassa is crowned

With the coronation of the self-styled 'Emperor' Bokassa (1921–   ), the Central African Republic became an Empire. Bokassa, the Republic's President, crowned himself at a lavish ceremony costing up to 20,000,000 dollars – a quarter of the country's annual income.

Conflict in Ethiopia

With full-scale wars in the Ogaden Desert against Somalia, conflict with secessionists in Tigre and Eritrea, a number of provincial uprisings and bloody civil war in Addis Ababa, Ethiopia was in utter turmoil.
Above: Militiamen parade in Addis Ababa before combat.

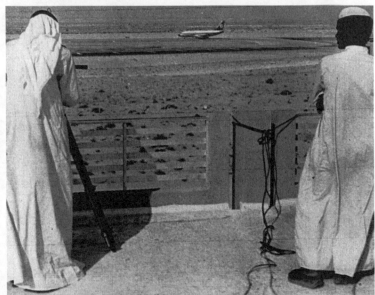

Mogadishu hijack

West German commandos ended the hijacking of a Lufthansa 737 in Mogadishu, Somalia, killing three of the four terrorists. The plane, seen here leaving Dubai, toured the Middle East as its captors demanded the release of 11 Red Army Faction members held in West Germany and two Palestinians in Turkey.

Pompidou Centre

The newly opened Pompidou Centre in Paris was already proving a popular attraction in a city known for architectural innovation since Eiffel built his tower there in the 19th century. The Centre, designed by Renzo Piano and the British architect Richard Rogers, consists of an enormous steel cage, constructed in rigid rectangles and supporting floor spaces capable of being used in many different ways. Through and outside the central cage, brightly coloured tubes carry services and convey people around the building, in the latter case often by escalator. This cultural and leisure complex, one of the great achievements of high-technology architecture, was to become the most visited building in Paris.

The boat people

Some 800,000 mainly Chinese and middle-class Vietnamese became refugees from the repressive communist regime of South Vietnam. The 'boat people', as they were known, took to the sea in whatever vessels they could muster for escape to the West. Left, 4000 people cram themselves aboard one ship. Many perished on their long, perilous journeys, falling victim to starvation, disease and piracy. Large numbers ended up in Hong Kong internment camps. The more fortunate landed in any country which would accept them, albeit unwillingly. Given the chance to settle, many not only survived but managed to thrive in various business enterprises.

Bravo blow-out

A serious blow-out in an oil well in the Norwegian sector of the North Sea caused widespread pollution in April. The accident, the first of its kind in almost a decade of offshore drilling in the area, happened at the Bravo Platform in the Ekofisk Field on April 22nd. Over the next eight days some 22,500 tons of oil escaped into the sea, covering about 4,000 square kilometres with a slick 1 to 2 millimetres deep and doing irreparable damage to marine life. A fire-boat sprayed water on to the oil, which was forced out almost at boiling point, in order to avoid an explosion (left). A subsequent inquiry blamed inadequate organisational and administrative systems for the disaster.

Air disaster in Tenerife

Five hundred and eighty-two people died on March 27th when two Boeing 747 jumbo jets collided on the runway at Los Rodeos airport, Tenerife. Both planes had been diverted to Tenerife. One, a Dutch KLM flight from Amsterdam, was taking off without final clearance when the accident happened.

The Grunwick dispute

Police clashed with trade union pickets outside the Grunwick film processing laboratory in Willesden, North London, in some of the bitterest scenes ever witnessed in a British industrial dispute. 'Flying pickets' from the Yorkshire coalfield lent their support to the striking workers. There were over 500 arrests.

Menachem Begin

Following the general election in Israel on May 17th, the right-wing Likud leader Menachem Begin formed a centre-right coalition government, ending 29 years of Labour domination.

Red Rum

Red Rum made horse-racing history when he won the British Grand National for the third time, ridden by jockey Tommy Stack. Red Rum's previous victories were in 1973 and 1974.

Zia ul-Haq

On July 5th, the Army Chief of Staff General Mohammad Zia ul-Haq (1924–1988) ousted Pakistan's Prime Minister Zulfikar Bhutto in a coup.

Maria Callas

The beautiful American-born operatic soprano Maria Callas (1923–1977) died this year. Born of Greek parents, her most famous roles included *Medea*.

Bing Crosby

The American Bing Crosby (1904–1977), who co-starred with Bob Hope in the famous series of 'road' films, died while playing golf. He was 73.

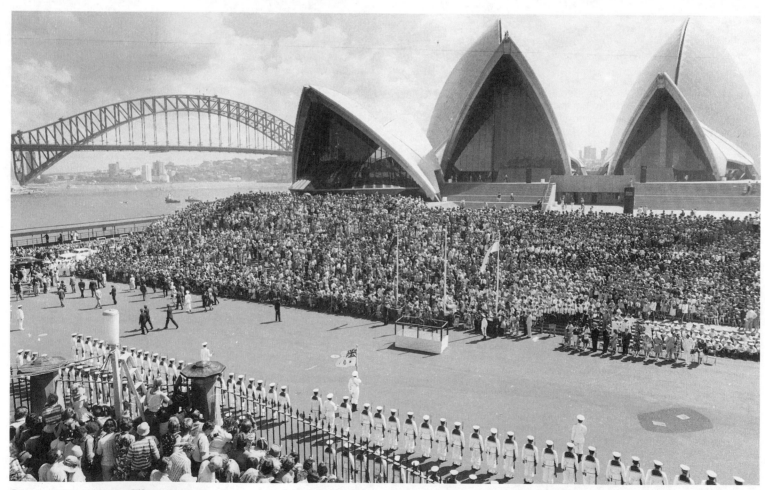

Queen Elizabeth's Silver Jubilee

Enormous crowds gathered outside the Sydney Opera House in Australia to welcome Queen Elizabeth II during her Silver Jubilee tour of the Commonwealth in February and March. In Britain celebrations for the 25th anniversary of her coronation were held in the summer with great pomp and ceremony. On June 7th, the Queen and Prince Philip attended a service of thanksgiving at St Paul's Cathedral before going walkabout in the streets of London. Street parties were held countrywide.

1978

Amoco Cadiz is wrecked

One of the world's worst oil pollution disasters occurred in March when the supertanker *Amoco Cadiz* ran on to rocks off Portsall on the coast of Brittany. The ship was on her way from the Persian Gulf to Rotterdam with 230,000 tonnes of crude oil when her steering gear failed in heavy seas. More than 100 miles of French beaches were polluted by the oil after the tanker broke in two. There was unprecedented destruction of marine and bird life, with millions of marine animals and molluscs being washed ashore. A subsequent inquiry criticised the vessel's captain, Pasquale Bardari, for his 'inexcusable delay' in asking for assistance.

Civil war in Nicaragua

The regime of General Anastasio Somoza came under increasing pressure, as workers and students went on strike and political alliances were formed to confront the government. The FSLN ('Sandinistas') fought Somoza's National Guard in a violent civil war and in August, 25 Sandinistas occupied the National Palace in the capital Managua. After securing the release of a large number of prisoners and a ransom, the Sandinistas fled to neighbouring Panama. They are seen (left) about to embark on their flight out of Nicaragua. The nature of Somoza's rule (described by local Roman Catholic bishops in 1978 as a 'state of terror'), and the depth of opposition to it, led the USA to withhold aid and to encourage a peaceful transfer of power to civilian elements.

Revolution in Afghanistan

Tanks and MiG-21 fighter planes attacked the presidential palace in Kabul as the government of Mohammed Daud was overthrown by a military coup in Afghanistan. The revolution erupted after a clamp-down on political dissent during which one opposition leader had been assassinated and others arrested. The President himself was massacred (together with members of his family) by the insurgents who assumed power as the Armed Forces Revolutionary Council on April 27th.

The Council, led by Colonel Abdul Qadir, appointed Mr Nur Mohammed Taraki as Prime Minister, banned all public meetings and announced that martial law would remain in force indefinitely. The new pro-Communist regime was recognised by the Soviet Union on April 30th and by Britain on May 6th.

The death throes of Rhodesia

After the failure of UDI – the Smith government's declaration of Rhodesian independence within the Commonwealth– pressure increased for an agreement to be reached with the moderate wing of ZAPU, under the leadership of Joshua Nkomo. By 1978 over 6,000 had been killed in the guerrilla warfare tactics of the ZANU, the militant group led by Ndabaningi Sithole. Smith's government and some Nationalist leaders finally agreed to form an interim government which would include black members, with majority rule as the eventual goal (see above right).

Ian Smith agrees timetable

In March Ian Smith, the Rhodesian Premier, agreed with Chief Chirau, Bishop Muzorewa and Mr Sithole a timetable for independence under black rule by December 31st, but civil war continued.

Golda Meir dies

The veteran Israeli leader Mrs Golda Meir died on December 8th at the age of 80. She had been Israel's Prime Minister from 1969 until her resignation in 1974.

P. W. Botha elected

P. W. Botha (1916–   ) was elected leader of the ruling National Party and the ninth Prime Minister of South Africa on September 28th. He succeeded B. J. Vorster who resigned for health reasons.

Ayatollah in waiting

As opposition to the Shah led to increasing unrest in Iran, calls grew for the return of the Ayatollah Ruholla Khomeini (above right), who had been in exile for 16 years. The 77-year-old spiritual leader of Iran's majority Shi'ite Muslims had transferred his headquarters to Pontchartrain on the outskirts of Paris, from where, despite repeated warnings from the French government, he issued regular directives to his militant followers in Iran.

Aldo Moro murdered

The body of the former Italian Prime Minister Aldo Moro was found in the back of a car in Rome on May 9th. He had been shot 11 times. Signor Moro had been kidnapped by members of the Red Brigades on March 16th.

Mass suicide in Jonestown

More than 900 members of a religious cult, the People's Temple, were found dead at their commune in Jonestown, Guyana. They had committed mass suicide by drinking cyanide at the behest of their leader, the Reverend Jim Jones.

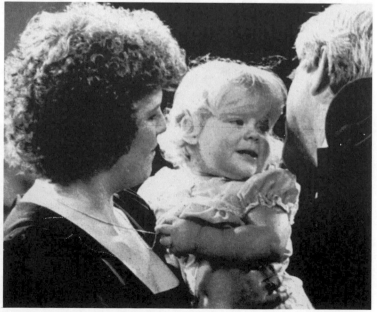

World chess champion

The temperamental chess grandmaster Viktor Korchnoi (1931–   ) (above right), who defected to the West in 1976, lost to fellow-Soviet Anatoly Karpov (1951–   ) in the world championship after a close match in the Philippines.

First test-tube baby

Louise Brown, the world's first test-tube baby, was born in a hospital in Manchester, England, on July 26th. The embryo had been implanted in her mother's womb after *in vitro* fertilisation in a pioneering operation by Dr Patrick Steptoe.

Three Popes in one year

The requiem mass for Aldo Moro was one of the last public appearances of Pope Paul VI (above left), who died of a heart attack on August 6th at the age of 80. In his 25-year reign he had taken an active role in international affairs and his funeral mass was attended by representatives of more than 100 countries.

On August 26th, a secret conclave of cardinals elected Cardinal Albino Luciani, the Patriarch of Venice, as the 263rd Pope (above right). His reign as John Paul I was to be very brief. On September 29th, he was found dead in his bed, apparently from a heart attack, after a pontificate of only 33 days – the shortest since 1605.

For the second time in a year, voting began in the Sistine Chapel to elect a successor to the throne of St Peter. On October 16th, the new Pope was named as Cardinal Karol Wojtyla, the Archbishop of Cracow. The 58-year-old Cardinal (left), the first non-Italian to be elected to the papacy for more than 400 years and the first Pole ever to hold the office, took the name John Paul II. The open-air mass celebrating his inauguration was attended by, among others, Dr Donald Coggan, the first Archbishop of Canterbury to attend the investiture of a Pope since England broke with the Roman Catholic Church in the 16th century.

1979

Jan	7	Cambodian capital Phnom Penh falls to Vietnamese
	16	Shah of Iran flees to Egypt
	25	Pope John Paul II visits Latin America
Feb	1	Iran: Ayatollah Khomeini returns after 16 years' exile
	8	US cuts military and economic aid to Nicaragua
	10	Pakistan: General Zia to introduce Islamic laws
	11	Iran: Khomeini's followers set up new provisional govt
	17	China invades Vietnam in retaliatory move
Mar	26	US: Egypt and Israel sign peace treaty in Washington
Apr	4	Demonstrations in Pakistan as ex-PM Bhutto is hanged
May	4	Margaret Thatcher elected first woman PM in UK
	29	Abel Muzorewa becomes Rhodesia's first black PM
Jun	2	Pope John Paul II visits his native Poland
	8	First direct elections for European Parliament
	11	US actor John Wayne dies
	18	US and USSR sign SALT II treaty
Jul	11	US space station *Skylab* returns to Earth from orbit
	19	Nicaragua: Sandinistas in control; Somoza regime ends
	23	Iran: Khomeini bans broadcasting of music

Aug	1	Commonwealth conference begins in Lusaka, Zambia
	23	Iran: Kurdish rebels clash with Iranian troops
	26	Rhodesia to be renamed Zimbabwe
Sep	20	Central Africa: Bokassa deposed; Republic restored
	29	John Paul II makes the first papal visit to Ireland
	29	China: Vice-Chairman condemns Cultural Revolution
Oct	11	US: Carter announces increased surveillance of Cuba
	15	El Salvador: President Romero ousted in army coup
	22	Deposed Shah of Iran Riza Pahlavi goes to US
Nov	4	Iran: Khomeini supporters occupy US embassy
	26	President Park Chung Hee assassinated by Korean CIA
Dec	2	Iran adopts new Islamic constitution under Khomeini
	7	Charles Haughey of Fianna Fail becomes new Irish PM
	27	Soviet troops invade Afghanistan, following coup
		The Arts
		James Bridges's film *The China Syndrome*
		William Styron's novel *Sophie's Choice*
		Peter Shaffer's play *Amadeus*
		Francis Ford Coppola's film *Apocalypse Now*

Conflict in Afghanistan

Throughout the year the security situation in Afghanistan worsened as government forces battled against Muslim guerrilla rebels in many parts of the country. Half the population were living in areas under rebel control or in disputed regions, ruled by the Army during the day and by the insurgents at night. The largely unco-ordinated Muslim groups, based in neighbouring Pakistan, mounted attacks on Soviet citizens, and the government increasingly turned to the Soviet Union for military equipment and supplies. In December a new Soviet-backed government was installed in Kabul (below), and some 5,000 Soviet combat troops were reported to have entered the country.

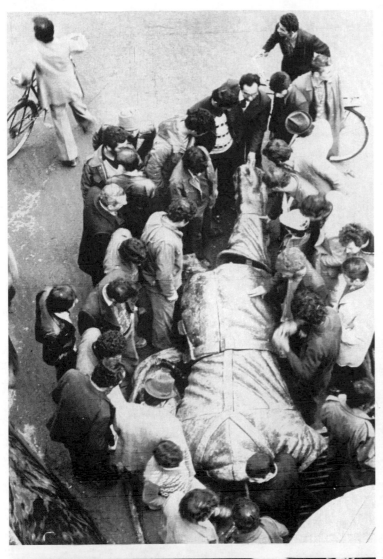

Revolution in Iran

Popular opposition to the regime of Shah Mohammed Riza Pahlavi reached fever pitch in Iran during the early months of the year. The streets of Tehran and other major cities became battlegrounds, as opponents of the Shah staged vast demonstrations to protest against poverty and repression, particularly by the hated national intelligence and security organisation Savak. Encouraged by taped messages from the exiled Ayatollah Khomeini (now in Paris) which were circulated among Iran's mullahs, a wave of strikes in major industries brought the country and its economy to a virtual standstill. Statues of the Shah were torn down (above left) and many people were killed as the security forces tried to contain the unrest.

The Shah leaves Iran

On January 16th, the Shah and the Empress Farah left Iran and flew to Egypt for what was described as a 'vacation' but was to become a permanent exile. On February 1st, Ayatollah Khomeini returned to his country after 16 years in the political wilderness to be greeted with adulation by the three million people who had crowded into Tehran to welcome him (left). Ten days later the military withdrew to their barracks and the post-Shah administration of Dr Bakhtiar fell. Revolutionary Islamic government in Iran had begun.

Demands for Shah's extradition

Demands for the extradition of the Shah intensified towards the end of the year. Muslims besieged the hospital in New York City where he had arrived for medical treatment. And in Iran itself a group of revolutionary 'students' occupied the American Embassy, taking its staff hostage and threatening to kill them unless the Shah was returned to face trial. The stage was set for a dangerous confrontation.

Vietnamese invade Cambodia

In Cambodia the tyrannical rule of 'Pol Pot' (real name Saloth Sar, above), was ended by Vietnamese invasion. The populace had suffered four years of assault from the Khmer Rouge and Pol Pot's legacy was appalling; all the towns had been emptied and the people subjected to psychological and physical torment with up to a quarter of them murdered. Despite this, the Khmer Rouge continued to represent Cambodia at the United Nations while Vietnam and the new Cambodian government were isolated by the international community. Above: Skulls piled up in a mass grave at a Khmer Rouge torture camp.

Nicaraguan revolution

On July 19th, after weeks of bloody civil war, the forces of the left-wing National Liberation Sandinista Front marched triumphantly into the Nicaraguan capital Managua. There were joyful celebrations in front of the Nicaraguan National Palace (top) as the dictator General Anastasio Somoza (1925–   ), deserted by his former allies the United States and by public opinion in Nicaragua itself, finally fled the country after 12 years of authoritarian power. During the bitter conflict Somoza's hated National Guard had been responsible for many atrocities, such as the machine-gunning of this couple's two teenage sons (above).

Fall of Amin

Following the Ugandan dictator Idi Amin's bloody incursion into neighbouring Tanzania in October the previous year, the Tanzanian President Julius Nyerere took spectacular revenge in January. Some 45,000 Tanzanian troops invaded Uganda, destroying the southern towns of Masaka and Mbarara before marching on the capital Kampala.

Despite aid from Colonel Gadaffi of Libya, Amin's forces could not resist for long and were soon routed by Nyerere's so-called 'army of liberation'. Amin himself fled the capital, leaving his incongruously suburban-looking house (above centre) and the

notorious State Research Bureau next door, where the flyblown bodies of Ugandans shot by his retreating men (above left) were only the last in a long line of people to be tortured and murdered there under his regime of terror. Widespread looting and lawlessness followed the arrival of the victorious Tanzanians, who then forged a path northwards into the West Nile district. Such resistance as they met was quickly overcome (top) and by June they had reached Uganda's northern border.

Meanwhile some 100,000 refugees, including many soldiers, had fled across the White Nile into southern Sudan (above).

Disaster at Three Mile Island

A wave of protests followed America's worst nuclear accident at a power station on Three Mile Island in Pennsylvania. Radioactivity was released into the atmosphere and the River Susquehanna when the uranium core of one of the plant's pressurised water reactors overheated in the early hours of March 28th. Thousands of people left their homes in the surrounding area as radiation inside the reactor building reached levels 75 times higher than those required to kill a human being. A subsequent inquiry criticised the National Regulatory Commission for its handling of the crisis.

SALT II

On June 18th, the US President Jimmy Carter and the Soviet leader Leonid Brezhnev signed the SALT II Treaty at the Hofburg Palace in Vienna. The treaty set equal ceilings for both sides on delivery systems for intercontinental ballistic missiles and established limits for the development of new weapons. Its 19 articles also made provision for the reduction of existing stocks of strategic offensive arms. Described by the two leaders as 'a substantial contribution to the prevention of nuclear war and the development of detente', the agreement was welcomed by NATO and the Politburo, but the US Senate refused to ratify it.

Airey Neave killed

On March 30th, Mr Airey Neave, Britain's Opposition Spokesman on Northern Irish affairs, was killed by an IRA car bomb as he was leaving the underground car park at the House of Commons in London.

Mrs Thatcher's triumph

On May 3rd, Mrs Margaret Thatcher, 53, became the first woman Prime Minister of Great Britain when the Conservative Party won the general election with an overall majority of 44.

Seb Coe

In just 41 days the 22-year-old British runner Sebastian Coe (1956–) broke three world records, for the 800 metres, the mile and the 1,500 metres, the last in Zürich (above) on August 15th.

Mountbatten murdered

Earl Mountbatten of Burma (1900–1979), the Queen's cousin, was killed on August 27th by an IRA bomb planted on his fishing boat at Mullaghmore in Ireland. He was 79.

Dame Gracie Fields

On February 20th, the much-loved singer Gracie Fields (1898–1979) was invested as a Dame Commander of the Most Excellent Order of the British Empire. She died on September 27th.

Death of a hero

John Wayne (1907–1979) died this year. The celebrated star of westerns and war films played his first major role in John Ford's *Stagecoach* (1939).

1980–1989

The 1980s

History may come to see in the 1980s a turning point not only in the relations between states, but also in the relationship between man and the natural world.

Perhaps the most remarkable changes in the international political scene came as a result of the accession of Mikhail Gorbachev to the leadership of the Soviet Union in 1985. The youngest member of Chernenko's Politburo, he brought with him an astonishingly fresh approach to the domestic and international problems of the Soviet Union, not least in admitting their existence and pledging himself to overcome them. The words *glasnost* and *perestroika* entered the international vocabulary as he launched his crusade for economic revitalisation and freedom from the bureaucratic and ideological shackles of the Brezhnev years, releasing in the process a dramatic tide of popular dissent in the satellite states of the Soviet bloc, which saw one entrenched Communist régime after another collapse in Eastern Europe in the closing months of the decade. The long-term effects of Gorbachev's policies have yet to be seen, especially in the Soviet Union itself, but their immediate effect has been to put East-West relations on a more constructive course than had seemed possible for many years.

Above all, though, the 1980s may come to be remembered as the decade in which concern for the environment soared to the top of the political agenda. The world's worst nuclear catastrophe, research into the so-called 'greenhouse effect' and revelations about the depletion of the world's ozone layer combined to bring green issues into the political mainstream after years of relegation to the margins of debate. Again, it is too early to tell what the long-term effects of this reappraisal will be, but there is now a widespread recognition that it is time to act. More immediate even than the issue of nuclear stockpiles, preserving the environment has become a matter of life and death.

Glasnost, perestroika and Eastern Europe

Glasnost – openness – and *perestroika* – reconstruction – are the terms which have come to be associated most closely with the campaign of the Soviet leader Mikhail Gorbachev to reform the economic and political machinery of the Soviet Union. Many of the traditional obstacles to East-West co-operation have been reduced in the years since he came to power. The release of such leading dissidents as Anatoly Scharansky and Andrei Sakharov reflected a wider relaxation of curbs on human rights – a relaxation that has brought its own problems for the Soviet Union in the upsurge of independence movements in the troubled Republics of Estonia, Armenia, Azerbaijan, Georgia, Latvia and Lithuania. Progress has also been made on the crucial issue of arms control, with the signing of the INF treaty, the first agreement ever to eliminate an entire category of offensive nuclear weapons. President Reagan's cold war rhetoric of the 'evil empire' thawed towards understanding at a series of superpower summits, and another major sticking point was removed with the withdrawal of Soviet troops from Afghanistan at the beginning of 1989.

Most dramatic of all, though, was the collapse of Communist rule in the Eastern European states during 1989 as, one by one, the governments of Poland, Hungary, Czechoslovakia, Bulgaria, East Germany, and even Stalinist Rumania toppled in the face of unprecedented public demand for democratic reform. Perhaps the most telling symbol of this remarkable torrent of change was the opening, after 28 years, of the Berlin Wall, which reunited thousands of East Germans with friends and family in the West and prompted serious discussion of German reunification.

Thatcher and Reagan

In Britain the country's first ever woman Prime Minister gave her name to a political movement. 'Thatcherism' has been defined in different ways by different people, but its effect on the fabric of British society is denied by no-one. Proclaiming the battle against inflation as her government's primary policy objective, Mrs Thatcher launched a campaign to regenerate Britain's recession-hit economy through control of the money supply, restraint of trade union power and a far-reaching programme of 'privatisation' of nationalised industries. Praised by many as achieving a new prosperity, her controversial policies were blamed by others for producing high levels of unemployment and a sharp division between the haves and the have-nots. One of the longest serving of Western leaders, Mrs Thatcher has also played a significant role on the world stage, perhaps most conspicuously in 1982 during the Falklands conflict with Argentina. In the United States the policies of President Ronald Reagan sought to effect a similar rebirth of national self-esteem after the setbacks of the 1970s, and the so-called 'special relationship' gained new life from the two leaders' personal closeness.

The environment

The Chernobyl nuclear accident, which left much of Europe contaminated by radioactivity, made many people realise that environmental crisis is no respecter of national borders. Concern about the natural environment has been further heightened by the discovery that damage to the earth's ozone layer by chlorofluorocarbons (CFCs) and other chemicals is much more serious than had previously been thought. Already there is evidence of an increase in cases of skin cancer as a result of depletion of the ozone layer, which screens out the sun's harmful ultra-violet rays, and concerted action is now being taken to restrict the use of the chemicals concerned. There are also moves to arrest the wholesale destruction of the earth's tropical rainforests. This is held partly responsible for the 'greenhouse effect', which could produce disastrous changes in climate. For the first time, the urgency of the challenge facing mankind has been recognised by the world's governments. It remains to be seen how we shall meet that challenge in the 1990s and beyond.

Pages 198–9: A refugee camp in Ethiopia, October 1984.

Jan	6	Indira Gandhi's Congress Party wins Indian election	Aug	2	Bomb blast in Bologna, Italy, kills 76
Feb	18	Pierre Trudeau is Canada's Prime Minister again		14	Polish workers strike and seize Gdansk shipyard
	24	US Eric Heiden wins 5 Olympic gold medals		15	Wreck of *Titanic* found
Mar	4	Robert Mugabe elected PM of Zimbabwe	Sep	12	Bloodless military coup in Turkey
	25	UK: Robert Runcie is new Archbishop of Canterbury		17	Ousted President Somoza of Nicaragua assassinated
Apr	7	US severs relations with Iran		21	Iraqui troops cross Iranian border
	18	Zimbabwe becomes independent	Oct	3	Terrorists bomb Paris synagogue
	30	Princess Beatrix becomes Queen of Netherlands		10	Algeria hit by earthquake
May	4	Yugoslav President Tito dies		21	US: Philadelphia Phillies win World Series
	18	Mt St Helens volcano erupts in US		23	Soviet Premier Kosygin resigns (dies Dec 19)
Jun	2	West Bank Arab Mayors maimed by bombs		23	Screen actors end 94-day strike in US
	7	US writer Henry Miller dies	Nov	4	Ronald Reagan wins US Presidency
	12	Japanese PM Ohira dies 10 days before elections		23	Severe earthquake hits S Italy
	13	Auto workers strike in USSR	Dec	2	Portugal's PM Francisco Sà Carneiro dies in plane crash
Jul	5	Björn Bog win 5th consecutive Wimbledon		26	Algerian ambassador to Iran visits US hostages
	11	Sick US hostage Richard Queen released by Iran			*The Arts*
	19	22nd Olympic Games open in Moscow			William Golding's novel *Rites of Passage*
	27	Deposed Shah of Iran dies in Cairo			Robert Redford's film *Ordinary People*
	30	Israel makes undivided Jerusalem its capital			Umberto Eco's novel *The Name of the Rose*

Oil rig disaster

Tragedy struck the booming North Sea oil industry in March when the semi-submersible mobile rig the *Alexander Kielland* capsized in heavy seas 200 miles off the coast of Norway with the loss of 123 lives. The 10,000-ton rig, which was being used as an accommodation platform for workers on Phillips Petroleum's Edda field at the time of the accident, keeled over and sank in 80 metres of water when one of its five supporting legs collapsed. The death toll made this one of the worst accidents in the history of North Sea oil exploration and urgent checks were ordered on rigs of a similar design. The photograph (below) shows the upturned feet of the rig, which was towed to Haugesund for examination.

Soviet troops in Afghanistan

Following the airlift of Soviet troops into Afghanistan in the closing days of 1979, some 85,000 men were reported to be operational in the country by the end of January. The Soviet intervention, which was denied by Leonid Brezhnev, was met by widespread condemnation in the West and by the imposition of sanctions against the USSR by the United States. As diplomatic activity intensified to try to find a solution to the crisis, Soviet and Afghan troops in Afghanistan itself attempted to consolidate their power over the country beyond Kabul. It was the beginning of what was to prove a long and bitter war against the Moslem *mujahedin* rebels, whose guerrilla tactics were to prove as damaging to the forces of the Soviet Union as those of the Viet Cong had to the United States in Vietnam.

The new US President

Relaxing on board an Air Force DC-9, President-elect Ronald Reagan and his wife Nancy fly across country to Washington, DC for the first time since Reagan defeated President Carter in the elections. Reagan won 489 electoral votes, far more than the 270 needed to win, while Carter got only 49, which was a big drop from the 297 by which he had beaten President Gerald Ford, four years earlier.

Birth of Solidarity

Poland was engulfed in a tidal wave of industrial unrest from July to September after strikes triggered by a rise in meat prices took on a political dimension which threatened the future of the government itself. Stoppages paralysed the shipyards of the Baltic coast, with 17,000 workers occupying the Lenin yard at Gdansk (above left). Panic buying led to food shortages in Warsaw as the strikers demanded the legalisation of independent trade unions, the end of press censorship and the release of imprisoned dissidents. In September the authorities were forced to concede and on September 17th the independent National Committee of Solidarity convened in Gdansk, electing the shipworkers' leader Lech Walesa (1947–   ), shown here (above right), as its Chairman.

The Iran hostage crisis

Relations between the United States and the regime of the Ayatollah Khomeini in Iran reached a new low when American action to end the hostage crisis went disastrously wrong.

Diplomatic measures

The 53 American hostages had been held by a group of revolutionary students in the US Embassy (top left) and the Iranian Foreign Ministry in Tehran since November 1979, their captors demanding the extradition of the Shah. Khomeini threatened to put the hostages on trial as spies and there was a flurry of diplomatic activity on their behalf by the USA, the Palestinian Liberation Organisation and even the Pope. In January the United Nations Secretary-General Kurt Waldheim visited Iran for talks, but the hostages remained incarcerated. On April 7th, President Carter broke off diplomatic relations with Iran and announced a further package of economic sanctions. On April 24th, he launched a raid to release the hostages by force.

The raid

The operation was a catastrophe. Ninety commandos from a special anti-terrorist unit called the 'Blue Light Squad' took off for Iran under cover of darkness with eight Sikorsky helicopters and six Hercules transport planes. However, they were forced to land in a remote desert in the east of Iran when three of the helicopters developed faults. Deciding to abandon the operation, they refuelled for take-off, but in the process one of the helicopters collided with a transport plane, killing eight people. The rest of the team flew out, leaving the desert sands littered with the burnt-out remains of their planes and the bodies of their colleagues (above).

In Iran, reaction to the failure of the raid was jubilant, with crowds chanting and cheering in the streets (bottom left). The remains of the dead men were flown to Tehran, where the Ayatollah Khalkhali displayed and mutilated them at a ghoulish press conference in the Embassy.

The Iranian Embassy siege

This year saw another dramatic operation to rescue hostages, again involving Iranians and again centered on embassy buildings. This time, however, the scene was a cream-washed Georgian villa in the fashionable West End of London and the operation was a striking success.

The terrorists' demands

The rescue was the culmination of six days of tense bargaining between the British authorities and a group of Iranian terrorists who had occupied the Embassy on April 30th. The gunmen, calling themselves the Group of the Martyr, belonged to a minority Arab group and were demanding the release of 91 fellow Arabs imprisoned under the Ayatollah Khomeini's revolutionary regime in the Iranian province of Khuzestan. They threatened to kill their 26 hostages and blow up the Embassy unless their demands, which included a plane to fly them out of the country, were met. Negotiations reached a stalemate, the terrorists extending their deadlines and reducing their demands, until finally they asked only for a safe passage out of Britain. On May 5th, however, the siege entered a new phase when the gunmen shot dead two of the hostages.

The SAS storms the Embassy

The same day astonished television viewers saw a crack squad of the British Special Air Service (SAS) storm the Embassy in a meticulously planned raid. Smoke and flames billowed from the elegant windows as the hooded black-uniformed SAS men used explosive devices to cover their entry, some bursting in from the balcony at the front of the building (above), while others abseiled down the walls and swung in through windows at the rear. In a matter of minutes, five of the six gunmen had been shot dead and all the surviving hostages were released. The building itself was gutted by fire from the explosions (right).

Daley Thompson wins gold medal

Daley Thompson (1958–   ) won the first ever British gold medal for the decathlon at the Moscow Olympics in July.

Alexandra Palace fire

Alexandra Palace in North London – which contained the largest concert hall in Europe – was burned out in July. More than 200 firemen fought the blaze.

Alfred Hitchcock

The British film director Alfred Hitchcock (1899–1980) died in April at the age of 80. A master of suspense, he was famous for films such as *The Birds* and *Psycho*.

Cecil Beaton

The British photographer and designer Sir Cecil Beaton (1904–1980) died at his home in Wiltshire, England, at the age of 76.

John Lennon murdered

The former Beatle John Lennon (1940–1980) was shot dead in New York City on December 8th. He was 40.

Elton John in Central Park

The colourful British rock musician Elton John (1947–   ) gave an open-air concert in New York City's Central Park.

1981

Jan	1	Greece joins EEC
	5	UK: Yorkshire Ripper murderer arrested
	25	Mao's widow and 'Gang of Four' sentenced to death
	25	US: Oakland Raiders win Super Bowl
Feb	9	General Jaruzelski becomes Polish Premier
	9	US rock singer Bill Haley dies
	22	Iran frees 3 British missionaries
Mar	2	Pakistanis hijack airliner
	26	UK: Social Democratic Party formed
	30	US: President Reagan shot
Apr	4	Italian Red Brigades leader arrested
	12	US launches first space shuttle *Columbia*
	12	UK: Race riots erupt in Brixton, London
May	5	Hunger striker Bobby Sands dies in Belfast prison
	10	Socialist François Mitterrand elected French President
	13	Pope John Paul II shot in Vatican City
Jun	7	Israel bombs Iraqi nuclear reactor
	22	Bani-Sadr ousted from Iran's Presidency
	29	China: Hu Yaobang replaces Hua as Party Chairman
	30	UK: Blanks fired at the Queen in London

	30	Ireland: Garret Fitzgerald becomes PM
Jul	10	UK: Widespread youth riots
	18	US: 111 killed when hotel collapses in Kansas City
Aug	3	US air traffic controllers begin strike
	19	US downs 2 Libyan jet fighters
Sep	15	President Sadat expels 1,500 Soviets from Egypt
Oct	3	Belfast Maze Prison hunger strike ends
	6	President Sadat assassinated in Cairo
	13	Hosni Mubarak elected as Egypt's new President
Nov	9	U San Yu elected President of Burma
	30	US and USSR begin arms talks in Geneva
Dec	10	USSR: Sakharovs end hunger strike
	11	Argentina's President Viola ousted
	13	Martial law imposed on Poland
	31	Jerry Rawlings directs successful coup in Ghana

The Arts

Salman Rushdie's novel *Midnight's Children*

Meryl Streep in film *The French Lieutenant's Woman*

Steven Spielberg's film *Raiders of the Lost Ark*

Andew Lloyd Webber's musical *Cats*

Royal wedding

In the media event of the decade, the Prince of Wales and Lady Diana Spencer were married at St Paul's Cathedral in London on July 29th. An estimated 750 million people worldwide watched the pageantry on television, and the day of the wedding was declared a public holiday in Great Britain.

The big day

The festivities began the previous day when Prince Charles lit the first of a chain of 102 beacons across the British Isles and thousands of people crowded into London's Hyde Park to watch a spectacular firework display in honour of the royal couple. On the morning of the wedding day itself, the streets of the capital were thronged with well-wishers, many of whom had camped out for days beforehand. The Royal Family left Buckingham Palace at about 10 a.m., Prince Charles travelling in the last of a procession of carriages. When they arrived at St Paul's, the bridegroom advanced to his place flanked by his two 'supporters', Prince Andrew and Prince Edward, and preceded by the Admirals of the Fleet. Lady Diana arrived with her father Earl Spencer in the Glass Coach used by King George V at his coronation in 1910. She was accompanied by five bridesmaids and two pageboys who carried the 25-foot train of her ivory silk taffeta dress, the design of which had been a closely guarded secret.

After the event

After the vows the Prince and Princess walked down the red-carpeted aisle together and waved from the cathedral steps (right) before riding back to the Palace in an open carriage. The newly-weds made the traditional appearance on the balcony of Buckingham Palace and delighted their audience with an unprecedented royal kiss before leaving in an open landau for the first stage of their honeymoon.

President Sadat assassinated

On October 6th, President Mohammed Anwar el Sadat of Egypt was murdered by Islamic fundamentalist gunmen in Cairo. The shooting happened at 1 p.m. during the annual military parade to commemorate the beginning of the Egyptian offensive in the 1973 Arab–Israeli war. A lorry in the procession stopped in front of the rostrum where the President and other luminaries were watching a fly-past of Egyptian Air Force jets. Armed men climbed out and ran towards Sadat, hurling grenades and opening fire with automatic weapons. The President and seven others fell, mortally wounded (left). Sadat was flown to the Maadi military hospital where he died an hour and 40 minutes later.

Sadat's funeral on October 10th was attended by only one Arab head of state. He had isolated himself in the Arab world by the rapprochement with Israel which had won him and Menachem Begin the Nobel Peace Prize in 1978 and led to a peace treaty between the two countries in 1979. Iraq, Libya, Syria and the Palestinian Liberation Organisation openly applauded his assassination.

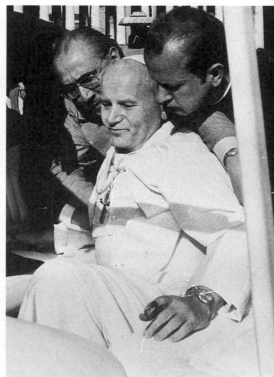

Reagan assassination attempt

Just ten weeks after his inauguration as President of the United States, Ronald Reagan became the victim of a bizarre assassination attempt. As the President left a hotel in Washington D.C., where he had been addressing a trade union convention, six shots were fired. Security men closed ranks around Reagan as he fell to the pavement (above). The President was rushed to the George Washington University Hospital where he underwent a two-hour operation to remove a bullet from his left lung. His assailant, John Warnock Hinckley, the 25-year-old son of an oil executive, was immediately arrested. He had apparently planned the shooting in order to impress the film actress Jodie Foster, whom he had never met but with whom he was obsessed.

Pope shot

Pope John Paul II was seriously wounded in a shooting incident in Rome on May 13th. He was hit in the stomach while driving in his open-topped 'Popemobile' among some 10,000 pilgrims in St Peter's Square. As he was driven to hospital for a five-hour life-saving operation, the gunman (a 23-year-old Turk named Mehmet Ali Agca) was apprehended by police.

Solidarity

Strikes and industrial unrest continued in Poland (top left:
Warsaw during a transport strike) where relations between the
government and the free trade union Solidarity deteriorated
badly towards the end of the year. In September the union held its
first national congress in Gdansk (left) and re-elected Lech
Walesa (top right) as Chairman. However, it also put forward
economic policies which the authorities saw as a bid for political
party status. When Solidarity proposed a national referendum on
a vote of no confidence in the government, the Polish leader
General Jaruzelski (above) arrested almost all the union's
leadership and declared martial law.

Vietnamese boat people

Refugees continued to risk death and piracy on the high seas in order to flee the new Communist regime in Vietnam. In the first eight weeks of the year, 451 boat people arrived in Hong Kong (left) – twice as many as in the same period in 1980. In neighbouring Macao, 240 refugees were arriving every day. Many of them came from China (which had taken 250,000 refugees since 1979), and the Hong Kong government asked the Chinese authorities to increase surveillance along its coast.

Unrest in Spain

It was a year of political violence in Spain. In February members of the Civil Guard burst into the *Cortes* (Parliament building) in Madrid in an attempted military coup. The following month there was trouble from the military wing of ETA, the Basque separatist movement. Ignoring the ceasefire declared by the political wing at their press conference (left), they murdered a police commissioner and two army officers. Troops were sent into the Basque provinces to assist the police but terrorist incidents continued, including a bank siege in Barcelona, a bomb attack on a car carrying the King's personal staff, and a number of kidnappings.

Bobby Sands dies

On May 5th, Bobby Sands became the first of ten Provisional IRA hunger-strikers to die in the so-called 'H blocks' of Belfast's controversial Maze Prison. Sands was serving a 14-year sentence for firearms offences; his protest was in support of demands for the reintroduction of special category status for Republican prisoners and had lasted 65 days. During that time he had been elected to the Westminster Parliament in a by-election in the Northern Irish constituency of Fermanagh and South Tyrone. On May 7th, he was buried in a Republican plot in West Belfast's Milltown cemetery (left).

US hostages released

Intense diplomatic activity by the Algerian government in the closing months of 1980 led to the release from captivity of the 52 US hostages in Iran (left). The end of their 444-day ordeal came on January 20th after the USA agreed to freeze the assets of the deposed Shah, end trade sanctions and unfreeze Iran's assets in the USA. They were released the day Ronald Reagan was sworn in as US President, but it was ex-President Carter who greeted the released hostages as they disembarked in Wiesbaden, West Germany.

Riots on streets of Britain

Serious unrest broke out on Britain's inner-city streets when police were attacked by black and white youths following an incident in Brixton, South London. Many buildings and vehicles were gutted (above left) and there were 779 reported crimes as Brixton was swept by three days of violence. In July the rioting spread to Southall in West London where fighting broke out between white and Asian groups. In Toxteth (above right), a dockland area of Liverpool, police used CS gas for the first time in mainland Britain to control gangs of youths who ran riot through the streets, throwing petrol bombs.

Tutu meets Runcie

In April Bishop Desmond Tutu of South Africa (1931–   ), General Secretary of the South African Council of Churches, visited London for talks with Dr Robert Runcie (1921–   ), the Archbishop of Canterbury, at Lambeth Palace. Tutu faced confiscation of his passport on his return to South Africa.

The Deptford fire

Thirteen black people died when fire swept through a house in Deptford, South London, during an all-night party on January 19th. Suspicions grew that the incident was a racist attack and the area became the focus of protests by members of the West Indian community. An enquiry began into the causes of the fire.

Yorkshire Ripper arrested

Four years of terror came to an end for women in the north of England when Peter Sutcliffe, 35, a long-distance lorry driver from Bradford, was arrested and charged with the 'Yorkshire Ripper' murders. Sutcliffe, seen here on his wedding day, pleaded guilty to 13 killings.

US space shuttle

The first flight of the US space shuttle *Columbia* began with a successful lift-off from the Kennedy Space Center in Florida on April 12th.

The 'Gang of Four'

In March the new Social Democratic Party was launched in Britain by four former Labour MPs: Roy Jenkins, David Owen, William Rodgers and Shirley Williams.

Natalie Wood

Natalie Wood (1938–1981) began her successful film career at the age of three. She died by drowning – thought to have lost her footing while boarding a dinghy.

Victory for Champion

British jockey Bob Champion, (1948–) who had been given eight months to live when diagnosed as having cancer in 1980, won the Grand National on Aldaniti.

Steve Davis wins

The 23-year-old snooker player Steve Davis (1957–) beat Doug Mountjoy to win the world championship in Sheffield, Northern England, in April.

McEnroe beats Borg

Temperamental young American John McEnroe (1959–) became the new Wimbledon tennis champion, beating Björn Borg.

1982

Israel in Lebanon

Months of mounting tension in the Middle East came to a head in June when Israel launched a full-scale invasion of Lebanon. The operation, code-named 'Peace for Galilee', had the declared aim of driving the Palestinian Liberation Organisation (PLO) out of bases near Israel's northern border. However, the invasion force of some 90,000 troops pushed on to Beirut in house-to-house fighting (above centre), leaving coastal cities in ruins and trapping many PLO fighters, including Yasser Arafat (top), in the capital as they surrounded it. By the time a ceasefire was declared on June 25th, Israeli tanks had advanced to the 'green line' dividing Christian East and Muslim West Beirut.

The Falklands conflict

From April to June the South Atlantic became the focus of world attention as Britain and Argentina went to war over the Falkland Islands. The conflict began on April 2nd when Argentinian forces invaded the islands in support of a long-standing claim to sovereignty. The 70 British Royal Marines stationed on the islands were overwhelmed. On April 3rd, the dependency of South Georgia was also occupied and by April 12th there were some 10,000 Argentinian troops on the islands.

Britain took swift action. A large task force was assembled and set sail for the South Atlantic. During the three weeks it took to cover the 8,000 miles to the Falklands there was intense diplomatic activity by the USA and others to find a peaceful solution to the crisis.

At the end of April British forces recaptured South Georgia and imposed a 200-mile total exclusion zone round the Falklands. On May 2nd, Argentina's second-largest warship the *General Belgrano* (top) was sunk 30 miles south of the zone, and on May 4th the British destroyer HMS *Sheffield* (above) was struck by an Argentinian Exocet missile. British troops established a bridgehead on East Falkland on May 21st from which they advanced over the next week to take Goose Green and Darwin after fierce fighting. A second bridgehead was established on June 8th near the capital Port Stanley, which fell after further heavy fighting on June 14th. The same day the Argentinian forces surrendered to the British commander of land forces. The hostilities had cost 254 British and 750 Argentinian lives.

Bombings in London parks

IRA bombs claimed 11 lives and injured more than 50 people in the centre of London on July 20th. The first of the two explosions occurred at 10.43 a.m. in Hyde Park as members of the Queen's Household Cavalry were making their way to Whitehall for ceremonial guard duty. Four soldiers were killed and many civilians wounded by the bomb, which was packed with four- and six-inch nails. The full force of the explosion was taken by the cavalry horses (left), many of which had to be destroyed. The second bomb went off at 12.55 p.m. under a bandstand in Regent's Park where members of the Royal Green Jackets were giving a concert. Seven soldiers died and 28 people were injured.

The Iran–Iraq War

With the beginning of 1982 the war between Iran and Iraq entered its 16th month. The military stalemate which had bogged the two sides down in a series of inconclusive battles, and which may already have claimed as many as 100,000 lives, was broken by a new Iranian offensive in March. The action was one of the most decisive of the war. Iranian troops recaptured some 850 square miles of land in Khuzestan which the Iraqis had gained after their attack on Iran in 1980.

At the end of March Iranian military officials claimed to have taken 15,500 Iraqi troops prisoner, some of whom are shown (left) at a camp outside Tehran. By May the Ayatollah Khomeini's forces had taken the key border town of Khorromshahr and invaded Iraq itself. Over the following months the Iraqis were driven out of Iran almost completely, and President Saddam Hussein reacted to his troops' losses on land by launching a series of air attacks on Iranian oil installations in the Gulf.

Meanwhile, all political and diplomatic efforts to put an end to the fighting seemed doomed to failure. Iraq called for a ceasefire as the war began to turn against it, but Khomeini was now determined to pursue the fight until he brought down President Hussein's regime. As the death toll mounted, and younger and younger recruits were sent to the front, it seemed as if the slaughter would continue indefinitely.

PLO leave Beirut

Some of the 1,500 Palestinian fighters forced to leave the war-torn city of Beirut give victory signs to supporters gathered to greet them at the harbour gate in Larnaca, Cyprus. In further attempts to destroy terrorist bases, Israeli jets had bombed Moslem West Beirut, despite appeals for restraint from the US government. The guerrillas were allowed to go with one gun each, leaving behind rocket-propelled grenade-launchers and other sophisticated weaponry.

It was hoped that the election of Bashir Gemayel, the Christian leader, as Lebanon's President would ease negotiations for the later withdrawal of the Israelis and Syrians, but he was killed by a bomb before he could take up the post. In the end his brother was sworn in as President.

Unrest in Poland

Following the imposition of martial law and the arrest of leading members of the independent trade union Solidarity at the end of 1981, there was continuing unrest in Poland. In May more than 3,000 people were arrested when police used teargas grenades and water cannons to break up anti-government demonstrations in Warsaw (left).

There were also serious disturbances in Szczecin, Wroclaw, the steel town of Nowa Huta and the Baltic port of Gdansk (birthplace of Solidarity) where some 10,000 people clashed with security forces in August. In October Solidarity and Rural Solidarity were outlawed by the authorities, but the Solidarity leader Lech Walesa, who had been held in isolation for almost a year, was finally released on November 12th.

Boat people rescued

On July 26th, the West German rescue ship the *Cap Anamur* (left) entered its home port of Hamburg. On board the converted freighter were 285 Vietnamese boat people, refugees from the Communist regime which succeeded the American withdrawal from Vietnam in 1979.

This was the *Cap Anamur*'s last rescue mission. For three years it had patrolled the South China Seas with a medical team from the Committee of German Emergency Doctors and had rescued a total of 9,500 refugees. It was estimated that as many as 80 per cent of Vietnamese boat people had been victims of acts of piracy on the seas, and stories of robbery, murder, abduction and rape were commonplace among those still arriving in many of the world's ports.

The *Mary Rose*

On October 11th, the *Mary Rose*, the flagship of Henry VIII's fleet, was raised from the seabed off Southsea in Hampshire, England. The operation was the culmination of 17 years of research on the wreck, involving almost 25,000 dives. At 9.03 a.m. the ship's hull emerged from the water for the first time since it sank 437 years earlier. There was a heart-stopping moment when part of the lifting frame gave way, but the ship was successfully mounted on a barge (above) and taken to dry land.

Potomac air crash

More than 70 people were killed when a Florida Air jet plunged into the frozen Potomac River in Washington D.C. during a heavy snowstorm on January 13th.

Birth of a royal heir

On June 21st, the Prince and Princess of Wales celebrated the birth of their first son. The young prince, second in line to the throne, was christened William Arthur Philip Louis.

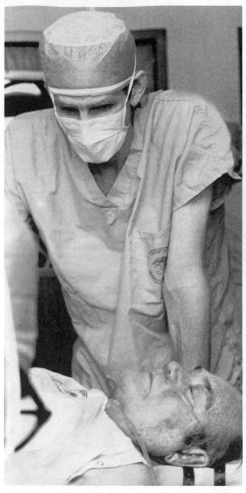

First artificial heart

Dr Barney B. Clark, 61, received the world's first artificial heart in a 7½-hour operation performed by Dr William DeVries in Utah, USA.

Pope at Anglican service

Pope John Paul II made history in Canterbury Cathedral on May 29th as the first Pope to attend an Anglican service in Britain.

Socialist landslide in Spain

Felipe González (1942–), aged 40, became Europe's youngest Prime Minister when his Socialist Workers' Party swept to power in Spain's elections on October 28th.

Rainer Werner Fassbinder

The German film director Rainer Werner Fassbinder (1946–1982) died at the age of 36. He had made more than 40 films.

Henry Fonda

The American actor (1905–1982), died in August after winning an Oscar for his last film *On Golden Pond*.

Princess Grace and Ingrid Bergman

The world of show business mourned the deaths of Princess Grace of Monaco (above left) and Ingrid Bergman (above right).

1983

Jan	3	Poland forms new labour unions
	7	Guatemala to get US arms
Feb	2	USSR and US resume START talks in Geneva
	25	US dramatist Tennessee Williams dies
Mar	2	Pope John Paul II visits Central America
	5	Labour leader Bob Hawke wins Australian elections
	8	UK composer William Walton dies
	14	OPEC forced to cut oil prices
	23	US: Reagan proposes 'Star Wars' defence system
Apr	12	US: Chicago gets first black mayor
	24	Turkey restores political parties
May	21	US makes AIDS top health priority
Jun	9	Tory Party led by Thatcher re-elected in UK
	9	Soares named Portuguese Premier
	16	Yuri Andropov elected Soviet President
	18	Sally Ride becomes first US woman in space
Jul	15	Armenians bomb Paris airport
	21	Poland ends martial law
	27	US: Pershing II missile fails test for third time
	29	UK: Actor David Niven dies
	29	Spanish film director Luis Bunuel dies
Aug	4	Bettino Craxi becomes Italy's first Socialist Premier
	5	Bomb kills 19 at Lebanese mosque
	21	Philippines: Benigno Aquino assassinated in Manila
Sep	1	Soviets shoot down S Korean airliner
	2	Israel's Premier Begin resigns; Yitzhak Shamir elected
	10	Peru lifts state of emergency
Oct	5	Lech Walesa awarded Nobel Peace Prize
	19	Grenada's PM Malcolm Bishop killed in coup
	23	Beirut car bomb kills US and French soldiers
Nov	14	First US Cruise missiles arrive in Britain
	24	Israel and PLO swap prisoners
	26	UK: £2.6 million in gold stolen from Heathrow airport
Dec	13	Turkey gets new government with Turgut Ozal as PM
	17	London: IRA bomb kills 5 in Harrods store

The Arts

Philip Roth's novel *The Anatomy Lesson*

Shirley MacLaine in film *Terms of Endearment*

US invades Grenada

In the small Caribbean island of Grenada, a military coup had ousted the moderate faction of the ruling New Jewel Movement. Prime Minister Maurice Bishop and members of his Cabinet had been executed and a 'Revolutionary Military Council' established.

President Reagan described the regime as a 'threat to the security of the United States', claiming that a new airport being built with Cuban assistance was a military facility. In October the United States mounted Operation 'Urgent Fury' and invaded the island, meeting unexpectedly fierce resistance from Grenadan troops. Here (below), a Chinook helicopter has been shot down on a Grenadan beach. American forces then left the island in the hands of a pan-Caribbean force, pending new elections.

Massacres in Assam

Thousands of people died as intercommunal violence swept the Indian state of Assam, focused on the State Assembly elections on February 14th. The bloodshed took place against a background of hostility to the estimated one million Bengali refugees who had fled to Assam before the formation of Bangladesh. Troops were sent into the Nelli area of the Nowgong district after hundreds of villagers were massacred on February 18th (above). Up to 500 Bengalis were reported killed on Oppidaya island and as many as 1,000 in the Mangaldoi district. By the end of March some observers estimated the total death toll as 3,000.

747 jumbo shot down

All 269 passengers and crew were presumed dead after Soviet fighters shot down a South Korean Boeing 747 airliner in Soviet airspace on September 1st. The Soviet Union accused the plane, which had veered off course after leaving Alaska, of spying and failing to respond to warnings. While relatives grieved, there was widespread Western condemnation of the shooting.

Contras in Nicaragua

In Nicaragua the anti-government Contra guerrillas continued their efforts to destabilise the country. The vital oil facilities at Corinto were attacked (above), leading to evacuation of the town and a fuel shortage. President Reagan attempted to increase funding for the Contras, but the House of Representatives reduced the appropriation and sought control over expenditure.

Beirut

Throughout the year anarchy reigned in the Lebanese capital Beirut, as opposing factions fought for supremacy on the streets, reducing the city (which had once been the playground of the wealthy in the Middle East) to a ruined shell.

Bomb attack against US Embassy

The international peacekeeping force, which had been stationed in Beirut since August 1982, was subjected to continual attacks and harassment by militia groups. Resentment at the presence of the US contingent culminated on April 18th in a suicide bomb attack against the US Embassy. Sixty people died and more than 100 were injured when a van packed with explosives was driven into the building, leaving it a smoking ruin.

Violence escalates

The general lawlessness escalated in May after Israel agreed to withdraw its troops. Druze militiamen stationed in the hills overlooking the city shelled Christian and Lebanese Army positions in the suburbs. Masked Shi'ite fighters put up barricades in the southern suburbs and heavily armed factions battled it out in alleys and burned-out buildings. Kidnappings became commonplace, and the government seemed powerless to control the spiralling violence.

A ceasefire declared in September proved to be only a brief respite from the bloodshed. On October 23rd, in an incident that sent shockwaves through the Western world, more than 300 American and French soldiers were killed in two simultaneous suicide attacks on their headquarters in Beirut. The majority of the casualties occurred at the US Marine Battalion HQ, where 260 men died when a lorry loaded with some 5,000 pounds of explosive crashed through the perimeter fence (above).

Violence in Sri Lanka

Official figures put the death toll at more than 380 as intercommunal violence swept Sri Lanka. There was criticism of President Junius Jayawardene (1906–   ) for the wide-ranging powers given to security forces to combat the terrorism of Tamil separatist guerrillas, as fighting erupted between the Tamil minority and the Sinhalese majority in July and August. Many Tamil refugees fled to the north as fire, looting and murder devastated parts of the capital Colombo (left). The violence spread to the island's central highlands, with reported revenge attacks by the Sri Lankan Army in the Jaffna peninsula and elsewhere.

Impasse in El Salvador

In the strife-torn Central American Republic of El Salvador, rebels of the FMLN (Farabundo Marti National Liberation Front) continued their campaign against the government. Both sides remained chaotically divided and unable to resolve the impasse. An FMLN offensive (the 'January Revolutionary Heroes' campaign) succeeded in capturing 12 towns in Morazan province. A bridge over the Torola River, bombed by the FMLN to slow government efforts to secure the province, is shown (left).

President Reagan attempted to increase aid to the government while the US Congress wanted assurances that human rights were being respected and that promised elections would proceed. Meanwhile, there were mounting protests at the numbers of deaths at the hands of government troops. The US Ambassador had noted in November 1982 that 30,000 people had been murdered since 1979.

Rebellion in Chad

In 1982 the Libyan-backed President of Chad, Goukouni Queddei had been ousted by the forces of Hissène Habré. Queddei formed a rival government in the north of the vast African nation and made a bid to regain power. Assisted by Libyan military units, the rebels moved south in the second part of 1983.

At President Habré's request, France came to the aid of its former colony and French troops and aircraft helped to repel the rebels. Here (left), a guard watches over captured Queddei supporters in the capital, Ndjaména. But large areas of Northern Chad remained in the hands of Queddei and his Libyan allies.

When the United States became involved on the side of the government, US-Libyan tensions were increased, especially in the Gulf of Sirte on Libya's Mediterranean coast.

The Harrods bomb

The scene outside Harrods, the prestigious London store, on Saturday, December 17 after the explosion of a terrorist car-bomb. Five people were killed and 91 injured on one of the busiest pre-Christmas shopping days. While the IRA claimed responsibility for the bomb, leaders of the organisation denied having given authorisation for the attack.

The America's Cup

Yachting history was made on September 26th when the USA's stranglehold on the prestigious America's Cup was broken for the first time in 132 years. The American defender *Liberty* (above left) was defeated by Australian millionaire businessman Alan Bond's *Australia II* (above right). The seventh and final race of the series was a close-run contest, with *Liberty* maintaining the lead from the early stages.

Klaus Barbie arrested

The former Nazi officer Klaus Barbie (1913–   ) was arrested in Bolivia in January on charges of fraud and organising paramilitary groups. Barbie was wanted in France, where he had twice been sentenced to death *in absentia* for war crimes committed during his time as Head of the Gestapo in Lyon. France demanded his extradition and on February 5th he was sent to Lyon to face trial.

Mass murder in London

Dennis Nilsen, one of the biggest multiple killers in British criminal history, was arrested on February 9th after the remains of human bodies were found at his house in Muswell Hill, North London (above). Police were astonished when Nilsen, a 37-year-old civil servant, openly admitted killing 15 men over four years. Dismembered human remains were found in plastic bags in his wardrobe and in drains under the house.

Neil Kinnock elected leader

On October 2nd, Neil Kinnock (1942–   ) was elected leader of the British Labour Party at its annual conference in Brighton. He succeeded Michael Foot, who had been leader since 1980. Mr Kinnock, 41, had been Labour MP for Bedwellty in South Wales since 1970 and Shadow Cabinet Spokesman on Education since 1979.

Raúl Alfonsín becomes President

Argentina returned to civilian rule on December 10th with the inauguration of President Raúl Alfonsín (1926–   ), following the victory of his Radical Civil Union Party in the general elections of October 30th. He vowed to curb the power of the military and to try those responsible for the 'dirty war' of the 1970s.

Arthur Koestler

The Hungarian-born writer and thinker Arthur Koestler (1906–1983) died in March at his home in London together with his wife Cynthia. They had both committed suicide. Koestler, a naturalised British citizen, was best known for *Darkness at Noon*, a searing critique of left-wing totalitarianism.

Face to face

Amid growing rumours that the Bulgarian security services might have been involved in the assassination attempt on Pope John Paul II in 1981, the Pope met his would-be assassin in his prison cell in Rome on December 27th after conducting a Christmas service at the gaol. Mehmet Ali Agca, a Turkish extremist, had been imprisoned for life in 1981 for an attempt on the Pope's life which led to the deaths of bystanders in St Peter's Square. The rumours, which resulted in Italy and Bulgaria breaking off diplomatic relations, originated in statements made by Agca himself.

1984

Jan	18	Gromyko and Shultz meet in Sweden		25	US author Truman Capote dies
Feb	7	US astronauts first to walk untethered in space		30	Space shuttle *Discovery* makes maiden flight
	9	Soviet leader Yuri Andropov dies	Sep	4	Beirut car bomb kills 23 at US Embassy
	13	USSR: Konstantin Chernenko succeeds Andropov		4	Canada: Prog. Con. Brian Mulroney is PM
	29	Canada: Pierre Trudeau resigns; John Turner PM	Oct	11	Kathryn Sullivan first US woman to walk in space
Mar	15	UK: Miners begin year-long strike		19	Polish priest Popieluszko kidnapped and killed
	21	French President Mitterrand visits US		24	French film director François Truffaut dies
Apr	1	US singer Marvin Gaye killed by father		26	US: Baboon's heart implanted in Baby Fae
	17	UK: Policewoman killed at Libyan Embassy siege		31	India's PM Indira Gandhi assassinated
May	1	Reagan concludes visit to China	Nov	5	Nicaragua: Daniel Ortega is elected President
	7	El Salvador: Jose Duarte wins Presidential elections		6	Ronald Reagan re-elected as US President
	19	British poet laureate John Betjeman dies		6	Chile's President Pinochet re-imposes state of siege
Jun	30	John Turner replaces Trudeau as Canadian PM	Dec	3	Toxic gas leak kills thousands in Bhopal, India
Jul	12	US: G. Ferraro first woman to run for Vice-President		7	South African Bishop Tutu meets President Reagan
	21	Poland grants amnesty to 652 political prisoners		23	Terrorist bomb kills 29 on train in Bologna, Italy
	27	UK: Actor James Mason dies			*The Arts*
	28	Olympic Games open in Los Angeles			David Lean's film *A Passage to India*
Aug	5	Actor Richard Burton dies			Roland Joffe's film *The Killing Fields*
	22	'Coloureds' allowed to vote in South African polls			Milos Forman's film *Amadeus*

Ethiopia's plight

Although famine ravaged many countries in Africa in 1984 it was the plight of Ethiopia which attracted global attention. The continuing failure of the rains had transformed once bountiful areas into virtual deserts. And as crops failed, families left their farms in search of food. Here (below), the search reaches one of Ethiopia's few roads.

The scale of the catastrophe was immense. The United Nations representative in Ethiopia calculated that between 600,000 and one million people had died by the end of the year and that up to eight million more were at risk. A BBC television report, in which a child died before the camera, finally moved the affluent West to act, and an immense relief effort began.

The Bhopal disaster

Two thousand people died and 180,000 were treated in hospital after poisonous gas escaped from a pesticide factory in Bhopal in the Indian State of Madhya Pradesh. The leak occurred in the early hours of December 3rd at the Union Carbide (India) plant. (In the photograph, left, the top of the three-flanged steel tank which leaked can be clearly seen.) It contaminated some 40 square kilometres of the city; many people died in their houses or in the streets as the cloud of highly toxic methyl isocyanate (MIC) moved over the shanty town around the plant, causing respiratory difficulties, foaming at the mouth and unconsciousness. The plant was immediately shut down and five Union Carbide officials were arrested for criminal negligence. The decision to reopen the plant a few days later in order to process the remaining MIC led to a mass exodus from Bhopal as up to 200,000 people fled.

Clashes in Amritsar

Sikh movements for greater political and religious autonomy in the Punjab became increasingly militant in the early months of the year. Violent clashes between Sikhs and Hindus claimed many lives throughout the region and the Prime Minister Mrs Indira Gandhi introduced wide-ranging powers of arrest and search.

A group of Sikh extremists led by Sant Bhindranwale took refuge in the Golden Temple at Amritsar (left), which became the focus of fierce gun battles with the security forces. During the night of June 5th, the Army stormed the temple complex and as many as 1,000 people were killed in the assault, including Bhindranwale himself.

The action, seen as sacrilegious by many Sikhs, was to lead to further bloodshed and claimed its most eminent victim in October when Mrs Gandhi herself was assassinated by Sikh members of her bodyguard in New Delhi (below right).

French farmers' protest

French farmers took disruptive action in January and February in protest against the importing of foreign meat into France during a glut in the European meat market. The protests were intensified when President Mitterand's government ended rail subsidies for the transport of agricultural produce from Brittany. Groups of farmers hijacked and burned lorries carrying lamb and pork from other EEC member states or gave their contents away to schools and hospitals. Others blockaded railway lines and Channel ports, and set up road blocks on major haulage routes. In one of the worst outbreaks of violence, a gang of angry farmers ransacked government offices in Brest, Brittany.

Father Popiełuszko murdered

Poland was swept by demonstrations in support of the banned trade union Solidarity after a Roman Catholic priest was found murdered in October. Father Jerzy Popiełuszko (on the right in the photograph), who had often been outspoken in his criticism of the Polish authorities, was kidnapped by three men on a road near Warsaw on October 19th. A full-scale manhunt led to the arrest of three members of the security forces on suspicion of murder, and on October 30th Father Popieluszko's body was found dumped in a reservoir west of Warsaw. He had been tied up, beaten and strangled. His funeral on November 3rd was attended by some 250,000 pro-Solidarity mourners.

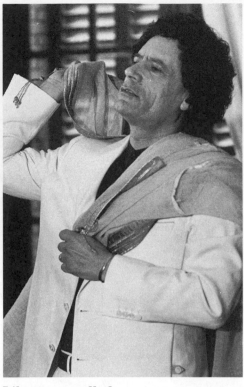

WPC Fletcher shot

Relations between Britain and Libya became very tense after a British policewoman was shot dead in St James's Square in London. The shooting happened on April 17th while WPC Yvonne Fletcher was policing a small demonstration outside the Libyan Embassy, known as the Libyan People's Bureau, by students opposed to the Libyan government. The gunshots came from inside the Embassy, which was immediately surrounded by armed police.

Above: The memorial unveiled to WPC Fletcher on the spot where she fell.

Libyans expelled

As a result of the shooting of Yvonne Fletcher, the British government broke off diplomatic relations with the Libyan regime of Colonel Gadaffi (above) on April 29th. Two days earlier the staff of the Libyan People's Bureau had been deported.

Mrs Gandhi killed

India's new Prime Minister Rajiv Gandhi – until now a commercial airline pilot – about to light the funeral pyre of his mother Mrs Indira Gandhi. Mrs Gandhi was assassinated by her bodyguards in the garden of her home in New Delhi on October 31st. Her killing was a direct response by Sikhs to her storming of their holiest shrine, the Golden Temple at Amritsar, regarded as a desecration even by Sikhs opposed to the extremists who had occupied the temple.

The Brighton bombing

Five people were killed and more than 30 injured when an IRA bomb devastated the Grand Hotel in Brighton, on England's south coast, on October 12th. The Conservative Party Conference was being held there.

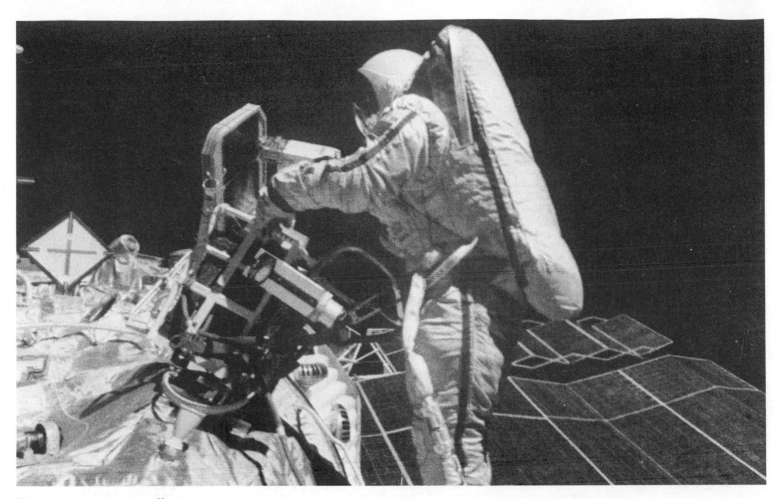

First woman spacewalker

In July the Soviet space programme achieved another 'first' when the cosmonaut Svetlana Savitskaya became the first woman ever to walk in space. She is shown working outside the Salyut-7 space station during the 12-day mission. Savitskaya and her fellow cosmonauts Igor Volk and Vladimir Dzanibekov returned to Earth on July 29th.

J. B. Priestley

England lost one of her grand old men of letters in August with the death, aged 89, of the author, playwright and essayist J. B. Priestley (1895–1984).

Richard Burton

The Welsh actor Richard Burton (1926–1984), seen here with Elizabeth Taylor, whom he married twice, died at the age of 58. His last role was that of O'Brien in the film *1984*.

1985

Jan	3	Ethiopian Jews settle in Israel
Feb	10	Mandela rejects offer of freedom from S African govt
	16	Israel begins withdrawal from Lebanon
Mar	3	UK: coal-miners end strike after 1 year
	10	Soviet Premier Chernenko dies: Gorbachev to succeed
	21	UK: Actor Michael Redgrave dies
	29	Spain and Portugal to join EEC
Apr	6	President Numeiry of Sudan ousted in coup
	11	Albania's Communist leader Elver Hoxha dies
	15	South Africa abolishes racial sex laws
May	10	India: Sikh terrorists kill 59, injure 150
	14	Tamil violence spreads in Sri Lanka
	20	Israel frees 1,150 Palestinian prisoners for 3 Israelis
	25	Lebanon: Hundreds killed in Chatila and Sabra camps
Jun	14	Terrorists seize TWA plane over Middle East
	23	Air India jumbo blown up in mid-air
Jul	1	USSR: Shevardnadze is Foreign Minister
	7	German Boris Becker, 17, is youngest to win Wimbledon
	10	Greenpeace *Rainbow Warrior* ship sunk in New Zealand
	13	US: Reagan undergoes surgery for removal of tumour
Aug	8	South African police kill 18 blacks
	20	Sikh leader Sant Harchand Singh Longowal killed
Sep	1	*Titanic* wreck found off Newfoundland
	2	Kampuchea: Khmer Rouge leader Pol Pot retires
	19	Earthquake devastates Mexico City
Oct	7	Palestinians seize Italian cruise ship *Achille Lauro*
	10	US jets intercept plane carrying hijackers
	10	US actors Orson Welles and Yul Brynner die
	27	El Salvador: President Duarte's kidnapped daughter free
Nov	6	General Jaruzelski elected Poland's head of state
	9	USSR: Gary Kasparov, 22, is world chess champion
Dec	2	UK: Poet Philip Larkin dies
	6	UK joins US Star Wars project
	30	President Zia of Pakistan ends martial law
	31	King Hussein and President Assad hold talks
		The Arts
		Kurt Vonnegut's novel *Galapagos*
		Sydney Pollack's film *Out of Africa*

Live Aid

On July 13th, an estimated 70 million dollars was raised for famine victims in Africa by a huge rock concert organised by the Irish musician Bob Geldof, seen at the event with the Prince and Princess of Wales (below). The all-day concert, which was broadcast to 152 countries by the largest ever intercontinental satellite link-up, took place simultaneously in Philadelphia and at Wembley Stadium in London (below right). It featured appearances by such stars as Mick Jagger and Tina Turner (above right), David Bowie, Paul McCartney, Bob Dylan, Joan Baez, Elton John, Madonna, and Phil Collins (who performed on the same day in both London and Philadelphia). More than 1½ billion people were believed to have watched the telethon worldwide, and switchboards in the UK and the USA were besieged with calls pledging money.

The Geneva summit

On November 19th Ronald Reagan and Mikhail Gorbachev met for the first time in Geneva for the first US–Soviet summit since President Carter met Leonid Brezhnev in Vienna in 1979.

The three-day meeting produced no striking new initiatives, but was generally seen as reducing international tensions by establishing a degree of personal rapport between the two leaders. The tone was set on the very first day when private talks between Reagan and Gorbachev overran their 15-minute schedule by more than three-quarters of an hour. The two men spent two hours in talks accompanied only by their interpreters in the Fleur d'Eau villa on the shores of Lake Geneva, an exchange which became known as the 'fireside chat'.

The talks were described as lively and businesslike, but differences of opinion remained on the crucial issues of arms control – where the US 'Star Wars' project proved a sticking point – regional conflicts and human rights. However, a number of agreements were signed on scientific and cultural matters in a televised ceremony attended by both leaders at the Geneva International Centre. A joint communiqué issued on November 21st pledged both countries to work for peace and the reduction of nuclear arsenals. President Reagan spoke of a 'fresh start' in East–West relations.

The Bradford fire

Fifty-six people died when fire engulfed a wooden stand at Bradford City Football Ground in the UK, on May 11th. The blaze, which began when a cigarette or match ignited accumulated rubbish under the seats, became an inferno within minutes. Many of the dead were trapped at the back of the stand when they found emergency doors locked.

Tragedy at Heysel

Another footballing tragedy occurred at Belgium's Heysel Stadium on May 29th when 41 people died and more than 400 were injured in crowd violence before the European Cup Final between Juventus of Turin and Liverpool. Most of those who died were crushed when a wall collapsed under the weight of supporters trying to escape rampaging British fans.

Colombian volcano

At least 25,000 people were believed dead when the volcano Nevado del Ruiz erupted near the town of Armero in Colombia on November 13th. The town and the surrounding area were devastated by the eruption, which lasted for several days and covered the area in a sea of mud. As rescue operations began (above), a national state of emergency was declared.

Earthquake in Mexico

Thousands of square miles of Mexico City and the surrounding area were devastated on the morning of September 19th by a massive earthquake which claimed the lives of up to 20,000 people. The quake, measuring 8.1 on the Richter scale, also left more than 30,000 homeless. And the rescue operation was hampered by a second earthquake which struck the following day.

Libyan hostages released

Four Britons held in detention in Libya for nine months flew home to England on February 7th. They are shown alighting at Gatwick airport after their ordeal.

TWA hijack

A US Navy diver, Robert Stetham, was murdered by the Lebanese hijackers of a TWA flight from Athens to Rome. Other hostages were released after two weeks of negotiations.

Clive Sinclair's C5

In January the British inventor and entrepreneur Sir Clive Sinclair (1940–   ), launched his electric vehicle, the C5. Looking rather like a large shoe, the C5 ran on a washing-machine motor and could travel at 15 miles per hour.

Pope in South America

Pope John Paul II visited Venezuela, Ecuador, Peru, Trinidad and Tobago during his 11-day tour of Latin America in January and February. He was met by vast enthusiastic crowds, but many clergy were upset by his rejection of 'liberation theology'.

Oil tanker explosions

Thirty people were killed and more than 40 injured when an explosion wrecked the Panamanian oil tanker *Petrogen-One* near the Rock of Gibraltar. The accident happened as the ship was unloading her oil at the Spanish port of San Roque, and set off a second explosion on board the Spanish tanker *Camponavia*, which was loading nearby.

Rainbow Warrior sunk

There was embarrassment among the French authorities after it was found that members of their security services had been involved in blowing up a ship belonging to the international environmental organisation Greenpeace. The attack took place in Auckland Harbour, New Zealand, on July 10th and one crew member died in the explosions from two limpet mines. *Rainbow Warrior* was due to have taken part in a protest against French nuclear tests on Mururoa Atoll in the South Pacific.

Robert Graves

The British poet and novelist Robert Graves (1895–1985) died on December 7th at Deya on the Spanish island of Majorca where he had lived since 1929. Graves, who was 90, was best known for his autobiographical work *Goodbye to All That* and his novels *I, Claudius* and *Claudius the God*.

Joan Collins

The career of 52-year-old Joan Collins (above), the British starlet of the 1950s, reached new heights with her portrayal of Alexis in the American television soap opera *Dynasty*. After her appearance in the series it moved rapidly into the top ten in American viewing ratings.

Marc Chagall

The Russian-born artist Marc Chagall (1888–1985) died in France, where he had lived since 1922. He was 97 and had been working almost to the end of his life. Chagall's brightly coloured paintings were marked by his use of often naive imagery from Jewish folklore and the natural world.

Unrest in South Africa

The South African President P. W. Botha declared a state of emergency in July as violence engulfed black townships in the Transvaal and the Eastern Cape. The rioting claimed hundreds of lives and was sparked off by the new constitution which gave political representation to coloured and Indian people but excluded blacks. There was widespread international criticism of the South African authorities when police shot at least 40 people during a funeral procession near Uitenhage on March 21st, the 25th anniversary of the Sharpeville massacre.

1986

Jan	8	President Reagan freezes Libyan assets in the US
	24	US spacecraft *Voyager 2* probes Uranus
Feb	7	Haitians overthrow President Duvalier
	11	Human rights activist Scharansky freed by Soviets
	25	Cory Aquino defeats Marcos in Philippine elections
	28	Swedish Prime Minister Olof Palme assassinated
Mar	17	US $ reaches lowest post-war rate against Japanese yen
	24	Libyan and US forces clash over airspace
	30	Actor James Cagney dies
Apr	2	Bomb explodes on TWA flight from Rome to Athens
	13	Jack Nicklaus wins US Masters golf, his 18th major
	15	US planes bomb Libya
	15	French dramatist Jean Genet dies
	24	Wallis Simpson, Duchess of Windsor, dies
May	1	1½ million blacks go on strike in South Africa
	14	President Gorbachev reveals Chernobyl facts
Jun	8	Kurt Waldheim elected President of Austria
	13	US jazz clarinettist Benny Goodman dies
	14	Argentine writer Jorge Luis Borges dies
	15	USSR: Chernobyl bosses dismissed
	25	Philippines gets US aid
Jul	2	General strike called in China
	4	US: Celebrations for reopening of Statue of Liberty
Aug	14	Benazir Bhutto of Pakistan is jailed
	31	British sculptor Henry Moore dies
Sep	5	Pakistan: Pan Am jet seized in Karachi
	6	Arab terrorists kill 21 at Istanbul synagogue
Oct	2	US imposes sanctions on S Africa
	7	Nicaragua captures US pilot delivering arms to rebels
	20	Israel: Shamir takes over as coalition PM
	22	US reforms tax code
Nov	3	Mozambique: President Machel killed in air crash
	4	Democrats to control US Senate
	10	Chemical spill pollutes River Rhine
	13	US violates Iran arms boycott
	30	British-born actor Cary Grant dies
Dec	12	Microlite aircraft circles earth non-stop
	19	Soviet dissident Andrei Sakharov freed from exile
	29	Britain's ex-PM Harold Macmillan dies
	30	US begins military exercises in Honduras
		The Arts
		Larry McMurtry's novel *Lonesome Dove*
		Woody Allen's *Hannah and Her Sisters*
		Paul Hogan in film *Crocodile Dundee*
		Oliver Stone's film *Platoon*

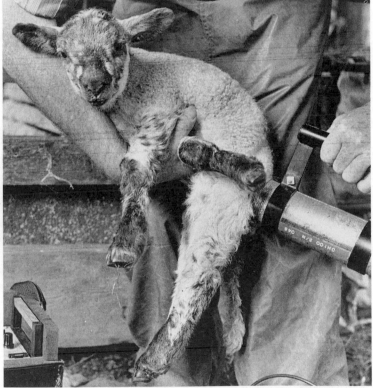

Chernobyl

The world's worst ever nuclear accident took place on April 26th when a disastrous fire at the Chernobyl nuclear power station in the Ukraine (top) contaminated much of Europe with radioactive fall-out. There was widespread international criticism of the Soviet Union's secrecy and slow reaction to the disaster, which came to light only after high radiation levels were detected in Sweden.

Meltdown was avoided by sealing the damaged reactor with concrete, but restrictions were imposed on the sale of animal foodstuffs in many countries as tests showed levels of radioactivity well above normal in grazing animals such as sheep, cows and reindeer (above). Doctors differed in their estimates of the number of additional cancer deaths likely to be caused by the disaster in later years.

The Gulf War

Despite diplomatic efforts to end the fighting between Iran and Iraq, the death toll mounted inexorably in what came to be known as 'the forgotten war'. Successes such as Iran's at Al Faw (above) were met by Iraqi counter-offensives and there were mounting rumours that Iraq was using chemical weapons.

Swiss chemical plant fire

Switzerland became the scene of a major environmental disaster in November when a fire at a chemical plant near Basle led to the discharge of thousands of gallons of toxic water into the Rhine. Half a million fish died after water which had become contaminated when it was used to control the fire (above) was pumped into the river.

The *Challenger* disaster

Tragedy struck the US space programme in January when the *Challenger* shuttle exploded shortly after take-off from Cape Canaveral, killing all seven astronauts on board. Well-wishers and relatives of the crew watched in horrified disbelief as the shuttle burst into flames just over a minute into its tenth mission. Media attention focused on the fate of Christa McAuliffe (top left, third from the back), a high school teacher from New Hampshire, who had won a contest to be the first ordinary citizen in space. The accident, which was traced to a fault in one of the twin solid-fuel booster rockets, led to staff changes at the top of the American space agency NASA.

US bombing of Libya

There was widespread criticism after US aircraft, flying from bases in Britain, launched bombing raids on targets in the Libyan cities of Tripoli and Benghazi, apparently in response to alleged Libyan involvement in a Berlin nightclub bombing.

South African pass laws

On April 23rd, President P. W. Botha announced an end to arrests under South Africa's hated pass laws, when a Bill was put before Parliament to abolish the requirement for black people to carry their passes at all times.

The Reykjavik mini-summit

In October President Reagan met the Soviet leader Mikhail Gorbachev for further talks almost a year after their famous 'fireside chat' at the Geneva summit. The meeting in the Icelandic capital Reykjavik took place during two days of talks on bilateral issues. A complete news blackout was observed, but there were rumours of a major agreement on arms control.

The Wapping dispute

Pickets clashed with police outside premises owned by Rupert Murdoch's News International Group after Murdoch moved production of his newspapers to a new plant at Wapping (in London's dockland) with the loss of 5,000 print jobs.

Royal wedding

On July 23rd, Prince Andrew married Miss Sarah Ferguson (known to friends and tabloid headline writers as 'Fergie') at Westminster Abbey in London. The Queen conferred on the royal couple the titles Duke and Duchess of York.

'People's power' in the Philippines

In an extraordinary upsurge of popular support, Mrs Corazon Aquino (1933–   ) (above left), widow of the assassinated Opposition leader Benigno Aquino, swept to power in the Philippines in February. Her inauguration as President followed a widely discredited election in which President Marcos, leader of the country since 1965, had claimed victory.

Kurt Waldheim elected

Dr Kurt Waldheim (1918–   ) the former United Nations Secretary-General, was elected President of Austria on June 8th after an election campaign dominated by questions about his war record. Dr Waldheim denied allegations that he had been involved in atrocities during his time as a Nazi lieutenant in the Balkans.

Death of Macmillan

Britain lost one of its elder statesmen in December with the death, aged 92, of the Earl of Stockton, who as Harold Macmillan had been Prime Minister from 1957 to 1963. Since acquiring his title in 1984, he had made controversial speeches in the House of Lords criticising aspects of government policy.

Swedish Prime Minister assassinated

Sweden was shocked by the assassination in February of the Prime Minister Olof Palme (1927–1986). Palme was shot dead as he was walking home with his wife after an evening at the cinema in Stockholm. Police investigations were slow to uncover his killer.

Oil and trouble

Oil prices took a battering in world markets in the early months of the year and on April 1st reached record lows after falling through the supposedly critical level of $10 a barrel. Next day trading in gasoline futures on the New York Mercantile Exchange (above) was heavy as prices staged a recovery. Saudi Arabia was alleged to have 'engineered' the price movements.

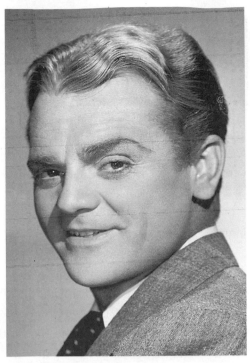

Andrei Sakharov released

On December 19th, the dissident Soviet scientist Dr Andrei Sakharov (1921–) and his wife Yelena Bonner were released from the closed city of Gorky where they had been in internal exile since 1980. Sakharov's return to Moscow on December 23rd was seen as a triumph for Mr Gorbachev's policy of *glasnost*.

Simone de Beauvoir

April saw the death of the French feminist writer and existentialist philosopher Simone de Beauvoir (1908–1986) at the age of 78. A long-time associate of Jean-Paul Sartre, she was the author of the influential works *The Second Sex* and *The Coming of Age*.

James Cagney

The American movie actor James Cagney (1899–1986) died in March at the age of 86. One of the most frequently imitated stars of all time, Cagney made his name playing tough guy roles in such films as *Public Enemy* (1930), *Angels with Dirty Faces* (1936) and *White Heat* (1949).

Henry Moore

The death of Henry Moore (1898–1986) in August robbed the art world of perhaps its greatest modern sculptor. Moore, seen here with the former British Prime Minister James Callaghan, worked in wood, bronze, stone and cement and was known for his smooth organic forms, often developing variations on the themes of the reclining figure and the mother and child.

1987

Jan	12	Britain's Prince Edward resigns from Royal Marines	25	Pope welcomes Austria's President Waldheim in Rome
	21	Archbishop's envoy Terry Waite disappears in Lebanon	28	Death of US film director John Huston
Feb	18	Ireland: Charley Haughey becomes PM	Aug 3	US: Irangate hearings end
	19	US lifts sanctions on Poland	Sep 19	Pope concludes US visit
	22	US pop artist Andy Warhol dies	21	US seizes Iranian ship in Persian Gulf
Mar	6	UK car ferry capsizes killing 184 at Zeebrugge	Oct 16	Widespread damage as Britain hit by hurricane
	16	Michael Dukakis enters US Presidential race	19	Stock markets collapse
Apr	17	US taxes Japanese imports	19	British cellist Jacqueline du Pré dies
	27	US bars Austria's President Waldheim from entry	19	US attacks Iranian boat base in Gulf
May	8	Gary Hart drops out of US Presidential campaign	Nov 8	UK: Bomb kills 11 at Ulster Remembrance Day Service
	15	Death of US actress Rita Hayworth	29	S Korean Boeing 707 disappears en route to Seoul
	17	Iraqi missiles hit US frigate	Dec 8	Reagan and Gorbachev sign arms treaty
	28	West German pilot lands in Moscow's Red Square	10	Russian-born US violinist Jascha Heifetz dies
Jun	2	Spanish guitarist Andrés Segovia dies	16	Roh Tae Woo wins Presidential election in S Korea
	11	Thatcher wins third term as Britain's PM		*The Arts*
	17	New York vigilante Goetz is cleared of murder		Van Gogh's painting *Irises* fetches £30 million
	23	Death of US dancer and actor Fred Astaire		Saul Bellow's novel *More Die of Heartbreak*
Jul	4	Nazi war criminal Klaus Barbie convicted in France		Arthur Miller's autobiography *Timebends*
	5	Martina Navratilova wins 6th consecutive Wimbledon		Bertolucci's film *The Last Emperor*
	11	Australians re-elect Hawke as PM		Richard Attenborough's film *Cry Freedom*

The *Herald of Free Enterprise*

One of the worst peacetime tragedies in the history of English Channel shipping occurred near the Belgian port of Zeebrugge on March 6th when a ferry with more than 500 people on board capsized.

One hundred and eighty-four people died when the 7,951-ton *Herald of Free Enterprise* keeled over in a matter of minutes just outside the harbour wall at Zeebrugge (left). Only a shallow sandbank prevented it from turning over completely. There were many stories of heroism during the rescue operation, one passenger being seen acting as a human bridge to allow others to escape to safety.

The ferry (run by Britain's largest ferry operator Townsend Thoresen) was of the roll-on roll-off kind, and doubts had been expressed in the past about the safety of this particular design. Initial investigations suggested that the ship had gone to sea with her bow doors open and had been destabilised by the resulting inrush of water on to the open car deck.

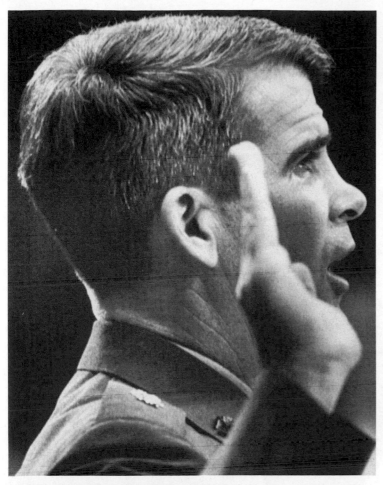

Irangate

Hearings began in May into the Iran–Contra affair which rocked the Reagan administration in the United States. In July the key figures in the case, Colonel Oliver North (top left) and his secretary Fawn Hall (top right) and Admiral John Poindexter (left) appeared before Committees of the House of Representatives and the Senate to answer questions on their part in the affair, in which profits from arms sales to Iran were diverted to support the Contra rebels fighting the Sandinista government in Nicaragua, thus bypassing a Congress ban on aid to the Contras.

The public hearings became a media event, with Oliver North in particular becoming something of a national hero for his uncompromising and unapologetic stance. Admiral Poindexter, who was widely expected to implicate the President himself in the scandal, in fact claimed that he had withheld information from Reagan in order to provide 'deniability' if the affair came to light.

Danny Kaye

Danny Kaye (1913–1987), born David Daniel Kaminsky in Brooklyn, died this year. He had a long career as one of America's best-loved entertainers and comedians, with an amiable, zany brand of humour all his own. He was also extremely popular in Great Britain, where he made frequent appearances at the London Palladium. Among Kaye's many films some of the best known are *The Kid From Brooklyn* (1946), *The Secret Life of Walter Mitty* (1947), *White Christmas* (1954) and *The Court Jester* (1956).

King's Cross fire

Thirty people died and scores were injured when fire engulfed London's busy King's Cross underground station at the end of the evening rush hour.

Survivors described the atmosphere of panic in which passengers ran back down the up-escalators as a fireball roared into the central ticket area, reducing the whole concourse to a mass of charred metal (above). Rescue operations were hindered by the intense heat and toxic fumes released by fittings in the station. Firemen at the scene of the disaster were unable to spend more than a few moments below ground without having to resurface for air as smoke poured down the tunnels.

When a public inquiry was launched into the causes of the tragedy there were indications that safety standards were inadequate, with no sprinkler system in operation and fire extinguishers locked up.

Mathias Rust lands in Moscow

People in Red Square were astonished to see a single-engined Cessna light aircraft land in front of the Kremlin on May 28th. Its amateur pilot, a 19-year-old West German, Mathias Rust, had flown from Helsinki straight through all the Soviet Union's air defences. He was immediately detained.

Mrs Thatcher and Mr Gorbachev

The British Prime Minister Mrs Thatcher and the Soviet leader Mr Gorbachev met twice during the year. In March Mrs Thatcher visited Moscow where talks with the Soviet leader lasted four hours longer than scheduled. She described the occasion as 'a big step forward', and despite their differences on a wide range of policy issues the two leaders evidently established a degree of personal rapport. The new atmosphere of mutual respect was confirmed in December when Mr Gorbachev stopped over in Britain for further talks with Mrs Thatcher on his way to a Washington D. C. summit meeting with President Reagan.

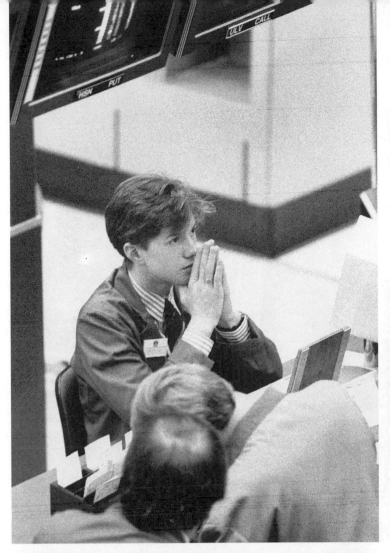

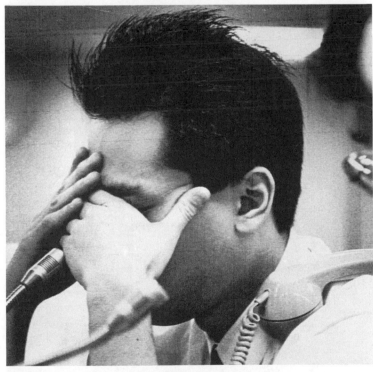

Black Monday

The long bull market in stocks and shares came to an abrupt end on Monday October 19th when the New York Stock Exchange registered a staggering one-day fall in values – twice that of the Wall Street crash of 1929. More than 600 million shares changed hands as investors scrambled to sell. The effects were felt from Tokyo (above) to London (top left), where the FT index fell almost 250 points, threatening the government's privatisation issue of British Petroleum shares.

Enniskillen

Eleven people died and more than 60 were injured when an IRA bomb exploded at a Remembrance Day ceremony in Enniskillen in Northern Ireland. The IRA alleged that the bomb had been detonated by British Army scanning equipment but the claim was dismissed by the British government. There was widespread condemnation of the killings, but many were moved by the words of Mr Gordon Wilson (top right), when he forgave the murderers of his daughter, who died in the explosion.

Tanker war in the Gulf

The Iran–Iraq War entered a new phase with a series of attacks on international shipping in the Gulf. Tension mounted after a Soviet freighter was attacked with machine guns and grenades by Iranian 'revolutionary guards' in speedboats. In May, 37 people were killed when the USS *Stark* was struck by two Exocet missiles from an Iraqi plane. Mines presented an additional hazard, and Britain and France sent minesweepers to the area for the first time.

Storms in Britain

Eighteen people died when unprecedented storms battered the south of England during the night of October 15th. Winds of up to 100 miles per hour tore trees up by the roots and the cost of the damage was estimated at between £100 and £600 million. Gusts of 94 miles per hour were recorded in the centre of London and at the Botanical Gardens at Kew a storm lasting a few hours destroyed trees which would take 200 years to regrow.

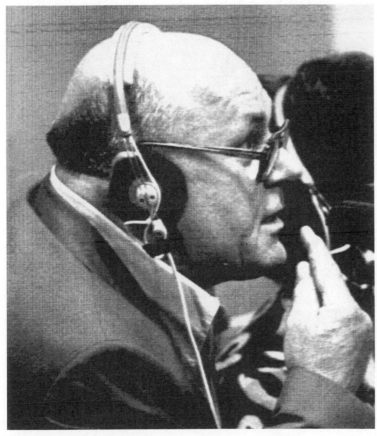

Ivan the Terrible trial

The trial began in Jerusalem of John Demjanjuk, who was accused of war crimes committed at the Treblinka concentration camp. The case turned on the question of whether or not Demjanjuk was the guard known as 'Ivan the Terrible'.

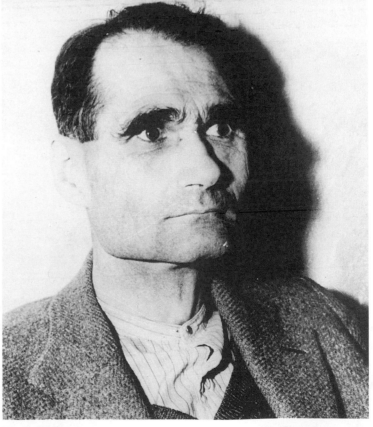

Rudolf Hess

On August 17th, Rudolf Hess (1894–1987), Hitler's former deputy, was found dead in Spandau Prison in Berlin where he was the only remaining inmate. He appeared to have committed suicide. Demolition of the prison began almost immediately.

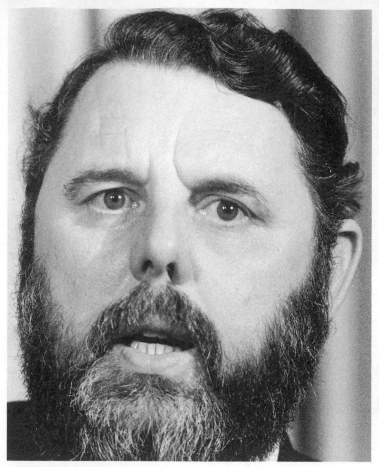

Terry Waite kidnapped

The Archbishop of Canterbury's special envoy, Terry Waite, who had been instrumental in securing the release of many hostages in Lebanon, himself became the victim of kidnappers when he disappeared in Beirut.

Spycatcher

On March 13th, an Australian Court rejected the British government's application for a permanent injunction against former intelligence officer Peter Wright (1917–   ) and the publishers of his controversial book *Spycatcher*.

Death of Andy Warhol

Leading pop art exponent and film-maker Andy Warhol (1931–1987), perhaps best remembered for his silk-screen images such as Marilyn Monroe (above right) and the Campbell's soup tin, died in New York on February 22nd. Despite his determination to remain an enigma, Warhol had a gift for personal publicity, perhaps developed from his background in commercial illustration. He claimed that 'everyone will be famous for 15 minutes' but his fame lasted well over 20 years.

1988

Jan	5	Austrian President Waldheim's war record investigated
	7	UK actor Trevor Howard dies
	15	Arab uprising in Israel begins
	29	Talks break down between Sandinistas and Contras
Feb	5	Panama's General Noriega on drugs charge
	11	UK: Marilyn Monroe's blouse fetches £7150 at Sotheby's
Mar	2	Tension growing between Armenia and Azerbaijan
	7	IRA bombers gunned down in Gibraltar
	19	Belfast: 2 British soldiers lynched at IRA funerals
	21	Nicaragua: Sandinistas open peace talks with Contras
Apr	7	Gorbachev to sign Geneva peace accord on Afghanistan
	16	Deputy PLO leader Abu Jihad murdered in Tunisia
	18	US Navy bombs Iranian oil base
	20	Kuwaiti jumbo hijack over after 16 days and 2 killings
May	10	France: Mitterrand wins 2nd term as President
	16	Soviet troops begin withdrawal from Afghanistan
	31	President Reagan visits Moscow
Jun	2	Ronald and Nancy Reagan visit Queen in London
	21	Western powers summit in Toronto
Jul	3	US warship *Vincennes* shoots down Iranian airliner
	11	Terrorists kill passengers on Aegean cruise ship
Aug	8	Iran and Iraq agree to ceasefire
	8	Angola, Cuba and South Africa agree to ceasefire
	11	Floods devastate Sudan
	14	Enzo Ferrari, Italian car genius, dies
	17	Pakistan's President Zia-ul-Haq killed in plane crash
Sep	4	Floods devastate Bangladesh
	17	24th Olympic Games open in Seoul
	24	Barbara Harris is first US Anglican bishop
Oct	2	Sir Alec Issigonis, inventor of Mini car, dies
	12	USSR offers $600 million reparations to Afghanistan
Nov	2	Israel: Shamir's Likud wins election
	11	George Bush defeats Michael Dukakis as US President
	17	Benazir Bhutto wins election in Pakistan
	23	S Africa: Botha reprieves Sharpeville Six
Dec	6	US rock singer Roy Orbison dies
	7	USSR cuts military strength by 10 per cent
	7	Yasser Arafat recognises existence of Israel
	10	USSR: Terrible earthquake hits Armenia
	22	Pan Am flight explodes over Scotland killing 270
	30	Yugoslav government resigns
		The Arts
		Bob Hoskins in film *Who Framed Roger Rabbit?*
		Salman Rushdie's novel *The Satanic Verses*
		Dustin Hoffman in film *Rain Man*

AIDS

Three major conferences in 1988 confirmed the seriousness of the threat posed to mankind by the rapid spread of AIDS (Acquired Immune Deficiency Syndrome). Delegates from all over the world met in London in January and March to discuss the global impact of AIDS. They called for urgent action by all governments to contain the disease which is spread through infected blood and other body fluids.

Another conference, in Stockholm in June, gathered some 6,000 experts from 125 countries, but delegates heard that despite the enormous international research programme scientists were as yet no nearer to finding a cure. Estimates suggested that five million people could be infected with the HIV virus worldwide, of whom 150,000 had already developed the full-blown disease. Experts predicted that this number would double by the end of the year and that there could be as many as a million new cases in the following five years. The largest number of cases had been reported in the United States, but the highest incidence of the disease was believed to be in Africa.

Ben Johnson

The Canadian athlete Ben Johnson (1961–   ) was stripped of his 100 metres gold medal at the Seoul Olympic Games after a drugs test proved positive.

The Eagle has landed

Great Britain's Eddie 'the Eagle' Edwards, seen here making the 120-metre jump in the World Cup ski jumping, came last in both the 89 and the 120 metre events in Thunder Bay, Canada.

The Klosters avalanche

Prince Charles returns to London after surviving an avalanche in the Swiss ski resort of Klosters which claimed the life of his friend Major Hugh Lindsay.

Michael Jackson

The reclusive American rock star Michael Jackson (1958–   ) did a world tour which was a spectacular success.

East and West

President Reagan speaks under a bust of Lenin at Moscow University during his five-day summit meeting with the Soviet leader Mikhail Gorbachev. Agreements were reached on arms control, human rights and regional issues.

Christina Onassis

The death was announced on November 19th of Christina Onassis (1950–1988), daughter of the millionaire Greek shipping magnate Aristotle Onassis (1906–1975). She was 37.

The INF Treaty

During the Moscow summit in June President Reagan and General-Secretary Gorbachev signed the historic INF Treaty. It provided for the elimination of all intermediate-range land-based nuclear weapons over three years. The first cruise missiles left Britain in September (above).

Save the whale

Campaigns by Greenpeace and other environmental organisations to save the whale from the ravages of international commercial whaling programmes met with some success during the year. Whales at Point Alaska were also given a helping hand by conservationists who cut breathing holes in the ice for them.

Clapham train crash

Thirty six people died and more than 100 were injured on December 12th when two trains collided during the morning rush hour near Clapham Junction station in south-west London. The accident happened when an express train ran into the back of a London commuter train which had stopped on the line to report a faulty signal. The impact hurled the two rear carriages of the train into the air and on to an embankment.

Rescue services were on the scene within minutes, but it took four hours to free all the surviving passengers. A third train was derailed and a fourth was stopped by a guard in time to avoid a further collision.

George Bush

George Bush (1924–   ) became the first sitting Vice-President of the United States since 1836 to win a presidential election when he defeated Michael Dukakis in November with 54 per cent of the popular vote.

Death of Zia

General Mohammad Zia ul-Haq (1924–1988), the President of Pakistan, was killed on August 17th when the *Hercules* transport plane in which he was travelling crashed near Bahawalpur in the Punjab. Sabotage was suspected.

Benazir Bhutto

Benazir Bhutto (1953–   ), leader of the Pakistan People's Party and daughter of the executed former Premier Zulfikar Bhutto, failed to win an overall majority in elections to Pakistan's National Assembly in November but became PM.

Gulf War ceasefire

The Iran–Iraq war neared an end with Iran's acceptance on July 18th of a ceasefire under the terms of the UN Security Council's Resolution 598. Peace talks foundered again in September over Iraq's claim to sovereignty over the Shatt al-Arab waterway.

Baroness Jennie Lee

The death occurred in November of the veteran British socialist Jennie Lee (1904–1988). The widow of Aneurin Bevan, she had been Minister for Education and Science under Harold Wilson and Chairman of the Labour Party from 1967 to 1968. She became a life peer in 1970.

Hurricane Gilbert

Thousands of people were left homeless and millions of pounds' worth of damage was done when Hurricane Gilbert hit Jamaica on September 16th. Here, the wreckage of planes lies scattered around Manley International Airport in the wake of the hurricane.

Australia's bicentenary

There were widespread festivities in Australia as the country commemorated the arrival of the first Europeans in 1788. The high point of the celebrations came on January 26th in Sydney when some two million people watched the arrival of a replica of the fleet (top) which had brought the first white convicts to the colony exactly 200 years before. The Prince and Princess of Wales (inserts) were present at the occasion, which was also marked by a march of 20,000 Aborigines, protesting against the celebrations and their poor living conditions. Above: Rockets light up the night sky in a celebratory fireworks display. Later in the year Queen Elizabeth and Prince Philip visited Australia for a 22-day tour, during which the Queen opened the Expo '88 Exhibition in Brisbane, Queensland.

Lockerbie

Two hundred and seventy people were killed in one of Britain's worst ever air disasters on December 22nd when a Boeing 747 crashed on to the small town of Lockerbie in southern Scotland. The accident happened at 7.19 p.m. as Pan Am flight 103 was on its way from Frankfurt to New York. After a mid-air explosion at 31,000 feet, the aircraft plunged to the ground, crashing across a major road before ploughing into the town. Eyewitnesses described how a fireball engulfed the plane, sending flames roaring 300 feet into the air. The impact demolished some 40 houses and left a crater 50 feet deep and 30 yards long. Many of those who died were Americans returning to the United States for Christmas. Investigations showed that the explosion had been caused by a bomb.

The Piper Alpha tragedy

Disaster struck on July 6th when fire engulfed the Piper Alpha oil rig platform in the North Sea. One hundred and sixty-six people died and many were injured when a series of explosions tore through the 12-year-old rig, which lay 120 miles north-east of Aberdeen. The blasts sent flames some 400 feet into the air above the platform, which was almost completely destroyed. Most of those who died were asleep at the time and there were only 62 survivors, most of whom escaped by leaping into the sea. Rescue operations were hampered by the extreme heat, which could be felt a mile away. The fire took several days to bring under control. An inquiry was launched into the circumstances surrounding the explosion.

Drought in the US

The United States suffered its driest spring since the dust bowl years of the 1930s. Many agricultural regions were designated disaster areas as some 30 states were struck by the worst drought since 1934. The areas most seriously affected were the mid-west and the south. Pasture lands became arid plains and waterways dried up as Montana, Minnesota, North Dakota, Tennessee, North Carolina and Georgia received less than a quarter of their normal level of rainfall. Dust storms scoured off topsoil across more than 13 million acres of land and the giant Mississippi River became unnavigable in places when the water level dwindled to a record low. Commodity prices soared as grain stocks fell, and financial support was planned for stricken farmers.

Earthquake in Armenia

At the end of a year of continued unrest there was tragedy and destruction in the Soviet Republic of Armenia when a massive earthquake devastated the cities of Leninakan and Spitak. As many as 100,000 people were believed to have died in the disaster, which left survivors huddled outside the wreckage of their homes (centre left) and hundreds of coffins piled in Spitak Stadium (centre right). A massive rescue operation was mounted, with many survivors scrabbling at the debris with their bare hands in the hope of finding missing friends and relatives (top left). The Soviet leader Mikhail Gorbachev paid a personal visit to the scene of the earthquake (above right). The disaster came at the end of a troubled year. In February the Southern Republics of

Armenia and Azerbaijan were racked by the worst outbreak of ethnic violence in the peacetime history of the Soviet Union after Azerbaijan rejected a call for the predominantly Armenian region of Nagorno Karabakh to be returned to Armenian control. Armenians accounted for more than three-quarters of the population of Nagorno Karabakh, which had been part of Azerbaijan since 1921. There were massive demonstrations and strikes in the Armenian capital Yerevan and throughout the disputed region, and more than 30 people were killed in intercommunal violence in the Azerbaijan city of Sumgait. In September tanks appeared on the streets of Yerevan (above left) as a state of emergency was declared.

Jan	7	Japanese Emperor Hirohito dies, aged 82
	9	British Midland Boeing 737 crashes on motorway
	20	George Bush sworn in as 41st US President
	23	Spanish surrealist painter Salvador Dali dies
Feb	2	Afghanistan: Last Soviet troops leave after 9 years
	3	S African National Party leader P W Botha resigns
	14	Iran: Khomeini orders Moslems to kill Salman Rushdie
Mar	25	Oil spill from Exxon Valdez tanker off Alaskan coast
Apr	15	UK: Football fans die in crush at Hillsborough stadium
	17	Polish Solidarity movement legalised after 8 year ban
	25	Japan: PM Takeshita resigns in corruption scandal
	27	China: Student demonstrators occupy Tiananmen Square
May	16	China: Mikhail Gorbachev and Deng Xiaoping hold talks
Jun	4	Gas explosion on trans-Siberian railway kills hundreds
	4	China: Army massacres pro-democracy demonstrators
	6	Iran: Chaos at Khomeini's funeral as crowds mourn
	22	UK: Bus, tube and rail workers on strike
Jul	4	Hong Kong: Protests against British immigration policy
	11	Actor Laurence Olivier dies, aged 82
	15	France celebrates 200th anniversary of Revolution
Aug	20	UK: Marchioness pleasure boat disaster on River Thames
	25	Voyager 2 spacecraft takes pictures of Neptune

Sep	11	Hungary opens border to East German refugees
	13	S Africa: 20,000 in anti-apartheid demonstration
	22	UK: IRA bomb blasts Royal Marines' School in Deal
	28	Ex-president Marcos of Philippines dies in Honolulu
Oct	19	US: Massive earthquake in San Francisco
	19	UK: Appeal court finds Guildford Four innocent
	23	UK: Ambulance workers begin work-to-rule over pay claim
	29	S Africa: 60,000 in ANC rally
Nov	10	E Germany: Berlin Wall opened
	10	El Salvador: Guerrillas battle with government forces
	24	Czechoslovakia: Communist leadership resigns
Dec	3	Malta: Mikhail Gorbachev and George Bush end summit
	13	Hong Kong: Forced repatriation of Vietnamese
	14	Soviet physicist and dissident Andrei Sakharov dies
	21	US invades Panama and ousts General Noriega
	22	Rumania: Ceausescu flees as civil war grips Bucharest
	26	Irish playwright Samuel Beckett dies in Paris
		The Arts
		Batman film starring Jack Nicholson as Joker
		Andrew Lloyd Webber's musical *Aspects of Love*
		Actors campaign to save Elizabethan Rose Theatre
		Kenneth Branagh's film *Henry V*

George Bush sworn in

On January 20th George Bush became the 41st President of the United States of America. A crowd of thousands cheered enthusiastically in front of the Capitol in Washington as the new President took the oath of office, laying his hand on the same bible on which George Washington had sworn the same oath two centuries earlier.

In what many people regarded as the most passionate and successful speech of his political career to date, Bush devoted his inaugural address to the themes of freedom, economic reform and the battle against crime and spoke of the need for co-operation to achieve these ends. Speaking of the 'new breeze' which he felt blowing, he called on Congress, where there was a substantial Democratic majority, to work closely with the government to reduce the enormous US budget deficit. He also called for a continuation of the war against drugs, crime and homelessness and voiced his confidence in the 'goodness and courage of the American people'.

After the inauguration ceremony, the celebrations continued all day, with a series of receptions and dances.

Soviet withdrawal from Afghanistan

On February 15th the last Soviet troops were airlifted out of Afghanistan ending nine years of bitter war against the *mujahedin* rebels. The previous few days had seen thousands of soldiers leaving the country, many of them crossing the Oxus River frontier in tanks and armoured personnel carriers. The phased operation, which had begun in May 1988, was completed exactly to schedule.

The withdrawal of Soviet troops was seen as another important indication of the new thinking resulting from Mikhail Gorbachev's leadership in the USSR and removed one of the longest standing causes of East-West tension. However, as the returning forces were greeted with a heroes' welcome in the border towns of Uzbekistan, tens of thousands of Afghan rebels were already massing outside Kabul and Jalalabad. The beleaguered regime of President Najibullah imposed virtual martial law in the capital as the first *mujahedin* rockets fell on the city.

Hirohito's funeral

On 24th February the funeral of the controversial Japanese Emperor Hirohito was attended by representatives of 163 countries. Half a million people lined the streets of Tokyo as the Emperor's coffin was taken to the Shinjuku Gyoen Imperial Gardens where he was entombed near his father's mausoleum. There were protests from US and British veterans of World War II, who objected to their countries honouring someone whom they considered a war criminal. His son succeeded him.

The *Exxon Valdez*

The worst ever oil pollution disaster in American waters took place in March when the 937 foot tanker *Exxon Valdez* ran aground and was holed in Prince William Sound off the coast of Alaska. A massive slick of some 10 million gallons of crude oil polluted 100 miles of coastline, causing irreparable damage to wildlife, including seals, otters and migratory seabirds.

The Salman Rushdie affair

Relations between Britain and Iran deteriorated sharply in February after Ayatollah Khomeini issued a death threat against British novelist Salman Rushdie. This came after months of controversy over Rushdie's novel *The Satanic Verses*, which had seen protests and demonstrations amongst Moslems worldwide. Speaking on Tehran radio, Khomeini urged all Moslems to carry out the death sentence against the author and his publishers, Viking Penguin.

Another football tragedy

Ninety-five Liverpool football fans were crushed to death on April 15th during the semi-final of the FA Cup at the Hillsborough Stadium in Sheffield, England. Fixed steel fences, designed to stop hooligans invading the pitch, had trapped people after police opened the gates.

Earthquake in San Francisco

Disaster struck San Francisco on 19 October when an earthquake, registering 6.9 on the Richter scale, devastated the Bay area of the city. The tremor caused more than 80 deaths, although early reports put the figure much higher. Most of the casualties occurred when the top deck of the double-decker Nimitz freeway fell onto rush-hour traffic travelling on the lower deck. The driver of the truck shown (left) had a lucky escape when the concrete slab poised above his vehicle miraculously failed to collapse.

The M1 air crash

Less than a month after the Lockerbie disaster, Britain experienced another major airline tragedy on 9 January when a Boeing 737 flight from London to Belfast crashed on the M1 motorway near the village of Kegworth in Leicestershire. Forty-four people died when the 12-week old aircraft ploughed into the motorway embankment just 15 seconds' flight from the runway at East Midlands Airport where it was attempting to make an emergency landing after engine trouble. Early reports suggested that the pilot might have shut down the wrong engine.

The Marchioness tragedy

Fifty-one people died when a pleasure cruiser sank after colliding with a massive dredger on the River Thames in the centre of London on 20 August. A birthday party was in full swing aboard the cruiser, the *Marchioness*, when she was struck by the 2000-ton *Bowbelle* under Southwark Bridge in the early hours of the morning. Survivors told of the dredger looming up out of the darkness without warning, prompting calls for urgent improvements in river safety standards.

Ten Years of Thatcher

The year that saw the tenth anniversary of Margaret Thatcher's election as the first woman Prime Minister of Great Britain was a troubled one for her Conservative administration. Opinion polls showed the Labour opposition gaining in popularity as public disquiet over proposed health service reforms, food safety standards and the poll tax seriously damaged the government's standing. Only two months after the anniversary celebrations (right), Mrs Thatcher found herself once more embroiled in controversy when she sacked her long-standing Foreign Secretary, Sir Geoffrey Howe, in a surprise cabinet reshuffle. Then, in October Chancellor Nigel Lawson resigned following differences with the Prime Minister over economic policy and Britain's role in an integrated European monetary system. This led to another significant slump in the government's popularity.

IRA bombing in Deal

This is the spectacle of destruction which confronted the rescue services as they hurried to the scene of a bomb attack on a British Army barracks in Deal, Kent, in September (right). The bomb, which exploded in the early morning at the Royal Marines' School of Music, killed ten soldiers and injured at least twice as many, some of them seriously. Most of the casualties were army bandsmen. The IRA claimed responsibility for the attack, prompting fears that the terrorist organisation was about to mount an intensive bombing campaign against military installations in mainland Britain. After questions were raised about the bomber's ability to gain access to the Deal barracks, there were calls for an urgent review of security procedures at military bases throughout the country.

Trans-Siberian railway disaster

More than 460 people were believed to have died in the Urals region of the Soviet Union after a massive gas explosion destroyed two trains travelling on the Trans-Siberian railway. The explosion, which reduced the trains to a heap of charred and tangled wreckage (right), occurred after a leak of gas from the huge pipeline which follows the railway for long distances as it crosses the wastes of Siberia. The gas was ignited by sparks from the line as the two crowded passenger trains passed each other some 1,200 kilometres east of Moscow. The tragedy shocked the whole country, and the Soviet leader, Mikhail Gorbachev, visiting the scene of the catastrophe, called for a full investigation into its causes.

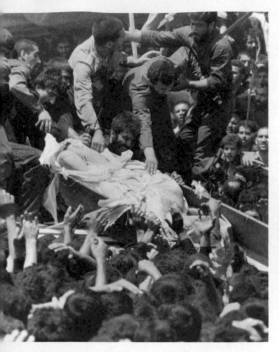

Khomeini's funeral

Crowds of hysterical mourners clutched at the coffin containing the body of the Ayatollah Khomeini as it was carried over the heads of the crowd to its final resting place on the outskirts of Tehran on June 6.

Death of Olivier

Lord Olivier, widely hailed as the greatest actor of the age, died at his Sussex home on 11 July at the age of 82. His roles included memorable interpretations of Richard III, Othello and Henry V (above).

F.W. de Klerk

The election of F.W. de Klerk (above) to the leadership of the South African National Party in February awakened hopes of serious reforms to the apartheid system and of the release from prison of the nationalist leader Nelson Mandela.

Farewell to Noriega

Manuel Noriega, the corrupt Panamanian leader, was finally ousted from power on 21 December when American troops invaded Panama, ostensibly in response to threats and violence against American citizens there. Troops loyal to Noriega staged a counter-attack and the fugitive President himself went to ground in the Vatican Embassy. Noriega, who had strong links with the CIA, originally came to power with the backing of the US government, but had long lost their support. President George Bush made known his desire to see him face drug trafficking charges in the United States.

Tiananmen Square

In the People's Republic of China hundreds of thousands of students, supported by others from all walks of life, gathered in Beijing's central Tiananmen Square to express their dissatisfaction with the country's ageing leadership and to voice their demands for democratic reform. The first mass demonstrations followed the death in April of Hu Yaobang, a former Communist Party leader widely seen as an advocate of reform, and soon developed

into a permanent presence in Tiananmen Square. In May, they overshadowed the visit to Beijing of the Soviet leader Mikhail Gorbachev, and later in the same month the students, some of whom undertook a hunger strike for democracy (above left), raised in the square a statue modelled on the US Statue of Liberty (above centre). Similar demonstrations were reported in other major cities throughout China.

On 4 June, the Chinese government decided to end the protests and detachments of the People's Liberation Army closed in on the square. Soldiers fired into the crowds and tanks advanced along the broad main streets of the capital. One brave student succeeded in halting a column of tanks in the Avenue of Eternal Peace (above), but hundreds of others were less lucky. More than 2,000 people are thought to have been killed in the ensuing massacre.

Eastern Europe

1989 witnessed changes in the political map of Europe more far-reaching than any since that map was first drawn in the aftermath of the Second World War. Spontaneous upsurges of popular dissent engulfed country after country in Eastern Europe, rocking to their very foundations the entrenched Communist régimes of the Soviet bloc. Despite the ominous shadow of the Tiananmen Square massacre, vast crowds appeared on the streets of the Eastern European capitals to demand democratic reform, and one by one the governments of the Warsaw Pact – Poland, Hungary, Czechoslovakia, Bulgaria, even East Germany – staggered and fell under the apparently unstoppable tide of their citizens' peaceful mass protest. In November, television viewers throughout the world witnessed emotional scenes in Berlin as the Berlin Wall – for so long the most potent symbol of East-West confrontation – was finally breached and tens of thousands of East German citizens crossed into the West to be reunited with friends and relatives from whom they had been separated by the closing of the border in 1961.

In Rumania, however, the story was tragically different. There the hard-line Stalinist régime of Nicolae Ceausescu met the first wave of street protests not with moderation, but with the gun. Thousands may have died as troops and secret police loyal to Ceausescu battled it out with demonstrators and pro-democracy factions in the army on the streets of Timosoara and Bucharest. In a period of less than two weeks the Rumanian people accomplished a revolution which swept Ceausescu from power, but the cost in human life was high indeed, the many victims including the former dictator and his wife, executed by firing squad in the last days of the year.

Meanwhile in the Soviet Union itself, Mikhail Gorbachev, in many ways the fountainhead of all the changes in Eastern Europe, faced similar demands for greater democracy both among his political colleagues and on the streets of the Soviet republics.

Opposite page, top: Former Czech Prime Minister Alexander Dubcek, exiled after the Soviet crackdown on his reform attempts in 1968, returns in triumph to address crowds in the capital, Prague.

Opposite page, bottom: In December President Gorbachev and Pope John Paul II met, ending 70 years of hostility between the Soviet Union and the Vatican.

Left: Souvenir hunters chip pieces from the newly-opened Berlin Wall.

Below: Polish Prime Minister Tadeusz Mazowiecki calls on Parliament to speed up the democratic process.

Bottom left: Nicolae and Elena Ceausescu shortly before their execution.

Bottom right: Crowds gather under the statue of Lenin in the capital of the Soviet Republic of Azerbaijan to demand independence from Moscow.

1990

German Unification

Amid large scale celebrations such as the spectacular rock concert in Berlin's Potsdamer Platz during which a giant mock-up of the Wall was demolished (below), the process of German reunification gathered pace throughout 1990. The first two-plus-four talks between East and West German, French, Soviet, US and UK foreign ministers were held at the beginning of May, and a few days later the East and West German finance ministers signed a treaty agreeing to the 'creation of a monetary, economic and social union' between the two countries and setting July 1st as the date for currency union. Full political reunification – a prospect hardly even dreamed of only a year before – officially took place at midnight on October 2nd.

Nelson Mandela Free

After much speculation, African National Congress leader Nelson Mandela finally walked free from Victor Verster prison in South Africa's Cape Province on the afternoon of February 11th. It was the end of 27 years in prison for the 71-year-old Mandela, who had been given a life sentence for treason in 1964. Widespread celebrations were followed by the beginning of serious negotiations between the ANC, of which Mandela was shortly elected Deputy President, and President F. W. de Klerk, but the process of effecting a peaceful transition to a multiracial society was threatened by escalating violence between the ANC and the rival Zulu-based Inkatha movement.

Reed and Polhill Released

In April 1990, the American hostages Robert Polhill and Frank Reed were released from captivity in Lebanon as a result of Syrian and Iranian mediation. Reed (above), a 57-year-old educationist, had been held, blindfolded 24 hours a day, for 3½ years after being kidnapped by the Organisation of Islamic Dawn.

Keenan Released

In August the Irish hostage Brian Keenan (above) was handed over to the Irish Foreign Minister in Damascus after being held for 4½ years by the Organisation of Islamic Dawn who kidnapped him in Beirut in April 1986. The 39-year-old teacher originally refused to leave captivity unless his fellow hostage John McCarthy was also released.

Stefano Casiraghi

On October 3rd Stefano Casiraghi, the husband of Princess Caroline of Monaco, was killed in a speedboat accident near Saint-Jean-Cap-Ferrat in the South of France. The 30-year-old Italian-born financier died instantly when his 5 tonne boat, *Pinot di Pinot*, turned over and sank after striking a wave at more than 125 miles per hour. Casiraghi and his co-pilot Patrice Innocenti, who ejected from the vessel and survived the accident, were defending their title (won the previous year in America) on the second day of the world offshore speedboat championships.

Greta Garbo

Greta Garbo, one of the greatest stars of Hollywood's golden age, died in New York in April at the age of 84. Garbo, whose real name was Greta Gustafsson, was born in Sweden, but moved to Hollywood in the 1920s to make such classic films as *Anna Christie* (her first talkie) and *Anna Karenina*. She went into intensely private retirement after making her last picture, *Two-faced Woman*, in 1930.

Leonard Bernstein

The music world mourned the death in October of the American conductor, composer and pianist Leonard Bernstein. Bernstein, a flamboyant public figure, was one of the greatest conductors of his generation as well as a composer who bridged the worlds of popular and 'serious' music with such scores as *West Side Story*, the Chichester Psalms and numerous orchestral and choral works.

Sammy Davis Junior

The singer, actor and entertainer Sammy Davis Junior died on May 16th after a long battle against throat cancer. He was 64. Davis started in show business at the age of three and became one of America's most successful entertainers in spite of racial prejudice and his own alcohol and drug problems. In addition to a spectacular stage career, Davis made more than 20 films.

World Cup

Emotions ran high in the 1990 World Cup competition. Paul Gascoigne ('Gazza') won hearts by crying openly after England's semi-final defeat (above), while Argentina were widely condemned for their indisciplined play during the final, which they lost 1-0 to West Germany.

Queen Mother is 90

Colourful celebrations in London to mark the 90th birthday of Queen Elizabeth the Queen Mother (above) provided temporary relief from widespread anxieties about Britain's declining economic performance and political arguments over domestic and European issues.

Turmoil in India

The government of the Indian Prime Minister V. P. Singh fell in November after the collapse of the coalition which had sustained his Janata Dal party in power. Controversy centred on Singh's caste policy, which aimed to set aside 49 per cent of all federal jobs for middle- and lower-caste Hindus. This challenge to India's ruling castes led in September to widespread protests and unrest in which many upper-caste students burned themselves to death. (Left, policemen scramble to extinguish a potential suicide.) Violence escalated with the attempt by thousands of Hindus to attack a mosque at Ayodha which they claimed had been built on the birthplace of the Hindu god Rama. Many people were killed as police sought to protect the mosque, and tensions between Hindus and India's minority Muslim community ran dangerously high. With civil war engulfing Kashmir and serious unrest in the Punjab, India, under a fragile coalition between the new premier Chandra Shekhar and Rajiv Gandhi's Congress (I) party, seemed to be spiralling towards anarchy.

The Junk Bond King

In April the American financial executive Michael Milken (right) pleaded guilty to six charges of criminal fraud and conspiracy arising from his time as head of the high-yield bond department at Drexel Burnham Lambert, the Wall Street investment bank. Widely seen as the inspiration behind the multi-million dollar US junk bond market, the 44-year-old Milken was fined $600 million after pleading guilty to the charges as part of a plea-bargaining deal by the prosecution. Part of the case against him derived from conversations secretly tape-recorded by Milken's erstwhile partner in arbitrage, Ivan Boesky. Later in the year Milken faced additional charges, and in November was sentenced to ten years in prison.

Guinness Scandal

In August the defendants in the Guinness trial were found guilty of charges arising from the conduct of Guinness' £2.7 billion takeover of the Distillers group in 1986. Former Guinness chairman Ernest Saunders (left) was sentenced to five years in prison and Gerald Ronson, the garage and property tycoon, was given a fine of £5 million, the largest in British legal history. The judge in the case spoke of 'dishonesty on a massive scale' in the mounting of an illegal share support operation during the takeover. The scandal rocked the City of London.

End of an Empire

On September 26th the Australian entrepreneur Alan Bond (above) finally resigned as chairman and chief executive of his beleaguered Bond Corporation Holdings after a two year battle to save the brewing, mining, media and property group, whose financial position crumbled from a profit of A$403 million in 1987-8 to a loss of A$980 million in 1988-9. A millionaire by the age of 21, Bond became an Australian hero after his boat won the Americas Cup in 1983.

Marion Barry

The problems of drugs, crime and racial tension in America's capital city were thrown into stark relief by the trial of the black Mayor of Washington, Marion Barry, on drugs and perjury charges. In August Barry (above) was cleared of 13 out of the 14 charges arising from a controversial police operation in which a former girlfriend lured him into a hotel room bugged by FBI agents. The case did irreparable damage to Barry's political standing.

Asil Nadir

In October the attempts of the Cypriot-born entrepreneur Asil Nadir (above) to save Polly Peck International, his troubled fruit and electronics company, failed when the company was put into administration. Rumours of financial malpractice at Polly Peck, once the most spectacularly successful share on the UK stock market, were investigated by the regulatory authorities and led to a collapse in investor confidence and the company's share price.

Resignation of Shevardnadze

In a move that shocked both the Soviet Union and the wider world, Soviet foreign minister Eduard Shevardnadze, one of the architects of the East-West détente of the 1980s, resigned on December 20th. In a dramatic speech to the Congress of People's Deputies, he cited the growing influence of conservative hard-liners for his decision, which was described by President Gorbachev as 'unforgiveable'.

Perestroika in the balance

In a grim reminder of the near collapse of the Soviet economy, food rationing was introduced in a number of the country's major cities, including Leningrad (above), in November and December. Despite record harvests, distribution networks had ground to a halt and, while millions of tons of grain rotted in the countryside, the international community, led by Germany, organised an airlift of emergency food aid.

New Prime Minister for Britain

Amid widespread unease about government policy on Europe and local government finance, the resignation in November of the long-time Thatcher loyalist Sir Geoffrey Howe prompted a challenge to Mrs Thatcher's leadership of the British Conservative Party by Michael Heseltine. Thatcher's majority in the first ballot was too small to avoid a second round and, despite her declared determination to fight on, she was persuaded to resign by members of her cabinet. Douglas Hurd and the Chancellor, John Major, then entered the race. Major came out on top in the ensuing vote and, following the withdrawal of Hurd and Heseltine, became the new leader of the Conservative Party and thus Prime Minister, ending 11 years of Thatcher government.

President Walesa

Against a background of soaring unemployment and plummetting living standards, Poland held its first direct presidential elections in November to choose a successor to the resigning President Jaruzelski. Lech Walesa, the leader of the Solidarity trade union, campaigning on a platform of accelerated economic and political reform, gained a narrow majority in the ballot, defeating the Prime Minister Tadeusz Mazowiecki, and the maverick self-made millionaire, Stanislaw Tyminski, whose emergence from exile in Canada to achieve second place in the ballot was a great political surprise. In the second ballot, however, Walesa was elected by a landslide and, at his inauguration on December 22nd, proclaimed the beginning of the 'Third Polish Republic'.

The Gulf Crisis

The cause of world peace, so dramatically advanced by the apparent ending of the Cold War during 1989, suffered a serious setback with the invasion of Kuwait by Iraq in the late summer of 1990. Following the breakdown of talks over territorial and commercial disputes between the two countries, troops loyal to the Iraqi President, Saddam Hussein (left), crossed the Kuwaiti border in force on August 2nd and quickly occupied the whole country, driving the ruling al-Sabah family into exile. Shortly afterwards Saddam Hussein announced the annexation of Kuwait as the 19th province of Iraq.

International reaction

The Iraqi action was met with unprecedentedly unanimous condemnation from the international community, a response no doubt sharpened by the commercial and strategic importance to the industrialised world of the Gulf's oil supplies. This opposition was expressed in the implementation of far-reaching economic sanctions against Iraq and a United Nations resolution demanding the immediate unconditional withdrawal of troops from Kuwait. Meanwhile, Iraqi forces had been gathering along the border with Saudi Arabia and, in response to an urgent request for help from the Saudi Government, the US President George Bush began a massive military build-up in the Gulf area as the spearhead of a multi-national force to defend against further Iraqi aggression and to enforce withdrawal.

Countdown to war

More than 200,000 US troops, supported by British and other contingents and equipped with the most sophisticated military hardware and material, had already been airlifted to the Gulf in Operation Desert Shield when Bush announced at the beginning of November that this force was to be more than doubled over the coming months, creating the potential for a massive counter-strike against Saddam. Thousands of Westerners and other foreign nationals initially held hostage in Kuwait and Iraq as a 'human shield' against UN attack had begun to be released by the end of the year, amid intense diplomatic efforts by individuals and governments to avoid the momentum of war becoming unstoppable. But with sanctions taking longer to bite than had been hoped, and with Saddam attempting to rally both the Islamic fundamentalist and Arab nationalist camps behind his cause by urging holy war against the US (above right) and linking Iraqi withdrawal from Kuwait with demands for Israeli withdrawal from the occupied territories of the West Bank and the Gaza Strip, a diplomatic solution to the crisis seemed more and more elusive. At the end of November United Nations Resolution 678 authorised the use of force by the 28-nation Allied coalition if Iraq had not withdrawn from Kuwait by January 15th, 1991.

Iraqi TV Taped Broadcast

Above: Saddam's use of foreign nationals as 'human shields' against the possibility of attack was condemned throughout the world, his appearance with Western children as part of Iraqi television's cynically euphemistic 'guest news' programmes, being especially deplored.

Top: Troops arriving in the Gulf, like this French detachment, were given anti-chemical warfare equipment. Saddam Hussein was widely expected to respond to any multi-national attack with chemical weapons.

Right: US marines reporting for duty in the Saudi desert. The airlift of forces to the Gulf was to reach a peak of 700,000 troops, including a larger percentage of the US armed forces than had served during the war in Vietnam.

1991

War in the Gulf

Less than 24 hours after the UN deadline of January 15th passed without seeing an Iraqi withdrawal from Kuwait, Allied forces launched a wave of massive attacks on targets in Iraq and Kuwait, initiating an aerial bombardment of military centres, command and supply networks, and civil infrastructure that was to continue relentlessly for more than a month. The Iraqi response to this phase of the so-called 'air war' was eerily muted, and by the end of January Allied commanders were able to claim air and naval supremacy throughout the Gulf theatre of operations. The effectiveness of the air campaign in eroding Saddam's vast technologically inferior military machine became only too apparent when on February 24th the long-awaited ground war began with a three-pronged attack into Iraq and Kuwait. Fears of enormous Allied casualty rates proved unfounded as Iraqi resistance crumbled before a textbook military operation which saw the complete liberation of Kuwait within three days. On February 28th President Bush called off the bombardment of Iraq's retreating forces and suspended hostilities. Allied casualties amounted to some 250 dead; Iraq's losses will probably never be known, but have been estimated at between 35,000 and 100,000.

Going the extra mile

Attempts to find a diplomatic solution to the Gulf crisis continued even after the breakdown of talks between US Secretary of State James Baker and Iraqi Foreign Minister Tariq Aziz in Geneva on January 9th and the beginning of hostilities on January 16th. On February 17th Aziz met President Gorbachev in Moscow (above) to discuss a Soviet peace-plan designed to avert the land war. Iraq's ensuing conditional offer to withdraw from Kuwait was rejected by the Allied coalition.

Stormin' Norman

As Commander-in-Chief of the Allied forces, US General H. Norman Schwarzkopf (above) was responsible for converting Operation Desert Shield, the defence of Saudi Arabia, into Operation Desert Storm, the campaign to liberate Kuwait.

Scuds and Patriots

Shortly after the outbreak of hostilities Saddam Hussein carried out his threat to retaliate against Israel in the event of attack by Allied forces by launching a number of Scud missiles at civilian centres including the cities of Haifa and Tel Aviv (above). Anxious to avoid Israel becoming drawn into the conflict the US stationed on Israeli soil a number of batteries of Patriot missiles, an anti-aircraft system which proved effective in countering the aged but politically dangerous Scuds.

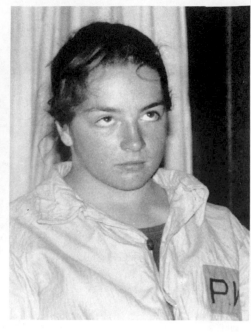

Surrender

The Allied ground offensive revealed the appalling conditions and pathetically low morale of the majority of Saddam's forces. Only the élite Republican Guard put up sustained resistance. Others surrendered in droves (above), and by the end of the war the Allies held some 175,000 Iraqi prisoners of war.

POWs

Melissa Rathbun-Nealy (above) was one of a number of Allied prisoners of war captured by the Iraqis during fighting at the Saudi border town of Khafji.

Scorched earth

Allied forces arriving in Kuwait City saw at first hand the human and economic cost of seven months of Iraqi occupation. Property had been looted and destroyed throughout the city and reports of atrocities committed against civilians were widespread. Almost all of Kuwait's 950 producing oil wells had been set on fire before Iraq withdrew (above), leaving a permanent pall of black smoke over the country and an oil-slick over hundreds of square miles in the waters of the Gulf. At the same time, members of the al-Sabah family returning from exile (including Crown Prince Saad (right), charged by the Emir with the task of imposing martial law) were greeted by determined demands for democratic reform.

The Kurds

Even before the end of hostilities, factions within Iraq had begun to respond to President Bush's call for the Iraqi people to overthrow Saddam Hussein. A Shia rebellion in the south and a Kurdish uprising in the north were both brutally suppressed by Saddam's remaining forces, creating a massive refugee problem as hundreds of thousands of people fled their homes. International attention focussed on the plight of the Kurds crowding the mountains above the Turkish border (right) in an attempt to escape Saddam's genocidal reassertion of power. Humanitarian aid was sent but calls for Allied military intervention remained unanswered.

The Baltic Republics

Further evidence of the new hard line on domestic dissent in the Soviet Union was provided in January when government troops began a military crackdown in the Baltic Republics. Civilians were killed as tanks appeared on the streets of Vilnius and Riga, the Lithuanian and Latvian capitals, and Black Beret paramilitaries stormed government, press and television offices held by supporters of the nationalist movements. President Gorbachev

denied ordering the use of force, but the bloodshed led to massive demonstrations in the Baltics, and in Moscow some 100,000 protestors demanded Gorbachev's resignation. Soviet paratroopers withdrew at the end of January, but tensions remained high in Latvia, Lithuania and Estonia. With Western governments anxious to retain Soviet support for the anti-Saddam coalition, however, international condemnation was muted.

Unrest in Albania

Relatively untouched by events in Eastern Europe at the end of 1989, Albania saw an upsurge of popular demands for democratic reform in 1990 and 1991. In the early months of 1991, President Ramiz Alia imposed presidential rule in an attempt to contain unrest in the capital Tirana, where students tore down a giant statue of the Stalinist leader Enver Hoxha, and, despite some liberalising measures, thousands of refugees fled the country for Greece and Italy.

Mandela and Buthelezi

The long-awaited meeting between ANC Deputy President Nelson Mandela and Chief Mangosuthu Gatsha Buthelezi, head of the rival Zulu-based Inkatha movement, took place in Durban on January 29th (above). The meeting, the first between the two leaders for 30 years, was seen as a vital first step towards the easing of tensions between ANC and Inkatha followers which had claimed thousands of black lives in the townships in the preceding months.

IRA attacks

In February the IRA launched a series of terrorist attacks in London, including the most dramatic strike at the heart of the British Government since the bombing of the Grand Hotel in Brighton during the Conservative Party conference in 1984.

Just before 10 o'clock on the morning of February 7th a van parked across the corner of Horse Guards Avenue and Whitehall, just 200 yards from Downing Street where the Cabinet was meeting. The roof opened and three mortar bombs were fired at Downing Street, one of them falling in the back garden of Number 10 and shattering the windows of the Cabinet room itself. The van then burst into flames (left). John Major's sang-froid under fire was widely reported, but the attack, coming as it did at a time when security had already been heightened in the light of terrorist threats from Iraq and its allies, raised serious questions about the vulnerability of the government machine.

In a further departure from recent strategy on the mainland, the IRA also planted bombs at mainline London railway stations a few days later. On February 18th one person was killed and many were injured when a bomb exploded at Victoria station at the beginning of a morning rush-hour. A similar bomb at Paddington station also exploded, but no-one was injured.

'The wrong kind of snow'

Heavy snowstorms and freezing temperatures wrought havoc in Britain in February. Many services ground to a halt in the capital (above), and British Rail came in for particularly sharp criticism for its inability to keep trains running in conditions far from uncommon in mainland Europe.

Death of King Olav

King Olav V of Norway (above), symbol of his country's resistance to the Nazis, died aged 87 and was succeeded by his son, Harald V.

Martha Graham and Margot Fonteyn

The world of dance lost two of its most celebrated figures with the deaths of Martha Graham and Margot Fonteyn. One of the most influential dancers and choreographers of the 20th century, Martha Graham (above right) was born in Pittsburgh in 1894 and first appeared on the American stage in 1920. She made her independent debut in 1926 and formed her own touring dance group in 1929. Known particularly for her interpretations of primitive or mythological subjects, she became a leading exponent of modern dance techniques, creating some 150 works during her long career.

Born Margaret Hookham in 1919, Margot Fonteyn (above left) made her debut with the Vic-Wells Ballet in the *Nutcracker* in 1934 and went on to appear in her first solo role as Giselle three years later. As prima ballerina of the Royal Ballet in London she worked closely with its Director, Frederick Ashton, to create roles in a number of ballets, including, in 1963, *Marguerite and Armand*, in which she danced with Rudolf Nureyev in one of the greatest partnerships of modern ballet.

Graham Greene

The death in April of Graham Greene silenced one of the most significant voices of modern English literature. Born in Berkhamsted in 1904, Greene published his first novel, *The Man Within*, in 1929, three years after his conversion to Catholicism, but critical acclaim eluded him until the publication of *Stamboul Train* in 1932. Much concerned with loss of faith and the problem of evil, Greene's novels proved enduringly popular and many, including *Brighton Rock* and *The Third Man*, were made into successful films.

The Birmingham Six

On March 14th the so-called Birmingham Six walked free from the Old Bailey in London after serving 16 years in prison for a crime they did not commit. John Walker, Paddy Hill, Hugh Callaghan, Richard McIlkenny, Gerry Hunter and William Power (seen, left to right, above, with Chris Mullin, centre, who campaigned for their release) were imprisoned after the IRA pub bombings in Birmingham in 1974 in which 21 people were killed. The case – the third to overturn convictions for terrorist offences in recent years – raised serious questions about the working of the whole criminal justice system.

Collapse of ILG

Hundreds of people were stranded at airports in the UK and thousands of others had their holidays threatened by the collapse on March 8th of the country's second largest travel organisation, the International Leisure Group. The company, which owned the airline Air Europe and the tour operator Intasun, had been hit by recession and the decline in trade during the Gulf War. The Administrator appointed by the High Court discovered debts of some £480 million.

New Archbishop

The 103rd Archbishop of Canterbury, the Rt Rev George Carey (above), was enthroned at Canterbury Cathedral on April 19th. Formerly Bishop of Bath and Wells, the Primate is associated with the Evangelical wing of the Anglican church.

282

Photographic Acknowledgements

The publishers would like to thank all those who have supplied photographs for use in this book and apologise to any whose contribution may have been inadvertently omitted from these acknowledgements. We are particularly grateful to picture researcher Julia Ruxton, Siobhan Hewitt and the staff of the former Keystone Collection (now part of Hulton Deutsch) and Liz Moore and the staff of Paul Popper Limited.

The majority of the photographs in this book are from the Hulton Deutsch Collection, London. Other sources are as follows:
Associated Press, London 155, 194b, 256t, 269b; Camera Press, London 266, 270br, Auscape-JPF 255t, 255b, Colman Doyle 267br, Erma 267bl, Snowdon 268bc, Vario Press 273br; Colorific, London/Zapruder 104b; Kobal Collection, London 32c, 38br, 64tr; Larousse, Paris 58br; Magnum Photos, London/Abbas 272b, 273t, Dimitri Erwitt 272tr, Stuart Franklin 263tr, 263b, Philippe Halsman 268br, G. Mendel 267t, 275b, Patrick Zachmann 263tl; permission of MGN-Syndication International Ltd, Los Angeles 486br; National Aeronautics and Space Administration, Washington, DC 80-1; National Film Archive, London 78br, 120br, 262tc; Phillips Collection, Washington, DC, 57bl; Popperfoto, London 12c, 19tl, 24tl, 24bl, 26-7, 31b, 32t, 32b, 40tl, 42b, 48bl, 53t, 55, 58c, 65t, 65b, 66tl, 66tr, 68t, 70t, 70bl, 72c, 72b, 73t, 73b, 78tr, 87tr, 95b, 96tr, 100bc, 100br, 102 (all), 103c, 103b, 105b, 106t, 106b, 109t, 110tr, 110br, 111tr, 111b, 112 (all), 113tc, 113bl, 113br, 114, 118 (all), 120t, 120bl, 121, 123tl, 123tr, 123bl, 124tl, 128tr, 128br, 130tl, 131t, 132tl, 132tr, 133tl, 133tr, 135r, 136tr, 137, 140tr, 140bl, 140br, 141b, 142-3, 147t, 156t, 156bl, 157t, 157tr, 158r, 165tl, 170 (all), 173tl, 174tc, 174bc, 177tl, 177br, 179bl, 180tr, 180bl, 183bl, 183br, 184c, 184b, 186tc, 188t, 188b, 190tr, 190br, 192, 193 (all), 194tl, 194tr, 194br,

195cl, 201, 202t, 203t, 204 (all), 208t, 210t, 210ct, 213c, 213b, 214t, 214c, 215 (all), 216 (all), 217t, 218tl, 219, 220t, 220bl, 221t, 221b, 222 (all), 223 (all), 224b, 226 (all), 227 (all), 228bl, 228br, 229t, 230, 231 (all), 232b, 233t, 233b, 234 (all), 235b, 236 (all), 237t, 237b, 238t, 238b, 239 (all), 240 (all), 241b, 242tl, 242tc, 242b, 243tl, 243tc, 243tr, 244, 245tl, 245tr, 245c, 246 (all), 247 (all), 248t, 248b, 249 (all), 250bl, 251, 252 (all), 253 (all), 254tl, 254tr, 254bl, 254bc, 254br, 256 (all), 257 (all); Press Association, London 211br; *Punch*, London 60tl; Rex Features, London 258, 260b, 270bl, 270bc, 278bl, 281br, Nick Bailey 279bl, Brooker/Jorgensen 269tr, Deis Cameron 264t, Thierry Chesnot/Sipa Press 271br, Delahaye/Sipa Press 259t, East News/Sipa Press 278t, ITN 272tl, Juhan Kuus 278br, Novosti/ Sipa Press 261b, Leon Schadeberg 277, Sipa Press 262b, 265br, 268t, 270t, 273tl, 275tl, 275tr, 276tl, 276c, *The Sun* 261t, A. Tavera/ Prisma 264b, *Today* 261c, 270c, Barry Wilkinson 259br; Royal Geographical Society, London 47r; Frank Spooner Pictures, London 259bl; Syndication International, London 255tl, 255cr, 260ct, 260cb, 268bl, 269tl; Topham Picture Library, Edenbridge 281bl, Associated Press 145, 259bc, 262tl, 262tr, 265tl, 265bl, 271tl, 271tr, 274, 276tr, 276b, Press Association 260t, 271bl, 279t, 281t.

Oskar Kokoschka's *Self-portrait* (detail 17bl) is © COSMOPRESS, Geneva/DACS, London, 1989.
Salvador Dali's *Laurence Olivier as Richard III,* 1956 (detail 64br), is © DEMART PRO ARTE BV/DACS 1989.
Grandma Moses' *McDonell Farm,* 1943 (57bl), is copyright Grandma Moses Properties Co., New York, 1987.
Andy Warhol's *Marilyn,* 1967 (detail 250br), is copyright the Estate and Foundation of Andy Warhol, 1989. Courtesy ARS, N.Y.